African Military History and Politics

African Military History and Politics

Coups and Ideological Incursions, 1900–Present

A. B. Assensoh
and
Yvette M. Alex-Assensoh

Foreword by Richard W. Hull
Introduction by Okey Onyejekwe

palgrave

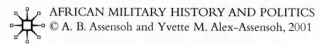

AFRICAN MILITARY HISTORY AND POLITICS
© A. B. Assensoh and Yvette M. Alex-Assensoh, 2001

First published 2001 by PALGRAVE™
175 Fifth Avenue, New York, N.Y.10010 and
Houndmills, Basingstoke, Hampshire RG21 6XS.
Companies and representatives throughout the world

PALGRAVE is the new global publishing imprint of St. Martin's Press LLC Scholarly and Reference Division and Palgrave Publishers Ltd (formerly Macmillan Press Ltd).

ISBN 0-312-23893-2 hardback
ISBN 0-312-24039-2 paperback

Library of Congress Cataloging-in-Publication Data

Assensoh, A. B.
    African military history & politics: coups and ideological incursions, 1900–present / A.B. Assensoh, Yvette Alex-Assensoh; foreword by Richard W. Hull; introd. by Okey Onyejekwe.
        p. cm.
    Includes bibliographical references and index.
    ISBN 0-312-23893-2 — ISBN 0-312-24039-2 (pbk.)
    1. Civil-military relations—Africa—History—20th century. 2. Coups d'etat—Africa—History—20th century. 3. Africa—Politics and government—20th century.
    I. Title: African military history and politics. II. Alex-Assensoh, Yvette M. III. Title.

JQ1873.5.C58 A77 2001
960.3'1—dc21   2001021863

A catalogue record for this book is available from the British Library.

Design by Westchester Book Composition.

First edition: January 2002

10 9 8 7 6 5 4 3 2 1
Transferred to digital printing in 2006
Printed in the United States of America.

This volume is dedicated to our son, Baby Livingston Alex, who is named for his maternal grandfather of blessed memory, Reverend Livingston Alex (1928–1998) of Breaux Bridge, Louisiana, USA; and also to Mrs. Thelma Coleman Alex and Mrs. (Nana) Enola Thomas for their inspiration and support at all times.

CONTENTS

Contents

PREFACE

A. B. Assensoh and Yvette M. Alex-Assensoh

A lot of historical-cum-political factors prompted us, as a historian–political scientist team, to write this book. The most recent factor which reinforced our interest to finish the manuscript appeared in the *Chicago Tribune* of December 25, 1999, titled: "General leads a revolt in Ivory Coast coup." As researchers, we could not believe that a stable French-speaking West African nation like the Ivory Coast could also fall prey to the incessant coups d'etat that have engulfed many countries on the African continent.

Expressing surprise, the Christmas day article from Associated Press correspondent Alexandria Zavis, in the Ivory Coast capital of Abidjan, began with these words:

> This African nation, long a bastion of stability in a region wracked by war, was riven Friday by an army revolt described by its declared leader as a coup d'etat. Army troops and civilians together looted parts of the capital, Abidjan, a day after soldiers went on a rampage. Many soldiers said they were owed back salary and perks, while others on Friday said the revolt was aimed at ousting the President [Konan Bedie].[1]

Ivory Coast Army General Robert Guei, who had been replaced as army chief in a 1995 reshuffling of officers, led the coup to topple the elected regime of President Konan Bedie. Characteristically, France, Ivory Coast's former colonial power, condemned the coup and reportedly "issued a statement calling for the immediate re-establishment of order and security in Abidjan."[2] This is one of the most recent events in which African army officers have toppled an elected or a sitting government, and one wonders about the political history of all of these incidents. Our study unfolds the stories behind many of the coups d'etat. In doing so, we have also traced how we began to show interest in the subject as well as behind-the-scenes antics that culminated into an entire manuscript for this study.

The Genesis of our Study

In the summer of 1994, we were ready to take overseas trips, first to several places in West Africa and, later, to the British capital of London, which once happened to be the nerve-center of the erstwhile British Empire and its African colonies. From the British capital, we were to frequent Oxford, and its Rhodes Scholar's Library, where Cecil Rhodes had the wisdom of leaving a vast legacy through the pecuniary bequest for his Rhodes Scholarship, of which many international students, at the undergraduate level and before reaching age 25, scramble to be an integral part, especially if they want to study at Oxford.

We were happy to be returning to Oxford, where this book's coauthor, A. B. Assensoh once held an important postdoctoral fellowship at the Center for Cross-Cultural Research on Women (CCCRW), which is based in Queen Elizabeth House. A. B.'s nostalgic view of Oxford included the fact that, during his University of Oxford Visiting Fellowship, he gave lectures on ethnicity to students of the famous anthropological seminars at St. John's College, Oxford, which was directed by the late anthropologist Edwin Ardener (whose wife, Shirley, a prolific writer and scholarly editor who was eventually knighted, headed CCCRW at the time). In 1994, both of us—Yvette and A. B.—were scheduled to give two separate lectures at Oxford, which made our business trip a pleasure!

While putting the finishing touches to our plans for the overseas journey, we promptly decided many helpful things. For example, having been married earlier in 1994, we decided to make the entire trip, as pointed out earlier, to be for business and for pleasure, partly to observe our deliberately-delayed honeymoon. That interest was coupled with plans to gather research materials for two books that we had earlier sketched out in our respective academic or teaching fields (history and politics). Yvette had written to make research contacts in several British cities, including Liverpool, where one of her academic advisers-cum-mentors at Ohio State University, Professor William E. Nelson, Jr., had done Fulbright-sponsored research at the University of Liverpool. (The outcome of Dr. Nelson's research is a very useful book on Black Atlantic politics in Boston, MA and Liverpool, England, published in 2000 by State University of New York Press.)

In the British cities, Yvette was to do a comparative study of the underclass and urban poverty among ethnic and racial groups. She, indeed, bore in mind that Charles Murray, a leading scholar in that area of research, was a formidable intellectual pillar in those places. In fact, Murray was the subject of a major British newspaper article when we were in Britain in the summer of 1997.

Our would-be sojourn in Britain was considered fine and safe by many people who knew that we were taking off that summer. Ironically, that was in spite of the British-Irish Republican Army (IRA) problems that, sometimes, escalated into unfortunate bombings of strategic targets in Britain and Northern Ireland. At the same juncture, however, many friends and some of our professional colleagues wondered if it would be very safe for us to travel to Africa in view of several political, military, as well as ethnic upheavals that were going on over there. As perfect examples, some friends sent newspaper clippings to us as unspoken warnings. As we read, the Rwanda-Burundi area was being suffocated by chaotic ethnic-cum-military struggles; the Congos were not at peace in a variety of ways; Somalia was still engulfed in ethnic warfare (about which A. B. and then U.S. president Bill Clinton had exchanged letters); and Liberia, a former jewel of American interests in Africa, was also in a hectic civil war, which was due to the intransigence of the West African nation's President Samuel K. Doe. Mr. Doe, who was later captured by some of his opponents and murdered, had refused to negotiate with military forces that his fragile regime in Monrovia could not easily defeat.

Since we were interested in visiting Liberia, where A. B. once served as an editor of three newspapers, we did anguish over the West African country's ongoing political problems. According to everyone we spoke to, Doe was to be blamed for most of Liberia's problems, not the Americo-Liberians (freed slaves from America) who had controlled the politics and economy of the country since the 1840s. Doe was unwilling to step down, even when America offered a ship to take him and his family from the Freeport of Monrovia to safety in America. This was despite the fact that Doe, a military man and Liberian President at the time, had mismanaged Liberian affairs in every way since April of 1980, when he led the coup d'etat that overthrew the True Whig Party regime of the late President William R. Tolbert, Jr. In Doe's so-called "enlisted men's coup," Tolbert and several of his cabinet members—including American-educated Foreign Minister C. Cecil Dennis, Jr., as well as the president's own brother, Senate President Pro-Tempore Frank Tolbert, both of whom were very well known to coauthor Assensoh as an editor in Liberia— were summarily killed during or in the aftermath of the military takeover.[3] Dennis' father, an elected legislator, owned the newspapers that A. B. edited in Liberia. Other places on the African continent in 1994, as amply demonstrated in our study, were also having their share of the ongoing coups and ethnic-induced instability, including countries with elected politicians in control of national leadership.

Everyone feared for our lives when we went to Africa, especially since we went during a turbulent period of the continent's political, economic, and social history. However, Yvette's political science mind worked magic on both of us, as she queried if it would not be auspicious—when we were in Africa—to study the very reasons that create the instability that our friends and some of our professional colleagues were afraid would engulf us. Yvette's desire was that we should utilize our historical and political expertise to dissect the reasons for the rampant military incursions into African political affairs and, to some extent, the roles that foreign ideological influences had played, over the years, in all of these scenarios. Working in the area of urban political behavior that is undergirded by theories of contextual influence, Yvette suggested that we should study the various contextual forces on the historical and contemporary plane that, unfortunately, often give birth to military and ethnic upheavals in Africa.

Although most of Yvette's scholarship is on political behavior in the American context, her graduate studies in the field of political sociology have often provided her with a broadened understanding of political behavior in general; that knowledge would be necessary to work on this study. A. B.'s background, including his extensive journalistic and scholarly writings on political leadership as well as conflict in America and Africa, would provide the central base of the scholarly knowledge and expertise that would serve as the wellspring for this project. Consequently, we were happy that we received the encouragement of several publishers and editors to expand the research project that we had originally had in mind to a book about the African military and its incursion into the continent's day-to-day politics through coups d'etat.

While our work covers a lot of ground, we still want to caution readers and researchers, who may rely on it for their own research that it is not, by any means, an exhaustive study. There is, in fact, a lot of room for scholars to build on, especially in terms of comparing African coups d'etat with those in Eastern Europe, Asia, and Latin America. We did only a brief comparison between African and Argentine coups d'etat, with doses of the most recent events in some parts of Southeast Asia discussed as well.

In a large measure, some readers may feel that our work is too heavily enveloped in events of the 1950s/1960s, although we are also very much aware that real coups d'etat and ideological events of Africa have a long history, dating back to precolonial times, when one looks at pockets of warfare and the reasons for them. However, our main interests rested in the notion that, in modern times, the roots of coups d'etat and ideological struggles on the continent date back to the 1950s, particularly in Egypt, Libya, and Algeria, and in the 1960s, whereby Sub-Saharan Africa is concerned. We therefore dwell heavily on the 1950s and 1960s. The importance of the 1960s has been captured in the following statement by Michael Colin Vazquez, executive editor of the prestigious Harvard-based *Transition Magazine:*

> It was the dawn of the 1960s, a time of transition: an era of youth and hope, has deferred dreams finally coming true, or starting to. John F. Kennedy was in the White House; Martin Luther King, Jr., was in Birmingham; and Africa was on the move. Decolonization was proceeding apace: in 1960 alone, seventeen new African states were admitted to the United Nations.[4]

Indeed, it is hoped that our emphasis on the military upheavals, decolonization, and ideological jamboree of the 1960s is both valid and useful, although we endeavored to discuss other relevant periods, whereby coups d'etat on the African continent were concerned. As Vazquez pointed out above, as many as 17 African countries broke free from the chains of *active* colonialism and imperialism in 1960 alone, hence our pointed stress on the 1950s or 1960s is neither an exaggeration nor a misplacement of priorities, especially when the years of military upheavals are concerned. Above all, our emphasis is on the fact that while some coups d'etat have served useful purposes, the rampant overthrows of some of the elected (civilian) regimes in Africa have often been a waste of taxpayers' funds, which are invested in elections, and, sometimes, a clear undermining of genuine exercises at democratic governance as well as of experiments in constitutionalism.

Succinct Chapter Descriptions

Apart from the authors' preface, an introduction, and a foreword, our study has eight chapters, including the short conclusion. Chapter one deals with Africa's recent colonial past, dating from 1900 to the 1960s. This past has been given an extensive coverage to help users of this publication who may not have a decent or an extensive grounding in African political history. We hope that we will not be faulted for the comprehensive nature of this chapter, which took quite some time to complete to satisfy our respective interests in history and politics. Chapter one has taken several subjects into account. The subjects that we plan to discuss in the subsequent pages include the evolution and roles of various types of religions, slavery, traditions, and customs (these later play decisive roles in the continent's coups d'etat). These and other events, indeed, account for part of the reasons for the chapter's intrusive length, and we hope that our readers would have the patience to bear with us before they reach the main part of our study concerning the African armed forces (including the police forces) and their evolutionary prowesses. Chapter two spells out the historical-cum-political evolution of Africa's armed forces, with specific examples from selected countries in particular regions up to the early part of the postcolonial period. What is unique is that we did not have to cite many specific examples because, in sum, what evolved of the military and police forces in one particular colonial entity was similar to what took place in the other colonies, and was in fact almost the same. Chapter three of our study discusses corrupt and dictatorial tendencies, which are known to tacitly invite military involvement in national politics, since such undemocratic tendencies make even the electorate see the need for a coup to end what is often seen as the rot and abuses on the part of elected or appointed politicians. Chapter four is an overview of several military leaders, especially those who have become civilian leaders, often upon either shedding their military garb or retiring from the armed forces, including the police.

Many of the coup leaders in Africa tasted the "sweetness" of leadership as well as of holding power, and, as a result, after their military reign they promptly returned to partisan politics, even if it meant forming their own political parties and running for civilian offices. An interesting exception was the case of the Ivory Coast, where General Robert Guei's plans to become an elected dictator were thwarted by the citizenry in an uprising in October 2000.[5] Chapter five discusses whether or not military involvement in African politics augurs well for stability or not with our conclusions; as shown in the study, there are many pointers to answer in the negative, especially as many military leaders became so "civilianized" (or no longer militiary men or women) that they repeated the very mistakes they took power to correct. Chapter six discusses the proliferation of coups as well as some of the foreign political or ideological involvement in some of these coups d'etat. This chapter also offers interpretations of various historical and political terminologies, including "ideology." Chapter seven is a discussion of these coups d'etat within their political and theoretical contexts. Chapter eight offers a conclusion, in which we have endeavored to tie up together the strings that, loosely, bind all of the events that can often lead to many of these armed interventions in African politics.

ACKNOWLEDGEMENTS

It is not very easy to acknowledge, by name, the numerous authors, colleagues, friends, family members, and, indeed, students whose discussions and ideas have helped in shaping this publication to its present form. To the pioneers of the study of African military and ideology, especially the various military scholars who wrote their memoirs to set records of their coups d'etat involvement straight, we are very grateful.

We are also happy and, most certainly, very blessed that two exceptional scholars in the study of African politics and history—Professors Richard W. Hull of New York University and Okey Onyejekwe of Ohio State University, a historian and a political scientist, respectively—promptly agreed to write a foreword and an introduction, respectively, to this publication. They are scholars that we have come to know and unlimitedly respect. Therefore, certainly, we want to thank them effusively for expending part of their tight professional schedules to provide their contributions for the successful completion of our own work.

Apart from his own research, teaching, and family responsibilities, Professor Hull, for example, was also directing the NYU History Department's undergraduate program. Also, Professor Okey Onyejekwe—apart from his own teaching, scholarly, and family capacities—has been directing the Center for African Studies at Ohio State University. In fact, as an instant example of how busy these two scholars can be, at the time that Dr. Onyejekwe agreed to provide an introduction to this study, he was actively involved in cross-Atlantic negotiations to set up exchange programs between his center and several African educational institutions, including Ghanaian colleges and universities.

In our discussions with Okey in Columbus, Ohio, we were impressed that he took those foreign exchange negotiations so seriously that, at a time when planes, sadly, were dropping out of the sky and resulting in the death of their occupants, he had flown twice by July 1999 to Ghana to concretize the plans for the proposed exchange program there. With his sterling expertise in African history and politics, it was clear that he was doing an excellent job for his university.

On the home front for us—at Indiana University—we are very grateful to several persons, including administrators, staff persons, and, indeed, colleagues in our two departments: Afro-American Studies and Political Science. We very much thank the former acting College of Arts and Science (COAS) Dean Russell Hanson, who promptly assisted coauthor A. B. Assensoh with part of the much-needed funds to take care of his research needs. Passionately and empathetically, Dr. Hanson agreed to help A. B. to continue research for this publication and others, which helped the coauthor's research planning stages to advance significantly.

It is, most certainly, correct that a true scholar understands the desperate needs of other scholars, and, as an administrator with open and patient ears, we expect Dr. Hanson to succeed very well in the realm of university administration and academia.[1] Hanson, as a man of transparent modesty and straightforwardness, revealed to A. B. that the financial help he was providing did not come from his office alone but partly from Associate Dean Jeffrey Alberts of the Research and University Graduate School (RUGS) at Indiana University. We are, therefore, effusively grateful to Dr. Alberts as well. Dr. Hanson chose not to become the substantive Dean of our College of Arts and Sciences but, instead, to return to the classroom as a professor of political science. His replacement as the substantive Dean, Dr. Kumble R. Subbaswamy, also arrived with a lot of vision and energy on the Bloomington campus of Indiana University, from where he had previously earned his doctoral degree; he has already shown a remarkable straightforwardness and the willingness to continue the good job that had been done in the College by Dr. Hanson and his chief lieutenants (including Executive Associate Dean David Zaret, a sociologist by training who also has the capacity to be a wise and patient listener).

Another Indiana University administrator who deserves applause is former Dean and academic Vice-Chancellor Debbie Freund. "Dr. Debbie," as we affectionately called her, looked for every legal way to help A. B. with his research needs, including helping him to acquire a new computer for home use in place of the one that was damaged in a fierce rainstorm.

As we were concluding work on the manuscript for the book, Dean Freund left Indiana University to become the new Provost and the Academic Vice-President of Syracuse University. We wish to thank her, for her forthright and excellent administrative skills as well as her willingness to bend backward, if professionally necessary, to help professors to whom she served as an "advocate" Dean and, indeed, academic chief. Her gentle and very warm ways, especially when holding professional discussions, will be sorely missed.

Additionally, Indiana University's former Bloomington campus Chancellor Kenneth R. R. Gros Louis deserves commendation for promptly approving A. B.'s request for sabbatical leave, which made it a lot easier for A. B. to concentrate on the final stages of his coauthoring role in this publication. As a scholar in his own right, with expertise in English literature, Dr. Gros Louis is an asset in varied ways to young and old scholars who work under him. Dr. Gros Louis began his letters approving the much-needed sabbatical leave as well as Dr. Alex-Assensoh's one-year leave of absence (as a result of her National Academy of Education/Spencer Foundation grant), with the fact that he was "very pleased" to approve our requests, as he knows very well, as a true scholar himself, that faculty members sometimes deserve a break—whether it is a leave of absence or a sabbatical leave—to embark on serious and uninhibited research to produce scholarly works.

Above all, A. B. wants to thank his intellectual colleagues and friends of the Association of Third World Studies, whose serious discussions of African political and historical issues, coupled with their own astute scholarship in the field, most certainly enriched this publication: Among them are Professors Julius O. Ihonvbere, John Mukum Mbaku, Harold Isaacs, Pita Agbese, George Kieh, E. Ike Udogu, Wafula (the future Mzee), Peyi, Anna, Uwadibie ("Governor"), Phillip Aka, Samuel K. Andoh (the future "Osagyefo"), Paul Kuruk, and Tom Leonard.[2] Indeed, outside ATWS circles, for research and consultation on African political, legal, and communications history, there were helpful scholars like Professors Victor K. Essien of Fordham University and Cecil Blake of University of Nebraska at Lincoln; journalists and editors Kaye Whiteman; Maxwell Nwagboso; Desmond Davies, of *West Africa Magazine* of London (what we used to call Methuselah), and then contributing writer Anthony A. Akinola of Oxford, England.

We are also grateful to the Reverend Livingston Alex of blessed memory (1928–1998), his better half and widow, Mrs. Thelma Coleman Alex, and attorney Joslyn Alex (Yvette's older sister) for their early and sustained encouragement. In the instance of Yvette, for the positive encouragement these persons have actively played in her life. In Dr. Alex-Assensoh's Political Science department, she is very grateful to colleagues and staff persons for the congenial scholarly atmosphere, under which she is thriving as a budding political scientist. She is particularly thankful to Mrs. Margaret Anderson and Mrs. Loretta Heyen for helping us to "untangle" several diskette problems that resulted from our using different computers and word processors at various places away from Indiana over a span of almost five years, including Ohio State University, where A. B. was on a summer NEH seminar, and Louisiana, Kansas, Virginia, and Florida, where Yvette spent summer research stints and had to use different computers to do her own part of the coauthoring process. Margaret has always been a very patient gem, whenever Yvette needed her assistance, and we are very grateful to her and Loretta. Many thanks to Bloomington-based *Herald-Times* newspaper editor Bob Zaltzberg and managing editor David Hackett for promptly allowing us to cull for reprint here one of our published guest columns.

We also thank the wonderful publishers and editors of Palgrave for their encouragement and assistance throughout the process; particularly we want to mention the hard work and exceptional cooperation of Karen Wolny, Gabriella Pearce, and production editor Donna Cherry. Our copy editor Jen Simington and production assistant Sabahat Chaudhary were both brutal and terrific; we thank them greatly as well!

Our three children, Akwasi (A. B., Jr.), Kwadwo, and "Baby" Livingston Alex Assensoh deserve our praise for their understanding that, sometimes, Mom and Dad needed some quiet scholarly periods to jump on the computer or word processor to work on the manuscript for the book. To them, we extend our unlimited thanks and appreciation for the much-needed cooperation. As an eleventh-grader at Bloomington High School-North, Akwasi was, himself, busy with classwork every evening and, sometimes, had to interrupt our work at dawn or during the wee hours of the morning for one of us to proofread a particular completed high school project. A. B. is grateful to Dr. Ego Onyejekwe, who assisted him in becoming very familiar with OSU computer networks, where he worked on part of the manuscript for this publication. We thank God that all of us survived the intellectual research as well as other pressures and, in the end, finished this book.

FOREWORD

Richard W. Hull

Tragically, Africa has been a continent under ideological and military siege for many centuries. Today, painful stories of endless civil wars, ruthless warlords, starving refugees, and random banditry continue to fill our mass media. A report issued by the United Nations in November 1999 notes "massive and blind atrocities" against civilian populations in the Republic of Congo (the former Zaire). There, Chadian, Angolan, and French mercenaries are fighting alongside government forces as well as with opposition rebels.

In many regions of Africa, as we read in newspapers and reports, people are being subjected to arbitrary executions, mutilations, rapes, and disappearances. With millions of displaced people, Africa has the world's highest refugee population. As Africanists, we complain that the press dwells too heavily on these disheartening themes and that the many positive events and trends evident to observers in the field are not brought to wider attention. Nevertheless, as historians and political scientists of Africa, we cannot overlook the sadly recurring theme of militarism and its destructive consequences.

Most people, even African leaders, like to think that the military siege began after the end of the Cold War or at least in the postcolonial era. In reality, its roots are to be found in the late sixteenth century, four long centuries ago. For a moment, let us take a snapshot of the year 1599. The frame looks depressingly familiar. The Turkish Ottomans had just conquered Mediterranean North Africa and transformed peaceful coastal states into garrison polities. Ruthless military leaders bearing the title of *bey* had gained ascendancy over the civilian *ca'ids*. Egypt, Tunis, and Tripoli had effectively fallen under the heel of military juntas. Westward, in the Sultanate of Morocco, Ahmad al-Mansur (1578–1603) had just defeated the Portuguese and his southern neighbor, the empire of Songhay, after creating a formidable war machine. The great intellectual centers and trade emporia of Timbuktu and Jenne were now ruled by military governors, who preyed upon the local merchants and farmers and harassed the Muslim intelligentsia.

To the east, near Lake Chad, the King of Borno, Idris Alooma (1564–1595), had expanded his territories by waging a series of bloody wars against the region's non-Muslim ethnic minorities. Alooma's biographer classed firearms high among the gifts God had given to his patron, the Borno ruler. Southward, at the forest edge in what is today Nigeria, the rulers of the nascent Oyo empire had just extended their authority over their Yoruba neighbors and Nupe.

The military element in government had achieved enormous power within Oyo and had challenged proud traditions of civilian control. In Angola, in West Central Africa, civil war had been raging for a quarter century, since the slave-raiding Portuguese irruption. By 1599, the vast Mbundu kingdom of Ndongo had become a battleground for local slave-trading warlords aided by avaricious Portuguese conquistadors. The entire region was torn by civil war, and the King of Kongo, whose predecessors had ruled democratically, boasted a standing army of five thousand, including five hundred mercenary musketeers. Deeper in the interior, the militarily minded Luba and Lunda warriors were destroying villages as they forced peasants into their new imperial state systems. Farther east, in what is today Uganda, warrior-king Ntare II (1582–1609) of Buganda was terrorizing the farmers of the Lake Victoria region. And along the once-tranquil coast of East Africa, the sophisticated Swahili city-states were under siege by Portuguese mariners from the Indian Ocean and Zimba marauders from the interior. By 1599, the Zimba were also spreading turmoil in the Zambezi River valley, disrupting the gold and copper trade and dislocating thousands of villagers. Under siege, Rusere (1596–1627) the *mwene mutapa,* or king, of a huge empire centered at Great Zimbabwe, had to turn to Portuguese gunrunners for military support. Not long afterward, the empire degenerated into a military state and eventually collapsed.

In what is today South Africa, the Sotho-Tswana, an Iron Age spear-wielding Bantu-speaking people, displaced ancient populations of peaceful Stone Age Khoi and San. By 1599, Sotho *indunas* had gained ascendancy over the civilian chiefs. Far to the north, in the Horn of Africa, General Sertsa Dingel by the end of the sixteenth century had thoroughly militarized the Solomonid kingdom of Ethiopia after a horrific war against the Muslim Eritreans and their Turkish allies.

These are but a few examples of the violence and mayhem that were so pervasive on the African continent four hundred years ago. In many communities, real power had passed to military figures embracing a warrior ethic. Today, Africa is at war with itself and even though the roots of contemporary military rule in Africa are found deep in history, before the sixteenth century Africa was a relatively peaceful and secure continent whose leaders were largely responsive to their clans and lineages. Power came from ancestral sanction, not out of the barrel of a musket or at the tip of a poison arrow or spear. True, there were incidents of warfare and ethnic conflict, and there had been several destructive Islamic *jihads* north of the Sahara. But for the most part, warfare was limited in scope and duration and people enjoyed a high degree of security. Casualty and mortality rates were extremely modest. Indeed, before the sixteenth century Africa was a far more peaceful continent than either Europe or Asia.

I would argue that the trend toward militarism began with the expansion and globalization of the oceanic slave trades, particularly in the Atlantic region, from the onset of the sixteenth century. The emergence of the labor-intensive American plantation system, the rising demand for slaves in the markets of the Ottoman Empire and in the Persian Gulf emirates, and the need for slaves along the west coast of India and on islands of the Indian Ocean all fed the ideology of slavery and the violent practice of slave raiding. With the era of the slave trade came new weapons of war, and civilian leaders were either overthrown or transformed into warlords. Christian and Jewish European mercenaries and Muslim Asians allied with African military leaders to bring down governments that refused to engage in the slave trades. Democratic regimes were subverted and destroyed. Different ethnic communities were pitted against each other, negating any possibility of a united front against European imperialism in future centuries.

Africa has never fully recovered from this terribly disruptive era. During the brief colonial interregnum in the first half of the twentieth century, African militarism receded. After the conquest and partitioning of the continent, Europeans replaced Africans as military leaders, but in most cases they were subordinate to civilian colonial authorities. However, the ideologies and institutions of indigenous militarism were never entirely destroyed and indeed they made a rapid recovery in the postcolonial era. Since then, civil war has returned to the very regions of Africa where the warlords once flourished, especially in Sierra Leone, Nigeria, Angola, the Sudan, the Horn of Africa, and the Zambezi River valley.

The book that Professors A. B. Assensoh and Yvette M. Alex-Assensoh have written is especially important because it provides us with a clear understanding of the nature and dynamics of military rule in Africa today. Clearly, if peace and security are ever to return to the African continent, its people—as well as those beyond Africa's shores—must be cognizant of the workings and destructive effects of militarism on human communities. Africa is indeed under military siege, even in countries such as Nigeria and the Sudan, where civilians are nominally in control. The Assensohs are to be commended for this ambitious undertaking, as the eight very useful chapters, coupled with the very relevant introduction and the detailed bibliographic information, will do very well to advance our knowledge of this important, fascinating, and timely subject.

INTRODUCTION

Professor Okey Onyejekwe

It is a great pleasure for me to be invited by my good intellectual and social friends, Dr. A. B. Assensoh and Dr. Yvette Alex-Assensoh of Indiana University, to contribute this brief introduction to the study of a Pan-African subject matter that is at the heart of my expertise on African politics and history: the African military and foreign ideological impact on African politics. My own 1981 book, *The Role of the Military in Economic and Social Development: A Comparative Regime Performance in Nigeria, 1960–1979*, offers an instructive guide and, indeed, an intellectual excursion into several aspects of the current area that Professors Assensoh and Alex-Assensoh have painstakingly delved into. Their work is a vital study that, in my opinion, will stand the test of research and make endurable contributions to several aspects of African studies, particularly where the continent's politics and history intersect.

Although through our respective research and writing activities we were very familiar with each other's penchant for research on Africa, Dr. Assensoh (who is affably called "A. B." by all of us) and I first met face-to-face in 1988, when he was appointed to a year's postdoctoral fellowship at Ohio State University. Ever since, we have remained great intellectual allies and friends in the inky fraternity.

Indeed, our brotherly discussions and bantering on African issues—sometimes at some of the heavyweight conferences that our OSU African Studies Center or the former Black Studies Department organized at the OSU campus—are always memorable, the latest conference being the memorial service at OSU to honor Mwalimu Julius K. Nyerere.

Dr. Yvette Alex-Assensoh later matriculated in the graduate program of OSU's Political Science Department, where I had earned some of my graduate degrees. Upon Yvette's graduation, she joined the faculty of the Bloomington campus of Indiana University, where she is making very useful contributions in the annals of our discipline. Since she is not very far away from the state of Ohio, Yvette makes a point of paying regular visits to Columbus, where she often conducts research. Her recent study was funded by the Pew Trust through a Morehouse College-based research program that is headed by the Reverend Dr. Drew Smith, a Yale-educated religious and political science scholar who originally hails from Indiana. Completing her portion of the Pew research as well as the coauthored manuscript for this book in the summer of 1999, I found Yvette's intellectual plate both hectic and full; yet, as always, she found time to smile!

To a large extent, my 1981 study has a specific emphasis on Nigeria, but in instances, general African political situations came into play. Also, where I treated the issues of colonial and postcolonial politics in Nigeria, and where I compared the country's civilian and military regimes, one can gauge a lot of similarities with other African countries, notably the former British-controlled areas of Ghana, Gambia and Sierra Leone. Africa's recent colonial past is a subject that Professors Assensoh and Alex-Assensoh handle very well in the first chapter of this book. As they explained to me, A. B. and Yvette have very generously made this first chapter a comprehensive introduction to several facets of African history and politics for anyone who wants to read the book but is not familiar with the continent's recent colonial past.

It is very fascinating to read the coauthors' discussion of the establishment and growth, in the realm of the overall evolution, of Africa's armed and the erstwhile colonial frontier forces. Since the colonial authorities created the forces in the mold of their own armed forces, they endeavored to instill values that, historically, did not include interventions in democratically elected political processes on the continent. Therefore, one wonders where military officers acquired the taste for politics through armed insurrection, or the coups d'etat that many of them have used to advance their political agendas.

Where corruption is concerned, one easily sees how some elected officials of various African nations would resort to nefarious or questionable—in any case, corrupt—practices, sometimes to take care of electoral process debts that had been incurred before their election to public offices, and sometimes because of mere greed.[1] As I have discussed in comparative terms in my 1981 book, as part of the economic and social development in Nigeria between 1961 and 1975, many factors accounted for the events that led to military interventions in the country, beginning in 1966 when the first full-fledged coup d'etat, the so-called majors' coup, took place there.

As A. B. and Yvette have also aptly concluded, in some instances, where respective African armed forces were concerned, it is a disturbing truth that some military regimes have performed better than some of the previous civilian governments. As I also underscored in *The Role of the Military in Economic and Social Development,* there is overwhelming evidence to show that the military regime under retired General (now Dr.) Yakubu Gowon achieved a higher rate of economic and social development than the overthrown civilian regime that ruled Nigeria from independence in 1960 to the time of the coup in 1966. The existing evidence is simply amazing, especially where Nigeria's gross indicators like the GDP and sectoral growth, as well as development in agriculture, industry, transportation, communication, education and health, were concerned.[2]

The foregoing conclusion is about oil-rich Nigeria alone. What, then, about other African nations, especially those countries that do not have oil wealth like

Nigeria? It is in attempting to offer an answer or answers to this question that we immediately need this book to cover several aspects of African politics within the contexts of military interventions and the exact roles that foreign ideologies played, and continue to play actively, in the equation. In all instances, there are precipitating reasons for whatever situation that cropped up before and after a coup d'etat took place. Again, in my own study of Nigeria, I further indicated that among the facts that accounted for the difference in performance of the two regimes or eras (civilian versus military) was the fact that the military regime had a preponderance of resources over the civilian regime. In relative terms, the resources and revenues available to the Gowon Administration, during the 1970–1975 period alone, were simply enormous.

What about the situations in Ghana after the overthrow of the regime of the late President Kwame Nkrumah on February 24, 1966? What about the aftermath of the earlier overthrow of the Togolese regime of President Sylvanus Olympio, who was assassinated in the coup like Nigeria's first Prime Minister, Alhaji Sir Abubakar Tafawa Balewa? What we know is that, where foreign ideological influences are concerned, immediately after the overthrow of a particular regime, the new leaders are showered with foreign assistance, sometimes supplemented by even heavy doses of international loans. To understand all of these intricacies, it is very rewarding and also reassuring that Professors Assensoh and Alex-Assensoh have undertaken this study, through which many issues have been dissected for the benefit of interested researchers, teachers, and students.

I very highly recommend this book, *African Military History and Politics* because, in my scholarly opinion, all of the eight chapters, including the conclusion, offer very useful explanations and facts about many of the coups d'etat that Africans and their foreign friends have tried to either understand or grapple with. The authors have taken time to research and bring to the fore some of the forces that either initially prompted or later instigated particular military interventions, sad events that have helped to bring a living situation that Richard Sklar and Larry Diamond have described thusly: "Metaphorically speaking, most Africans today live under the dictatorship of material poverty."[3]

Should Black scholars, no matter where they come from, not take the time—as Drs. Assensoh and Alex-Assensoh have done in this lively study—to research and then explain some of the reasons, including coups d'etat and ideological interferences, that bring about these dictatorships existing among their people in Africa and also in the diaspora? In this book, one is bound to come across several examples and explanations that are very instructive, for which researchers, students, and the general reader should be grateful. For, apart from the "dictatorship of material poverty" that has confronted Africans for far too long in and outside of the continent, there is also the detailed discussion of the sad dictatorship of the military and police forces of Africa.

Above all, the authors have demonstrated that African nations had no business allowing the Big Powers of the former East-West paradigm to interfere in their political affairs, ideological considerations notwithstanding. Toward this end, I conclude with an axiomatic statement from Professor Ali A. Mazrui's *Cultural Forces in World Politics* (1990):

Before the East-West rapprochement Africans used to emphasize that side of their ancestral heritage which affirmed [that] "when two elephants fight, it is the grass which suffers." The rivalry between East and West, the two elephants, sometimes hurt the grass of the Third World. Korea, Vietnam, Afghanistan and Latin America have been hurt even more directly than Africa by the rivalry between the superpowers.[4]

In the foregoing context, Dr. Mazrui's words are very instructive, as they reaffirm that African countries should not have allowed foreign ideological concerns to play the known and, sometimes, unknown or covert roles that have led to most of the military interventions that the continent has endured in its postindependent era. These interventions date back to the 1950s, as the authors have amply demonstrated, beginning with one of the early coups in Egypt, which is considered a cradle of civilization. Again, Professors Assensoh and Alex-Assensoh deserve a pat—a mighty one, indeed—on their backs for this extensive study of a subject that is both intricate and, sometimes, vexing to undertake. It can be daunting because, in studying the African military and foreign ideological roles in these coups d'etat, an African patriot sees how the continent has become a political football for all sides to kick at will in the East-West conflagration of the 1950s and 1960s. However, it is also a fact that nonpatriots and some scholars with anti-Africa perspectives would, instead, place most of the blame for the continent's monumental problems at the doors of only the citizenry.

Indeed, thanks to the rapprochement—as Professor Mazrui put it—between the East and West, coupled with either the crumbling or minimizing of active ideological wars, Africa seems to be at some peace to develop economically and politically at its own pace. In doing so, as I emphasized in my 1981 study, there can be the notion of political development in Africa, which is predicated upon the premise that most nations aspire to be modern and also that modernity is a very desirable phenomenon that Third World societies, including Africa, must embrace vigorously.[5] Most certainly, Africa and its widely spread citizenry on the continent and in the diaspora need true political development as well as growth if these coups d'etat, which some cynics refer to as military adventurism, may be abated. Transparently, this is possible in the absence of either serious or active foreign ideological interference, particularly after the demise of the Soviet Union as we knew it in its Marxist-Leninist terms and as a result of the lack of any meaningful competition between Russian and American leaders, who get along much better today than in the years of the Cold War.

CHAPTER ONE

Africa's Recent Colonial Past, 1900–1970

A major goal of this book is to analyze the historical foundations and contemporary manifestations of the various armed forces (including the police) in Africa and their role in the political history of the continent, with an emphasis on coups d'etat. However, a valid assessment of the African military (or armed forces) cannot be attempted without first describing the social, political, and economic contexts in which they evolved. Consequently, this chapter provides a detailed analysis of Africa's recent colonial past, paying very close attention to how actions and circumstances led to the emergence of the African armed forces, again as we see them in the modern history of each country on the continent between 1900 and 1970.

In discussing the importance of historical factors that preceded the emergence of military coups d'etat, we focus in this section on the following issues: the consequences of colonial rule for African politics and stability; the role of religion in African politics; and the complexities of various postindependence issues, whereby various military factions have witnessed their greatest presence in internal and external matters. Indeed, the analysis of the foregoing factors is based on a theoretical framework that posits that all of these factors combined to shape the very environment in which African military forces and the regimes they installed through coups d'etat and other forms of military upheavals have existed.

The Influence of Colonialism:
Artificial Borders, Instability, and the Emergence of Ethnic Strife

Certainly, it is a historical as well as political fact that Europeans, out of colonialist and imperialistic interests, began their ideological and economic foray into Africa long before the advent of the twentieth century. Typically, formal British colonialist and imperialist interests in West Africa began in earnest in the 1800s when, for example, "the Bond of 1844 gave Britain a political footing in the country [the former Gold Coast, which was renamed Ghana at independence on March 6, 1957], and led to the forming of the Fanti Confederation in an effort to oppose British imperialism."[1]

As in several other African countries, including Nigeria, Sierra Leone, Kenya, and Uganda, there were "trade links [and interests] with the early merchant adventurers."[2] However, in the specific case of the former Gold Coast, the initial formal British–Gold Coast relationship "was effected by the famous Bond of 1844, which accorded Britain trading rights in the country. But from these humble beginnings of trade and friendship, Britain assumed political control of this country [as the Gold Coast]."[3]

Indeed, it was not only the British that had an economic, political, and ideological foothold in African nations, as there were the French, the Germans, the Portuguese, and the Spanish. Historically, the then-estimated 13,041 square miles of land lying between the Gold Coast and the French Togo (now called the Republic of Togo after independence) was a German Protectorate from 1884 until the outbreak of World War I in 1914.[4]

To these colonial and imperialist masters, it became a prime issue that the ownership of the land should be determined before the Gold Coast would be given its independence in 1957. Subsequently, it was decided that there should be a United Nations-supervised plebiscite "to indicate whether they [Togolese nationals of the 13,041 square miles] wanted to be united with an independent Gold Coast or to remain under British administration until such time as their political future could be determined."[5]

As the historical records have shown, the British in 1954 placed the issue of the land between the Gold Coast and French Togoland, then called British Togoland, before the United Nations Trusteeship Council. In August of that year, the Council—now in charge of parcels of land taken over from the vanquished Germans in World War I—decided to send a visiting mission to British Togoland in August 1955, to find out about the wishes of the inhabitants concerning their future status. They finally decided, however, that a plebiscite should be held in Togoland under British administration as soon as possible in order that "the people themselves should decide whether they wanted to unite with the Gold Coast at the time of Gold Coast independence or where the territory should be separated from the Gold Coast and continue under Trusteeship."[6]

The resulting vote was supervised by United Nations-appointed Plebiscite Commissioner Senor Eduardo Espinoza y Prieto, who was aided by U.N. observers from several other member nations. The plebiscite took place on May 9, 1956. Eighty-two percent of the registered voters did cast their votes, with 93,095 Togolese voting for and 67,492 of them voting against a unification with the then Gold Coast upon its attainment of independence in barely a year's time (on March 6, 1957).[7]

Similarly in Tanganyika, Dr. Julius K. Nyerere—who retired as Tanzanian leader and later died in London in October 1999—became President, after becoming the new leader of united Tanzania, but first as Prime Minister of former Tanganyika on May 1, 1961. Yet, he still faced the problem of uniting mainland Tanganyika with the island called Zanzibar. Subsequently, Tanganyika became independent on December 9, 1961 without Zanzibar as an integral or geographic part. However, as Dr. Nyerere had predicted, "Zanzibar posed a lot of problems for Tanganyika, including the 1964 coup d'etat that ended the Sultanate for [Sheik] Karume and [that allowed] other radicals to become the new leaders of the island."[8] Before then, on April 23, 1964 Nyerere and Karume had signed articles of union for Tanganyika and Zanzibar to be united. Subsequently, the new union would be called Tanzania, an amalgamation of the names of both nations.[9]

Issues of territorial integrity and unity, for some fortunate emergent African nations, were settled peacefully during or immediately after the receipt of the much sought-independence. However, some countries had to settle scores on the battleground through ethnic strife and even bloodbath. What happened in Nigeria, Africa's giant nation in terms of human and natural resources, was one such unfortunate example. The West African nation was, from July 1966 to July 1975, under the leadership of the youthful General Yakubu Gowon, who was variously described as a soft-spoken but dynamic military ruler, a real gentleman, a level-headed army boss, and, above all, as an almost faultless administrator.[10] To safeguard Nigerian unity, the country had to fight the Nigeria-Biafra civil war, a necessity epitomized by its national slogan, "to Keep Nigeria one is a task that must be done."[11]

The war ended on Nigerian terms, with the breakaway eastern region, the so-called Biafran Republic, returning to the national fold. However, on July 29, 1975, Gowon, who had become Nigeria's youngest head of state, was overthrown in a palace coup led by General Murtala Muhammed, one of his northern Nigerian military officers. Still young, deposed General Gowon was able to go to Britain, where he entered Warwick University and began undergraduate studies, later, earning a doctoral degree in political science. The Nigerian situation, created by political imbalance from the colonial period, was chaotic, and interethnic rivalries did not augur well for national unity and stability. Consequently, General Muhammed, who was considered a very strong military leader, was himself assassinated on February 13, 1976, in an unsuccessful counter-coup. He was replaced by his deputy, the retired General Olusegun Obasanjo (who is now Nigeria's elected president).

Why Nigeria Started the Civil War: A Succinct Account

In the late 1960s, General Gowon, in the words of Professor J. Isawa Elaigwu, "had been driven to the wall" by Colonel Odumegwu Ojukwu. Gowan therefore used his May 27, 1967 military decree, known as "Decree 8, of 1967," to declare a state of emergency throughout Nigeria,[12] granting himself the requisite military powers to thwart the secessionist effrontery of then eastern regional Governor Odumegwu Ojukwu and his fellow Igbo ethnic officers.

After the foregoing actions, a fierce and very bloody civil war (with ethnic dimensions) was started on July 5, 1967, on General Gowon's orders as a so-called "police action to capture Ojukwu."[13] It was a military order that eventually escalated into a full-scale civil war that would claim military, civilian and

even innocent children's lives. Eventually, on January 15, 1970, Nigerian and
Biafran leaders met at Dodan Barracks, the Nigerian Head of State's official residence, so that the secessionist leaders could "renounce secession."[14] The war
was an event that was bound to happen in Nigeria, because the British colonial
authorities reportedly encouraged ethnic rivalry between the predominantly
Islamic (or Muslim) north and the Christian south.

Methods of Colonial-Cum-Imperial Rule and
Their Accompanying Problems in Africa

What has not been widely documented is the manner in which colonialists from
Europe acquired their vast parcels of land and economic interests, coupled with
the policies they put in place. Professor S. C. Saxena, an Indian scholar who
holds the position of Reader in African Studies at University of Delhi, India,
offers an elucidation. He underscores that "the European colonial powers,
which ruled over various parts of Africa, adopted different methods of adminis-
tering their territories," and that "their colonial systems differed both in respect
of form and the underlying philosophy."[15]

As Dr. Saxena has further confirmed, the British authorities "believed in a
decentralized nature of their administrative set-up."[16] That accounted for the
systems of governance based on appeasement, by which they entered various
colonies and still allowed both good (or well-meaning) and inimical indigenous
customs or practices to flourish. They also practiced indirect rule, which was
widely used in East Africa, West Africa, and North Africa, specifically in Egypt,
where—as Saxena has indicated—the indigenous leaders, the Khedive and the
Egyptian governments were ostensibly in control, although the real power was
vested in the British Consul. The British Consul worked behind this facade of
Egyptian and Turkish legalism.[17] Egypt was a clear example of the indirect rule
system of governance introduced by British colonial leaders, led by Lord Lugard,
who moved from East Africa to West Africa.

Interestingly, the British (who used the methods of appeasement) were unlike
the French, who used outright methods of assimilation whereby they—as
French men and women—socialized and intermarried with colonial citizens. As
colonialists, the British were mindful of the fact that they possessed (1) settler
enclaves, like the Natal and Cape colonies in South Africa; as well as those in
Northern and Southern Rhodesia and Kenya; (2) Lord Lugard's indirect rule in
Uganda and Nigeria; and (3) the colonies acquired during the scramble for
Africa at the 1884–85 Berlin Conference, during which—as Professor Boniface
Ihewunwa Obichere of UCLA wrote unequivocally— "the question of the hinterland of West Africa was raised . . . during the discussions of the second and
third bases of the conference."[18]

Also, Dr. Saxena underscored the following about these territories:

These territories were acquired by Britain. . . . Prior to the scramble, Britain
had some coastal areas or enclaves under its occupation. These enclaves
were designated as "colonies," while the hinterland territories, which were

much larger, were called "protectorates." A crown colony was "an annexed territory" and an integral part of the king's dominions acquired by conquest, settlement or cession. . . . All subjects born in it enjoyed the status of British subjects.[19]

Furthermore, as Saxena has indicated, France controlled many colonies in Africa, with French West Africa alone comprising 4,600,000 sq. km., nine times the area of France. As indicated earlier, "the cornerstone of French native policy, in earlier stages, was the policy of assimilation."[20] In elaboration, that policy—which was also used by colonialists from Italy, Portugal and Spain—was categorized in the following terms:

> Assimilation was the most striking legacy which the first colonial empire left to the second. It was the pillar of French colonial policy. Assimilation in politics and law, the subordination of the "Pacte" Colonial in economics—that was the well-defined theory of the first colonial Empire; and it was also the theory on which the new French colonial empire was raised, at least until 1910. The actual basis of the new French colonial empire was given by Jules Ferry. . . . Ferry's theory rested on four elements which, according to him, were closely linked, namely, to industrialization, protection, markets, and colonies. Ferry wanted France to go in for massive industrialization as the United States and Germany were doing.[21]

The French applied the principles of Roman law, which included the contention that a vacant land belonged to the State, and hence such "vacant" parcels of land were declared French-owned in West Africa. The ownership was effected through an October 23, 1904 decree. An earlier March 28, 1899 decree did the same thing in Equatorial Guinea. According to Saxena and other scholars, the French unilaterally adopted and applied these self-centered policies in Africa, knowing very well that no land had been lying fallow without ownership.[22]

Indeed, it was recorded that French officials supposedly injected into the agenda of the Berlin Conference on Africa the Niger question, whereby "freedom of navigation on the Niger River was not sought for its own sake but for the commercial intercourse with the inhabitants of the Niger basin to which it would lead."[23] It was known by the British delegates to the Berlin meeting that Africa, as a continent, was being placed on the chopping board to be sliced up into pieces like apple pie or cake. Yet, they wanted to prevent the Niger basin (or Lower Niger) from becoming an international property. Instead, the right to determine navigational regulations, the first of such rights, was granted to only the British and French authorities.[24] Certainly, this selfish colonialist action was one of several unilateral events that would confirm that late Ghanaian President Kwame Nkrumah's contention that neocolonialism, as the last stage of imperialism, still served its own interests at the expense of the exploited.[25]

Other colonial powers—including the Portuguese, the Belgians, and the Spanish—had interests and policies that were similar to those of the British and the French, most of which were implemented in Africa during active colonialism. For example, Portugal controlled five major colonies on the continent: Angola, Cape Verde Islands, Guine Bissau, Mozambique and the islands of Sao Tome and Principe. It has been recorded that between 1830 and 1930, the Portuguese government in Lisbon, with limited success, did make strenuous efforts to encourage a settlement of many Portuguese citizens in Angola and in the other colonies. Similar to the French system of assimilation, the Portuguese colonial authorities saw their colonies in Africa as extensions of the mother nation of Portugal that merely happened to be separated by distance or an accident of geographic location. In fact, Dr. Antoniode Oliveva Salazar, a former Portuguese leader, made it abundantly clear that his country and its colonies "were a political and judicial unity, and [that] we desire to go along the road to economic unity."[26]

Professor Harry A. Gailey, Jr. of San Jose State University offers an excellent historical discussion of the Portuguese colonial case in his 1989 book, in which he also showed, as follows, "the Portuguese colonial system as it existed in the early 1950s," adding that "the real authority in the Portuguese government is the council of ministers controlled by the prime minister":

The experiences and tactics of the European colonial authorities were so similar in content, approach and over-all interests that, again, Nkrumah was on target in saying, in 1957, that he had "always regarded colonialism as the policy by which a foreign power binds its territories to herself by political ties with the primary object of promoting her own economic advantage."[27] Nkrumah was deemed prophetic in the context of the mother country syndrome, when, on the eve of Ghana's independence on March 5, 1957, he indicated the following at the Ghana National Assembly:

One of the spurious axioms of colonialism is that those who carry out the policy of the colonial power, however well intentioned they may be, almost always subconsciously seek a solution to the problems of the colonial territory in terms of a solution which was applicable to the so-called mother country.[28]

In Nkrumah's opinion, for example, neocolonialism—which is seen as the new form of colonialism—"acts covertly, maneuvering men and governments, free of the stigma attached to political rule. It creates client states, independent in name but in point of fact pawns of the very colonial power which is supposed to have given them independence."[29]

Professor Samir Amin, an Egyptian scholar, in 1973 contended that the origin of Africa's present problems "is often to be found in that decisive period which preceded the colonial conquest: between 1830 and 1880."[30] Amin also notes that two French citizens, Henri Brunschwig and Catherine Coquery, understood the importance of the 1830–1880 period, and that Brunschwig wrote that, as a result of colonialism, "Black Africa was shaken and changed, just as Europe had been by the coming of the inventions and discoveries which brought it out of the Middle Ages . . . [however that] the European conquest did not give a different direction to the path on which the African had now started . . ."[31]

In cataloguing the dilemmas of colonialism, several historians, including Nigeria's history Professor Kenneth O. Dike,[32] Amin and others, share the contention that "the accelerated colonial exploitation of this postwar period produced a crisis in the public finances of the colonies even before independence. Growth always lagged behind the current public expenditure that it [the colony] made necessary."[33] As a result, Nkrumah captured the historical mood very well and when he asserted that "imperialism, which is the highest stage of capitalism, will continue to flourish in different forms as long as conditions permit it," and that "imperialism knows no law beyond its own interest and it is natural that despite the pretensions of its agents to justice and fair play, they always seek their interests first."[34]

Certainly, in post-independence Africa, some of the interests of colonialist and imperialist forces would manifest themselves in a glaring and stubborn fashion. New regimes and their indigenous leaders were made to seem either outright incompetent or unprepared to shoulder the leadership affairs of their respective nations. To accomplish this, political opponents and even mere critics of these post-independence regimes would be propped up financially and otherwise by former colonial powers, either from inside the new nations or from political exile. They would be exploited to undermine the obvious nationalist efforts of the new leaders. This was typical in many of the postcolonial regimes, including that of Nkrumah's Ghana. In Ghana, the leadership of the National Liberation Movement (NLM) and, later, the United Party (UP), both of which were ethnic-based opposition political parties, was approved by former colonial powers.

Sometimes, the true nature of the external power behind a political and ideological opposing force in an African country becomes clear only after the overthrow of a particular regime through an armed insurrection or a coup d'etat. Indeed, in his book, *Dark Days in Ghana* (1968), Nkrumah made this point clear in the following words:

> The members of the "old opposition" with whom the "N.L.C." [the army-police council that ruled Ghana after the February 24, 1966 coup] are closely associated, are the same people who tried to sabotage the winning of our independence ten years ago [in 1957]. They struck on 24th February 1966, just as we were about to break through and win our economic independence. . . . They shouted from the rooftops that they acted spontaneously to save Ghana from "economic chaos." But as everyone who has studied the history of Ghana over the last fifteen years or so knows, their action was only the culmination of a whole series of actions aimed against my government and against myself. They have a long record of go-slow policies, of subversive activity and of alignment with imperialists and their agents.[35]

Also, Nkrumah used his book to discuss specific aspects of the military-cum-police overthrow of his government in 1966 as well as a few other relevant coups in other African nations, a subject that will be fully covered in another area of this book. However, the above quotation buttresses the intellectual arguments of some of the previously quoted authors, supporting the idea that the attempts at the overthrow of Nkrumah and several other African leaders were actions that followed a culmination of economic and political woes that dated back to the countries' colonial periods. To an extent, it is obvious that most of the grievances of coup leaders have often had their roots in the colonial periods of the nations concerned. Subsequently, from December 1962 to March 1967, there were 18 coups d'etat and coup attempts, a number that has been described in Nkrumah's book as a "record of military action in Africa."[36]

Yet, the colonial powers and their agents have often made it clear, that in wherever they did, especially during active colonialism and in postcolonial dealings, they meant well for the colonies. The Oxford-educated late Ghanaian leader, Dr. Kofi Abrefa Busia, discussed this in his 1962 study, in which he categorized examples of the modes of colonial rule.

According to Dr. Busia, who was well-known for his expertise in sociology at Oxford and at other institutions of higher learning, "the European powers that colonized Africa adopted different policies and evolved different administrative systems in the pursuit of their different objectives."[37] Indeed, several postcolonial African leaders and scholars have lamented the fact that the policies and systems utilized by the colonial powers were so tailored to "their different objectives," as Dr. Busia confirmed, that bequeathing these systems to independent African nations created nothing but economic, political, social, and cultural chaos. In *Revolutionary Path,* a 1974 posthumously published book, Nkrumah made the foregoing point much more clearly,[38] similar to what Tanzania's late President Julius K. Nyerere also stated about socialism in what his critics have labeled as his failed attempt at practicing a variation of socialism.[39]

It is not fair for critics of the late Premier Busia of Ghana to see him as either defensive of or apologetic for some aspects of colonial exploitation, although he points out in his 1962 study that many of the various colonial administrations, by their own definitions, were in Africa for good purposes. He cites the British as having "frequently insisted that their policy was to train the subject peoples of their colonies for self-government."[40] He was merely re-echoing the obvious facts defined by the colonialists themselves.

Busia, who was known to abhor all brands of socialism, was often seen as a champion of capitalism and, as a result, stayed in only capitalist countries when he went into voluntary exile abroad before the 1966 coup d'etat overthrowing Nkrumah's regime and, later, after his own 1969–1972 regime was overthrown in another coup in Ghana. From those capitalist countries, Dr. Busia reportedly collaborated with anti-Nkrumah forces in and outside Ghana to undermine the socialist regime that he vehemently detested. This ultimately resulted in the successful February 1966 coup, which sent Nkrumah into exile in Conakry, Guinea. That was a reversal of political fortunes, as Busia was then able to return to Ghana to play an active role in the new military regime.[41] He was Ghana's Prime Minister from 1969 until 1972, when Colonel Ignatius Kutu Acheampong removed him from power in a coup, and established the National Redemption Council (NRC) of Ghana's Armed Forces and the Police. Busia offered an explication of colonial policies and what they really meant in the colonies when he wrote the following about the French, the Belgians, the Portuguese and the Spanish:

> When one examines French colonial policy, one discerns running through it a conception of some kind of union between metropolitan France and its colonies. Belgian policy has been aptly summarized by G. Malengreau, himself a Belgian and an authority on the subject (in an article he wrote for a conference held in Washington, in 1954, under the auspices of Johns Hopkins University, and published in *Africa Today*), as one of "patient empiricism." It is a policy that has been marked by concentration on economic development rather than on training colonial subjects for political responsibility. The Policy of Portugal has been to regard its African colonies as extensions of the Portuguese, a policy emphasized by designing the colonies as "provinces" of Portugal. As for Spain, what is apparent in its colonial policy is the close economic integration of the African colonies with metropolitan Spain.[42]

In contrast to the foregoing assertion by Busia, other African political leaders, including Nkrumah, saw nothing good in colonialism, neocolonialism, or imperialism. It was, therefore, not surprising that Nkrumah called on his fellow Ghanaians to seek the political—instead of economic—kingdom first, and to move from there. Furthermore, he did not mince words when he spoke about colonialism or foreign domination, especially when he addressed the April 15, 1958 conference of independent African States. Among other details, Nkrumah felt that the only solution to the colonial problem was the complete eradication of the entire economic system of colonialism, gained through complete political independence. He promptly added the following details about foreign domination:

> We have, for too long, been the victims of foreign domination. For too long we have had no say in the management of our own affairs or in deciding our own destinies. Now times have changed, and today we are the masters of our own fate.[43]

Pan-Africanists from Africa and the Diaspora: A Succinct Overview of the Interaction of Black Leaders from Africa and America

After reading the writings of Busia and Nkrumah, younger generations of Africans and Pan-Africanists have often compared or contrasted the respective procapitalist and prosocialist leadership styles of the two political stalwarts of Ghana. In doing so, they have wondered about which was the better ideological inclination: Nkrumah's scientific socialism or Busia's capitalism? On the Pan-Africanist plane, for example, world-famous black leaders like Paul Robeson, Dr. W. E. B. DuBois and others have shown their own affection for socialism and, indeed, suffered for it in a variety of ways, just as Nkrumah, Nyerere, and others did.

In Robeson's 1958 publication, *Here I Stand,* he showed his relentless belief in scientific socialism. Robeson, who was internationally famous for his stage and

concert career,[44] knew Nkrumah and Kenya's President Jomo Kenyatta very
well from their sojourns in Europe. All three Pan-Africanists, along with
DuBois, Nyerere, and others, were known for their early anticolonialist stance
and their lifelong prosocialist interests. Like Nkrumah and Nyerere, Robeson
did not hide his socialist beliefs, writing the following in 1958:

> On many occasions, I have publicly expressed my belief in the principles
> of scientific socialism, my deep conviction that for all mankind a socialist
> society represents an advance to a higher stage of life—that it is a form of
> society which is economically, socially, culturally, and ethically superior to
> a system based upon production for private profit. History shows that the
> process of social change have nothing in common with silly notions about
> "plots" and "conspiracies."[45]

Several of Africa's post-independence socialist leaders suffered a countless number of coup plots and successful coups d'etat, partly because of their socialist
beliefs and economic programs. Some of the plots were because of ideological
reasons, similar to what Robeson espoused above. On the other hand, their kith
and kin in the diaspora, including Robeson, DuBois, and other Pan-Africanists
from Western societies, were penalized differently for their prosocialist views and
beliefs. Robeson and DuBois, both Americans, were denied passports and hence
overseas travel, mainly for what their antisocialist critics made out to be "un-
American" activities. Yet, Robeson said publicly that at the heart of the refusal
to reissue him a passport was his "concern for Negro rights."[46]
Nkrumah won the 1956 elections to become the leader of independent
Ghana. He had invited to Ghana's planned March 6, 1957, independent calibra-
tions several leading African-American leaders, including Dr. DuBois, Rev. Dr.
Martin Luther King, Jr., and his widow, Coretta, A. Philip Randolph, and Pennsylvania-based Lincoln University President Horace Mann Bond, along with
others from the Caribbean. But the U.S. State Department prevented their trip
to West Africa, by refusing to reissue American passports to some black leaders,
including Robeson. It was to the same meeting that U.S. Vice-President
Richard Nixon went to represent the administration of President Dwight Eisenhower. When DuBois and others were earlier denied U.S. passports to travel,
Robeson publicly and angrily denounced the action, saying that "of all the
Americans who traveled to the Ghana celebration there was not one man by far
who was as worthy of being there as was DuBois. For over forty years, he has
championed the cause of African freedom, and his books were the first to reveal
the truth about the relationship of Africa with the modern world."[47]
Robeson was further infuriated by other facts of passport denial involving
DuBois. They included Dr. DuBois's qualifications, which, in Robeson's summation, made DuBois the most qualified person to participate in Ghana's 1957
independent festivities:

> DuBois presided over the fifth Pan-African Congress in Manchester, Eng-
> land, in 1945, that was attended by Kwame Nkrumah, who later became

the first prime minister of free Ghana, by Jomo Kenyatta [of Kenya] and two hundred other leaders from every section of Africa, the West Indies, British Guiana, British Honduras, Brazil and the United States. Truly, Dr. DuBois' travels have been in the best interests not only of the people of the United States but in the best interests of the people of the world.[48]

Apart from the obvious personal wrongs Robeson himself suffered for being denied an American passport, he also disclosed an economic loss. He said it included "the loss of many thousands of dollars in fees offered to me as an artist in contracts that I have been unable to accept; and the legal expense of fighting my case for the past seven years has been considerable."[49]

Surprisingly, however, Robeson's closeness to radical African leaders of the anticolonial struggles has not been widely documented until recently, in the celebration of the centenary of his birth, in scattered publications. Yet, it is historically known that some of the numerous honors he publicly received in his lifetime were in recognition of those relationships. For example, as far back as January 29, 1950, Robeson, Nkrumah, and Dr. Nnamdi Azikiwe were honored by the National Church of Nigeria in a ceremony held at Aba, in the then eastern region of Nigeria. In front of an estimated 5,000 people, the three black leaders received the church's "Champion of African Freedom" award. Their citations indicated that Robeson was being an honored as a giant of the arts; Nkrumah spearheaded the modern phase of Africa's decolonization struggles with Ghana's independence in 1957; and that Azikiwe was one of the principal leaders of Nigeria's anticolonial struggle, which culminated in Nigeria's independence from Great Britain on October 1, 1960. At that point Azikwe became the country's first indigenous Governor-General and, later, ceremonial President. Both Azikiwe and Nkrumah had a lot in common earlier on, as they were both graduates of Lincoln University, and in fact Nkrumah went to Lincoln on Azikiwe's recommendation.[50]

In the mindset of colonialists and neocolonialists, Blacks in Africa and those in the diaspora deserved similar treatment for their radicalism, and that is why the examples of DuBois, Robeson, and others are very important here, if just for illustrative purposes. Indeed, while not necessarily extolling Robeson's socialist values but merely appreciating his Pan-Africanist and anticolonialist zeal, the way he was humiliated was unfortunately similar to the sad circumstances of other socialist leaders of the Third World during the Cold War era, including Chile's overthrown and murdered President S. Allende. Indeed, until recently Robeson was simply like a prophet without honor in his own country, although he was not murdered.

In the centennial observance of his birth, Robeson has been showered with honors, some of which were public honors in televised and published documentaries. For example, the *New York Times* was often selective in publishing news items about Robeson in his heyday and during his legal battle to recover his withdrawn American passport. However, the newspaper has now done a lot to rehabilitate Robeson's image since his death. The newspaper, during his centennial celebrations, wrote the following about Robeson:

This amazing man, this great intellect, this magnificent genius with his over-whelming love of humanity is a devastating challenge to a society built on hypocrisy, greed and profit-seeking at the expense of common humanity.[51]

As confirmed by historical events, Robeson genuinely felt that the actions of several African-American leaders of his generation—including his own and those of the New York-based Council on African Affairs—were geared toward Africa's struggles for decolonization, freedom, and justice. Also, American Black leaders simply wanted to lend a hand to the fierce decolonization struggles of their Africa-based cousins. Many Africans and Pan-Africanists have been happy that, in 1998, Robeson has been the subject of numerous distinguished honors, including a recent sobering *New York Times* article entitled "A Giant Denied His Rightful Stature in Film." The write-up spotted an imposing pictorial illustration of him in his title role as Othello at the play's showing in London and Broadway.[52] In the past, the article and picture would not have been published. The author was a dis-tinguished history professor of City University of New York, Martin Duberman, who is also the author of one of Robeson's latest biographies, *Paul Robeson*.

Indeed, it is now obvious that one cannot objectively appraise colonialism and its demise without necessarily touching on the noble roles played by Pan-Africanists and Blacks of African descent, including African-Americans of the Robeson and DuBois generation. That, certainly, is how and why Ghana's dis-tinguished historian, Professor Albert Adu Boahen was correct and forthright in his 1985 historical and political assessment of Blacks in general that there is no "theme in African history on which more has been written than that of the rise and fall of colonialism in Africa, [although] most of these authors have looked at the subject primarily from an Euro-centric point of view."[53]

It is, however, in handling the history of colonialism from a Euro-centric per-spective that a lot of the black diaspora contributions are left out. Professor Boa-hen has termed researched principal preoccupations as "the origins, structure, operation, and impact of colonialism." Such writers left out what the erudite historian has termed as "the crucial questions of how Africans perceived colo-nialism, what initiatives and responses they displayed in the face of this colonial challenge, and above all how they [the Africans] reacted after the forcible impo-sition of colonialism."[54]

Helpfully, Professor Adu Boahen relied on his own as well as other credible research sources in emphasizing some of the main reasons prompting formal colonial rule in Africa. Among these reasons were what he saw as a major change in the balance of power in Europe following the rise of Germany and increasing political instability occasioned by African wars in the nineteenth century that came to threaten peace in the African interior and consequently European trade on the coast."[55] While the so-called "scramble for Africa" or "partitioning of Africa" at the Berlin Conference could be seen as a crucial apex in the colonial epoch, Dr. Boahen quoted Nigerian history professor A. I. Asiwaju as asserting that the partition of Africa "cannot become fully intelligible except in terms of the convergence between the new situation in Europe and the prevailing politi-cal conditions in particular parts of Africa."[56]

In their responses to queries from younger scholars and students about African reactions to the conquest of their continent and its subjugation by colonialist interests, several historians of the European colonial experience in Africa have demonstrated that the colonized Africans did not sit unconcerned and allow their lands and people to be colonized by the imperial powers of Great Britain, France, Portugal, Spain, Italy, and Germany. For example, Professor Boahen has confirmed that, in fact, at the end of the first decade of the twentieth century, "despite the spirited defense and opposition put up by the Africans, the colonial imperialist conquest and occupation had been almost completed; and the continent of Africa had been carved up into colonies of different sizes and shapes among the imperial powers."[57]

It has also been demonstrated that the colonial powers showed a measure of efficient colonization by establishing, in the instances of British and Germanic rule, different systems of administration for each colony that came under their control. The French did so for several colonies that they grouped together. While there were municipal or regional governors and district officers (or commissioners) in all the colonies there were also executive, advisory, or legislative boards and councils, the membership composition of which depended on the mode of colonization, whether by indirect rule, assimilation, or appeasement. Again, Dr. Adu Boahen has clearly explained that while the British relied heavily on the use of traditional rulers (including local chieftains and members of royalty), the French, in their pursuit of complete control, "abolished most of the traditional ruling dynasties or, like the Belgians, drastically reduced their number and instead appointed educated Africans as chiefs to control local areas."[58]

Although there was a tight colonial hold on Africa, upheld by a crafty and very elaborate colonial administrative apparatus, Professor Samir Amin again points out that, "The origin of the [continent's] present problems is often to be found in that decisive period which preceded the colonial conquest: between 1830 and 1880."[59] Toward that end, Adu Boahen has described L. H. Gann, Margery Perham, P. C. Lloyd, D. K. Filedhouse, and P. Duignan as both European and Euro-centric historians who "have contended that the impact [of colonialism] was both positive and negative, with positive aspects far outweighing the negative ones."[60]

On the other hand, the argument continued that many indigenous African and Marxist scholars—particularly those that Professor Adu Boahen has described as underdevelopment and development theorists—often maintained that colonialism made little or no positive impact on Africa. The Ghanaian scholar disclosed that "the great exponents of this rather extreme position are Walter Rodney, the black Guianese [Guyanese] historian and activist, and the Ugandan historian T. B. Kabwegyere."[61]

Interestingly, the Rodney-Kabwegyere histo-political school of thought have maintained that the colonialists, out of selfish interests, hastened to dismember and balkanize Africa into small or fragile pockets of nonviable nation-states. Several liberal historians have also agreed that the first three decades of the colonial era introduced into Africa far more violence, instability, anarchy, and loss of African lives than probably any other period in its history. Conversely, others saw as the first obvious positive legacy of colonialism "undoubtedly the estab-lishment of continuous peace and stability in Africa, especially after the First World War."[62]

Defiantly, Ghana's Kwame Nkrumah in *Neo-Colonialism: The Last Stage of Imperialism* (1965)[63] saw Africa as having suffered balkanization, which, by defi-nition, meant that the continent was "clearly fragmented into too many small, uneconomic and non-viable States, many of whom are having a very hard strug-gle to survive."[64] In fact, Nkrumah went on to lament the fact that West Africa alone was divided, by departing colonial rulers, into 19 separate nations that, by his estimation, included two colonial enclaves possessed by Spain and Portugal.

Geographically, it was pointed out that in total sum, the population of West Africa was about a third of Africa's total population, although the average popu-lation of most of the independent [West African] countries, if Nigeria were excluded, was about 2.3 million each. It was further noted that: "It is, however, illusory to regard even Nigeria as an exception to the balkanization policy prac-ticed by the departing colonial ruler."[65]

However, Professor Adu Boahen, with the eye of a good historian, saw mat-ters differently, as he wrote in 1987:

> The second positive political impact has been the very appearance of the independent African states of today. The partition of Africa by the imperial colonial powers led ultimately to the establishment of some forty-eight new states, most of them with clearly defined boundaries, in place of the existing innumerable lineage and clan groups, city-states, kingdoms, and empires without any fixed boundaries. It is significant that the boundaries of these states have been maintained ever since independence.[66]

While both procolonialist and anticolonialist historical and political schools of thought have scored useful points and made meaningful their respective cases, it is still a historical as well as political fact that, in Pan-Africanist terms, colo-nialist powers, after years of cozy exploitation, had self-serving reasons to exit Africa as well as other Third World areas of the Middle East, Asia, the Caribbean, and Latin America. What, however, should be a minimal credit to these imperial powers was the fact that if they had left Africa as a monolithic cul-tural, political, and ethnic entity for the postcolonial politicians to carve into nation-states or countries, per se, the world would have seen more bloodshed, confusion and utter anarchy than has ever been recorded by Adu Boahen and other liberal historians.

Indeed, this is what has happened in boundary clashes among several African countries, particularly where there is ample evidence—or even a mere suspi-cion—that an area is endowed with rich natural resources, including petroleum products and such minerals as gold, diamonds, bauxite, iron ore, and uranium. On that score, it was good that the imperial powers carved up or partitioned Africa into the economic and political interests that we see today, even—as Nkrumah and others had lamented—if many of these African nations are "hav-ing a very hard struggle to survive."[67]

The Role of Christian and Islamic Religions:
The West African Examples

In many instances, colonialism and imperialism were seen in such negative terms by colonized peoples in Africa and other Third World places, including Asia and the Middle East, that even the religious aspirations of most of these colonized people were affected. That was particularly so where Christianity was concerned, as several postcolonial African leaders used their rhetorical skills to undermine the work of Christian missionaries, sometimes with a measure of justification, as these emerging indigenous leaders recalled their early experiences with Christian missionaries, educational systems, and/or churches as colonial subjects or citizens had been forbidden from speaking their indigenous languages or dialects in schools.

Moreover as, this book will show later, religion is sometimes the spark that ignites the unpopularity of corrupt politicians to help bring about military insurrections or coups d'etat. Several African leaders felt that way. In fact, in an address to the delegates of the April 15, 1958 Conference of Independent African States in Accra, Ghana, Nkrumah said the following about precolonial Africa:

> The stage opens with the appearance of missionaries and anthropologists, traders and concessionaires, and administrators. While the "missionaries" with Christianity perverted implore the colonial subject to lay up his "treasures in Heaven where neither moth nor rust doth corrupt," the traders and concessionaires and administrators acquire his mineral and land resources, destroy his arts, crafts and home industries.[68]

Apart from the foregoing and other unflattering aspersions cast about Christianity, several of Africa's scholars have seriously studied the role that both the Christian and Islamic religions have played in various facets of African life. Sometimes it is both instructive and disarming to note how some of the political leaders attempted to balance religious interests with ideological inclinations. While Nkrumah was making the foregoing tough but eye-opening statement about the exploitative nature of Christian missionaries, he still held steadfast to his Christian beliefs. Hence he made his 1957 assertion: "Today I am a non-denominational Christian and a Marxist socialist and I have not found any contradiction between the two."[69] To many of his political opponents and critics, it was hypocrisy dressed up in fine clothes, as they did not expect the Ghanaian leader to hold any meaningful Christian beliefs.

Like other indigenous educational products of the Christian experience, Nkrumah further made it clear that, in his youth, he took his Christian religion so seriously that, indeed, he "was often to be found serving [Roman Catholic] Mass." The future leader of Ghana added that, as he grew older, "the strict discipline of Roman Catholicism stifled me."[70] Certainly several future leaders of independent African nations felt that way as well.

To many non-Africans as well as to those opposed to Africa's traditional and customary practices, the talk against the imported Christian religion was the expected response of both the highly educated and the less educated, or the unenlightened, Africans. After all, as a way of finding anthropological reasons for every woe or shortcoming in the colonies, the Africans were seen as being both ungodly persons and animists who would worship anything. Yet, the truth was that these Africans still believed in God and shared most of the Christian beliefs with which they had been imbued.

Most nationalists, who might appear to be ungodly because of their anti-Christian assertions, had once either attended or taught in Christian missionary schools. In the early 1930s, for example, Nkrumah taught in the Catholic Seminary at Amissano, near Elmina[71] in the former Gold Coast before leaving for the United States in search of a college education, which included theological studies at the Lincoln Theological Seminary in Pennsylvania. Among the academic qualifications that he earned was the Bachelor of Sacred Theology degree, in 1942, for which Nkrumah graduated at the head of his class.[72] Later, in Nkrumah's adult life, he seemed to be frustrated with the Christian religion, including what he termed as "the strict discipline of Roman Catholicism."[73]

Yet, Nkrumah offered a further cogent explanation for his reaction in the following statement:

> It was not that I became any less religious but rather that I sought freedom in the worship of and communion with my God, for my God is a personal God and can only be reached direct. I do not find the need of, in fact I resent the intervention of a third party, in such a personal matter.[74]

Certainly, it is sometimes confusing to put a leader like Nkrumah in a specific ideological or religious mold. For, apart from his own 1957 written admission of being a Christian and a Marxist socialist, there were instances in his later life, particularly during his exile years in Conakry, Guinea (1966–1972), whereby he saw himself—as Kofi Buenor Hadjor quoted him as saying—only as "a convinced Marxist socialist."[75]

However, in discussing African religion—whether within the context of the colonial or postcolonial periods in African historical and political periods—many writers have tended to see the entire continent of Africa in monolithic terms. Instead of dealing with each region or nation on its own terms, some of the Euro-centric commentators have discussed such religious issues as if the continent is one entity. To deviate from that practice, especially since the African continent is a vast area of multiethnic and multicultural backgrounds, specific, brief, and very relevant examples of external religious influences on some African regions or nations will be offered in this book.

For example, the religious experiences of colonial and postcolonial Nigeria in the West Africa subregion have often raised thorny issues that have continued to cause a lot of anguish and even sectarian bloodshed. Various aspects of the Christian and Islamic religions have been researched in detail by several area scholars, from whose works this study plans to draw specific examples to buttress our independent research work and assertions.

For example, it has been shown that in Nigeria "the successful penetration of

Christianity began in southern Nigeria in 1842, with the arrival of the Wesleyan Mission Society (WMS) and the Church Missionary Society."[76] They were the first missionaries, but not the last, because several other expatriate Christian missions followed suit, "turning the region into a beehive of missionary work."[77]

Also, the modern religious conflagration and deadly clashes in Nigeria have their roots in the earlier ethnic suspicions and intolerance in the country. Nigeria, by all accounts, is considered a giant nation because of its size, well-educated human resources, population, and oil wealth. However, it has had its share in sectarian squabbles, although it is a historical fact that the Islamic religion was very successful, in the Kanem Borno Empire and, later, in the Hausa-speaking areas, in missionary work, since the eleventh century.[78]

However, the expeditions of the Christian missionaries to the Islamic northern areas of Nigeria were either unsuccessful or rebuffed because of "the deepseated fear of Christianity by the Islamic elite who regarded it [Christianity] as a subversive religion, and the ambivalence of the representatives of the Royal Niger Company (RNC) and later the colonial government."[79] An essay by Michael Amoah, a sociologist and theologian from Ghana, showed the early deep roots of both Christianity and Islam. He wrote:

> In the period before the 14th century, Christian activity on the African continent declined (although not to zero) because of the advent of Islam as the politico-religious power and dominant ideology. As Islam was challenged by another political power with the beginnings of European contact with Africa, Christianity revived.[80]

To Amoah, Africa deserves credit, for embracing various religions, especially Christianity. Hence, it is not surprising that religious issues have tended to take on sensitive and serious meanings in many places on the continent. Furthermore, Amoah went to the extent of making the controversial claim that "Christianity first of all went to Europe from Africa and that Judaism—the precursor of Christianity—does not originate from Europe, but from the geographical region currently known as the 'Middle East'."[81]

Interestingly, it is also a political fact that Nigeria has not been officially designated as an Islamic country but rather as a nonsectarian or nonreligious one. Yet several events there have often shown religious undertones, including the January 15, 1966 assassination of two major leading political leaders who were devout Muslims: the much-respected Prime Minister Alhaji Sir Tafawa Balewa and Alhaji Sir Ahmadu Bello, the Sardauna of Sokoto, who, as the leader of the Nigeria People's Congress (NPC) and Premier of Northern Nigeria, has been described as an Islamic crusader. Consequently, Muslim nations in and outside of Africa showed their open anger.[82] To translate the anger into action, therefore, in the Sudanese capital of Khartoum, a Muslim group staged a public protest at the Nigerian Embassy, describing the two dead men as Islamic martyrs who, as they claimed, had been killed by Zionism and imperialism. Also, in Egypt, the Cairo-based national radio station referred to the first Nigerian military coup d'etat as a "Kafferi onslaught" on Nigeria's main Islamic region or citadel.[83]

It is always very significant to cite Nigeria's Christian-Islamic divide because it is such an explosive issue that the two early coups in the country had religious undertones. The first coup, in January 1966, was seen as having been led by Christian army officers from the southern belt of the country; the second coup in July 1966—although led by General Gowon, a thoroughbred Christian—was, however, seen as having been Muslim-inspired because he was born and brought up in the-then Islamic northern region of Nigeria.

It is, however, an undeniable fact that religion played a role in the deep-seated problems that prompted the young army officers of Nigeria, in 1966, to over-throw elected Prime Minister Balewa's regime. Mr. Okion Ojigbo, the former Principal Private Secretary to then retired General Olusegun Obasanjo, put it well when he offered the explanation that problems other than religiosity nearly dismembered his country. In his study of Nigeria's first Republic, which lasted from 1960 to 1966, he explained that "teething problems of nationhood, mostly revolving round the issue of power-sharing, had brought Nigeria to the brink of fragmentation and disintegration after independence in October 1960."[84]

Ojigbo further explained that the immediate problems of Nigeria in the 1960s had religious undertones in terms of the years' coup officers but, indeed, that religion was not the main predicating issue at stake. This assertion is in line with the popular contention of many Nigerians and several experts, who write that, as a unified nation, Nigeria is too big to be governed from the center by an individual political leader. Again, Ojigbo was on target when he added:

> The most pressing issues of nation-building which Nigeria faced were the question of defining the new nation and the consequent issue of creating an effectively integrated polity. This was because the concept of the nation among Nigerians, as in many Third World countries, was still largely elu-sive and unconcretized—indeed fragmentary.[85]

As eloquently illustrated by Professor Rupert Emerson, it is the problem of chasing not religiosity per se, but a nonexistent nation that has led to the issues that would bring about the downfall of many countries in Africa and in other Third World nations. Emerson axiomatically uses the illustration of making a rabbit pie, whereby one first needs to catch the rabbit, adding that it is by the same token that, to engage in nation-building, one must first find the nation.[86] Ojigbo, in relying on Emerson's earlier assertion within the context of African political history, made the observation that "this is likely to be a more hazardous and uncertain venture than anywhere else."[87]

Certainly, religion has played a very decisive role in the evolution of many African nations, but it is still not correct historically or politically to assert that all crippling problems on the African continent have had their teething roots in religious missions and their leaders. A leading and prolific African historian, Pro-fessor J. F. Ade Ajayi, has estimated in his own pioneering study on Africa's Christian religion that Christianity was imported into Nigeria, for example, about half a century "before the establishment of British rule in Nigeria."[88] In observing religious trends, many Africans have wondered if the Christians came to prepare the way for the active colonialism that followed!

Professor Ajayi added:

1841, the year of the first Niger Expedition, marked the beginning of the movement to re-establish Christianity in this country [Nigeria], following the failure of earlier Catholic missions in Benin and Warri. 1891, the year of Bishop [Samuel Ajayi] Crowther's death, marked the end of the first phase of this new movement, the phase when the success of the missionary enterprise was associated largely with the creation and the encouragement of a Western-educated and Christian middle class. For the history of Christian missions in Nigeria, the first phase was only the "seedling" time in preparation for the great expansion that came later with British rule.[89]

In the West Africa subregion, Liberia is another nation in which the indigenous citizenry saw religious movements as playing major and even intertwining roles in its national evolution. Liberia-born Professor Amos J. Beyan of Youngstown State University, Ohio, offered a major perspective in his 1991 study, which showed the admixture of the development of political, economic, as well as religious institutions in his birth country. In his view, those institutions "were largely extensions of the institutional values inherent in the ACS [American Colonization Society] and the economic and social forces at work on the coastal region that became Liberia in the nineteenth century."[90]

Beyan and officials of the American Colonization Society (ACS) have documented that it was in November of 1817 that the society appointed Reverend Samuel J. Mills, to be accompanied by Ebenezer Burgess, a mathematician, to travel to West Africa, via London, to help "locate a suitable site for the proposed colony."[91] Traveling from Britain in November 1817 on the ship *SS Electra,* Mills and Burgess, on March 13, 1818, arrived in the West African coastal nation of Gambia, where "they saw a few European missionaries converting the coastal Gambians to Christianity."[92] Gambia, which, as discussed elsewhere in this book, has also fallen prey to Africa's incessant coups d'etat, was, as author Alex Haley made famous in *Roots,* one of the "gold mines" for the capture of Blacks for enslavement during active slavery.[93]

Although Christianity and Islam became the dominant religions in several areas of Africa, it is also a fact that the indigenous African populations, often referred to negatively as "natives", had their own traditional religions within the context of animism, not necessarily the same thing as paganism. It was, therefore, not very surprising that upon their arrival in Sierra Leone on March 20, 1818, via Gambia, Mills and Burgess were amazed by the indigenous religious practices of the native Sierra Leoneans. To show official connections back home, both men had expected to present a favorable letter of introduction from Earl Bathurst (whose name had been given to the early capital of Gambia) to the governor at the time, Sir Charles McCarthy, who was out of Sierra Leone upon the two voyagers' arrival. Mills, according to an 1818 ACS report, wrote that they saw on the mountains of the West African nation "altars that the natives had dedicated to the devils."[94] Therefore, he subsequently predicted that such non-Christian altars would fail "before the temples of the living God, like the image of Dagon before the ark [of Noah]."[95]

The available records, including those of the ACS, have shown that the notion of American manumitted freed slaves being shipped back to settle in West Africa, particularly Liberia, dates back to 1714. This factor has also been recorded by Professors John Hope Franklin and Alfred A. Moss, Jr., in their coauthored cele-brated study, *From Slavery To Freedom* (1998). Among other details, Franklin and Moss wrote that "as early as 1714 a 'native American,' believed to be a resident of New Jersey, had proposed sending Blacks back to Africa."[96] They added that the idea did not die with its originators, as "in 1777 a Virginia legislative com-mittee, headed by Thomas Jefferson, set forth a plan of gradual emancipation and deportation."[97]

Professors Franklin and Moss, as well as A. B. Assensoh, have, in their respec-tive studies, confirmed the active role played in the early "Back to Africa" move-ment by a prominent black shipowner from New England, Paul Cuffe (whose surname was sometimes spelled as Coffie, and derived from the Akan name of *Kofi* from Ghana). As reported, Cuffe as early as 1815 transported 38 freed slaves from America to West Africa at his own expense,[98] an act followed by Bishop Daniel Coker of the African Episcopal Church in 1820, who sailed with 90 other freed slaves to West Africa.[99] Since the number of these manumitted slaves was not huge, no big deal was made in the history records of their arrival in either Sierra Leone or Liberia.

Specifically, it was in 1851 that freed slaves from America—who would be called Americo-Liberians—began to travel directly to Liberia. For example, Augustus Washington, a wealthy black businessman, in that year left America for Liberia. On the eve of his departure, with many other freed slaves, he blasted the U.S. government, as he declared publicly that he "was leaving [for Africa] to escape from the prevalent racial injustice in the country of his birth."[100] Num-bering about 1,420, these Blacks who first traveled directly to Liberia as Americo-Liberians received so much material support from the political admin-istration of American President James Monroe that, as recorded by Assensoh and Franklin and Moss, the capital of Liberia was later named Monrovia.[101]

Indeed, the importance that religion played in all aspects of the lives of the new black arrivals in the former colonies of Africa had roots in the fact that most of the arriving manumitted slaves, called "expatriates" by other Blacks that they encoun-tered, happened to be either Christians or Muslims, putting both religions on equal footing in the new worlds. Circumstances in worshiping situations in sev-eral West African and North African countries would offer ample examples of the religiosity of these men and women. In the specific instance of Liberia, Pro-fessor Beyan has confirmed how "many observers [had] noted the tremendous impact of American religious values on nineteenth century Liberia."[102]

In fact, Sir Harry Johnston, a British specialist on Africa and later a colonial administrator, observed the following in his 1906 study of the impact of religion on Liberia:

With a few rare exceptions, the America-Liberian community suffers from religiosity. They are Episcopalians, Methodists, Baptists, Presbyterians, Lutherans, Zionists, and so forth. . . . They exhibit the puritanism of New England in the eighteenth century almost unabated. Their average morality is probably no higher than that of the European nations or even of the Negroes indigenous to Liberia. But so far as outward behavior, laws, and languages go, they are prudish to a truly American extent. . . . The America-Liberian still worships cloths as an outward and visible manifestation of Christianity and the best civilization.[103]

The Americo-Liberians wanted to make sure that their American values, particularly where the Christian religion was concerned, were made manifest so that the "natives" that they came to rule would benefit from and adopt their values (among these natives were such ethnic or tribal groups as the Kru, Krahn, Kpelle, Vai, and Grebo). At least the imposition of the Christian religion on the natives helped make life a lot easier for all, as Nigeria's first indigenous president, Dr. Nnamdi Azikiwe, in his pioneering 1934 study on Liberia, confirmed several aspects of the foregoing details. Also, in terms of the colonization of the West African nation, Dr. Azikiwe concluded: "It was by no means an easy task [for the Americo-Liberians] to colonize in those days."[104]

Finally, the Americo-Liberians had made up their minds to settle in Liberia and make it their home. To them, it was the only place that, given the prevailing circumstances, they could aspire to national leadership and international prominence. Therefore, it was in their best interests to ensure that lasting Christian values and civility were put in place from the beginning, as a way of influencing the native Liberians to love their neighbors as themselves. In fact, Azikiwe underscored how the native Liberians—or, in his own words, the "pristine inhabitants" of the country—showed an incessant hostility toward the Americo-Liberians. However, Americo-Liberian Elijah Johnson had the boldness to say about his arrival in Liberia from Fourah Bay, Sierra Leone: "For two long years have I sought a home; here I have found one; here I remain."[105] This showed that, in spite of the reported hostilities showed by the native population, the freed slaves felt much more at home than they had in America.

As shown by the prevailing facts, the Americo-Liberians did import Christianity to their new home in Liberia, but they did not necessarily continue to practice it. Instead, in trying to accommodate their hosts (native Liberians), and to blend into the indigenous culture, some of the leading officials in business and government allegedly got involved in typical traditional practices already in existence in the country, including human sacrifices and outright ritual murders. They believed that such events would help them to secure and eventually fortify high governmental positions. These anti-Christian practices have continued from the 1800s to present-day Liberia. In fact, the issue of human sacrifice got so out of hand that, in 1974, it was alleged that the Liberian President William R. Tolbert, Jr., had direct involvement in investigating such murders. As reported by the *Liberian Star,* newspaper of Monrovia, "President Tolbert had urged the Superintendent of Marshall Territory, F. O., Lawrence, to investigate the alleged ritual murders of some persons who got drowned in the Farmington River in the territory."[106]

About the wanton murders of innocent Liberians by those in authority for ritual purposes, it was further reported:

> And last month, the ruling True Whig Party bi-weekly newspaper, *The Liberian Age*, reported the discovery of the mutilated remains of one of two men who had mysteriously disappeared in Harper City. The newspaper reported that the abdomen had been removed from the body. . . . The story that is going the rounds is that the alleged reluctance of the [Liberian] authorities to give publicity to a whole series of ritual murders stems not only from a natural unwillingness to wash Liberia's dirty linen in public but also because of the motives for some of the murders. It is said that the mutilated bodies are being used to supply essential ingredients for black magic rites aimed at advancing the chances of certain politicians— including some prominent ones—in the nominations and elections due next year.[107]

In Liberia, the spate of ritualistic murders was allegedly black magic and other traditional or customary practices. Murders reached such high proportions that President Tolbert decided to take further stringent measures to abate them. That led to the arrest, prosecution, and conviction of several prominent persons and even leading governmental officers, including the eventual hanging of a county superintendent (whose title was similar to a state governor in America). President Tolbert was so serious about upholding Liberian laws dealing with ritual murder that he signed many death warrants, sanctioning the hanging of several convicted murderers; in 1971, he approved the public hanging of Dr. Justin Molokai Obi, a Nigerian chemistry professor at Cuttington University College in Suaccoco, Liberia, for murdering Episcopal Bishop Browne in Monrovia.[108]

Unfortunately, observers and critics of the ruling True Whig Party regime felt that President Tolbert, the son of Americo-Liberians, sanctioned the public hangings of convicted murderers to put fear in his political opponents and would-be coup plotters. Such criticism not withstanding, as an ordained Baptist Minister and onetime President of the World Baptist Alliance, Tolbert's sanctioning of the public hanging of Dr. Obi was reportedly a popular action that pleased Christians in Liberia. After all, Obi was convicted of murdering resident African-American Episcopal Bishop Browne, an American citizen, during Tubman's administration; he remained on death row for several years. His 1971 hanging, which was a horrible scene, as coauthor Assensoh observed it, was aimed at placating or pleasing the Liberia-based foreign clergy and, as rumored, the United States government.[109]

It is very essential to point out that Liberia was not the only African nation that was rife with ritualistic murders, as Guinea, under President Sekou Toure's leadership, Nigeria on various occasions, and other countries on the continent had their share of the problem. Many of these murderous activities were shrouded in both secrecy and cult violence. However, Liberia was also famous for the high-profile role that Freemasonry, or Masonic activities, generally played in local politics. The late Professor Tuan Wreh reported in *The Love of Liberty* (1976) that "The role of freemasonry in Liberian politics since the founding of the nation in 1847 and up to the end of the Tubman Administration cannot be underestimated."[110] Where ritual murders were concerned, Masonic murders were erroneusly suspected of involvement before the 1980 coup.

Although Freemasonry (specifically Prince Hall Masonry in the case of Liberia) was a social and service-oriented organization in America and other Western societies, it took on a different political meaning in Liberia. (It was popular only before the April 1980 military coup d'etat that toppled Americo-Liberian political and administrative leadership in the country.) Wreh further observed:

> Freemasonry used to be the exclusive preserve of the light-skinned [biracial] settler group to whom political power fell, by virtue of their superior education and connection with the American Colonization Society, when Liberia declared itself a sovereign and independent State.[111]

Indigenous Liberians—including Wreh, who was from the Kru ethnic group— were not happy with the Freemasonry influence in Liberian politics in particular and national affairs in general. Wreh, as the grandson of Kru Paramount Chief Doe Te Tuan Nyanati of Sasstown, Liberia, felt that, by its constitution, Freemasonry was a highly discriminatory organization in that only those who were highly connected with certain influential light-skinned families and who also occupied top governmental positions were encouraged to join. He added that just as the biracial population of Americo-Liberians readily controlled successive Liberian governments, from the 1847 regime of the first president Joseph Jenkins Roberts, to the end of the 1870 administration of the fourth president, James Spriggs Payne, biracial persons firmly dominated the Masonic fraternity organization and, basically, utilized it as an extension of their political prowess.[112]

On the political scene, Professor Wreh added:

> When concerted action at the polls by the dark-skinned settlers and the coming to power of the Fifth President, Edward James Roye, the first dark-skinned settler to hold the presidential office, broke the mulatto hegemony, freemasonry ceased to be the exclusive preserve of the mulatto settlers. . . . The masonic roster is shot through with such names as Tubman, Tolbert, DeShield, Cooper, Harris, Martin, Mitchell, Gibson, Pierre, Greene, Goodridge, Grigsby, Richardson, Grimes, Tyler, Stubblefield, Richards, Phillips, Duncan among others—descendants of the settler group who have served and are still serving as cabinet ministers, senators, representatives, judges and military commanders.[113]

Indeed, it was not only the Christian presence that constituted the religious influence of Africa's colonial era, as the Islamic (Muslim or Moslem) presence was evident in various places on the African continent. Toward that end, when French colonial interests called for additional expeditions in the 1890s, the main reason, as Professor Obichere described, was "to occupy effectively the territory lying between the eastern and western lines of posts already established."[114] There was an earlier fear of Muslim resistance, which did not take place.

As confirmed by other scholars, even during this period of authorized expeditions by the French authorities, there were already Islamic activities in the Niger area that the French expeditionary force, led by French Governor Victor Ballot, encountered.[115] However, similar to the opposition to Christianity in several areas of Africa, Obichere and other writers have shown that although Islam was, for example, notably making a very serious progress in the area that the late UCLA professor termed as on the right bank of the Niger River, the indigenous populace—described by him as the "fetishist" populations—still opposed it. The reason was that, like the receptive attitude of the colonized people in the Niger area to French civilization,[116] many other Africans in the colonies preferred the imported civilization, including Christianity, of the colonialists.

Apart from the Christian and Islamic religions, there were several animistic and African traditional practices that researchers like Professors John Mbiti[117] and J. Jahn, a German, have discussed in various studies. In fact, even during years of enslavement in America, some of these practices were prevalent, hence Jahn has documented that there was an interrelatedness between religion and the early politics.[118]

Jahn went on to reveal that during slave times such traditional dances, within the context of what he termed "voodooism," had their cultural value or political side, stating that these "dances were all the slaves had to remind them of their home. . . . In their possession, surrendered to the old gods, for a short time they could feel themselves free once more. Where they could come together to be near to Africa."[119] Such traditional practices were so deeply seated in the black culture during slave times that, in the words of Jahn, even "their enforced baptism after the most superficial instruction in the Catholic faith could not replace the old gods. And the more the slave-owners suppressed and punished the dancers, the dearer, the more sacred did they become to the slaves."[120]

Historically, it has been demonstrated that for Blacks both in Africa and during enslavement, traditional religious ways—including what Western writers have labeled voodoo practice—were liberating forces. Hence Jahn documented a particular August 14, 1791 rebellious incident in Haiti: A slave by the name of Boukman came to Haiti through Jamaica, and his master, Turpin, found him to be so good, or herculean, that he made him an overseer and a coachman. Reportedly, "Boukman came into contact with many slaves, swore them in, and at a Voodoo ceremony in the night of 14 August 1791 gave the signal to rebel, which after twelve years of war led to the liberty of Haiti. And when the war years were over the African cult and the African gods gave the fighters the courage, toughness and faith which were necessary to inflict upon the First Consul Napoleon Bonaparte his first defeat."[121]

An Overview

From all this information, therefore, we can see that it is not very unusual that emancipated slaves from America came to Liberia as Americo-Liberians and inherited the mantle of the nation's political leadership; they brought with them the Christian religion. Yet, it is also a known fact that some of them, for ritualis-tic and black magic reasons, did resort to ritual murders that, as reported in 1974 by the London-based *Africa Confidential* periodical, President Tolbert became so worried about—as earlier reported in detail—that he had to take a firm action to either minimize or stop them outright.[122]

The apparent existence of magical powers, as they apply to African religious practices, has been documented by other researchers. In Kenyan President Jomo Kenyatta's University of London anthropological study, *Facing Mount Kenya* (1965), he discussed several aspects of African magic. In fact, he devoted an entire chapter to the subject.[123] For Kenyatta, who died in 1978, African magic was a form of religion.

While African traditional religious practices vary, especially from country to country, Oberlin College Professor Calvin C. Hernton noted in 1990 that Jahn defined in his book *Muntu* the four basic categories and two basic principles of traditional religions—Muntu, Kintu, Hantu, Kuntu, NTU, Nommo—plus all the sub-categories and other concepts and principles. Hernton described Jahn's work as "a cartography of traditional African and neo-African culture"[124] that has complemented other African and Christo-Islamic studies by John Mbiti, Ghanaian Catholic Bishop Peter K. Sarpong, and several other authors. At least, these studies have helped in shedding positive light on several aspects of African traditional practices. These practices, in addition to the discussed pervading impact of the Christian religion, are also discussed by historians Adu Boahen and Ade Ajayi.

In his 1987 study, Dr. Adu Boahen has confirmed that, by 1880, "all the vari-ous activities of Christian missionary societies had a profound impact on African societies."[125] Among what Adu Boahen saw as part of the positive aspects of the imported missionary activities were the changing of the economic standards of living of the converted Africans, access of the converts to modern medicine as well as Western-style houses, modernization of marital ties, and, access to West-ern education.[126]

As expected, many radical African scholars wonder about the usefulness and, therefore, the positivity of Adu Boahen's insistence that Africans, converted to Christianity, begin the practice of monogamous marriages and, also, began "feel-ing contemptuous of their own traditional institutions, their traditional polyga-mous system of marriage, and their traditional religion."[127] However, what some of the radical proponents of African traditions tend to forget, in colonial and postcolonial African contexts, is that, by practicing monogamous marriages, Christianized African couples were introduced to a "natural way" of benefiting from birth control. In polygamous relationships with multiple wives from which countless children were produced, many male Africans were unable to adequately economically provide for their families. This circumstance is unlike the Mus-lims, whose holy Koran allowed them to have up to four wives only if the husband had the economic means to meet their needs and to take care of the expected offspring.

In fact, in her journeys to Africa and Great Britain to complete research for this publication,[128] Dr. Alex-Assensoh took an extra interest in this aspect of African tradition because of her own African-American as well as Judeo-Christian background, whereby polygamous marriages were an anathema, in her opinion, to civilized and Christian ways of living. She wondered how one man could, possibly, marry more than one wife under African customs or traditions, have so many children and still be happy.

Although there were occasional tensions and petty jealousies among the wives and children in African polygamous relationships, what we saw in our research was that many polygamous husbands had to be efficient managers of their households, particularly in their earning capacities, in order to take care of their immediate as well as extended families within African settings (the wives lived in separate homes or on farms owned by the husband). In that context, the men worked hard with their multiple families to earn their keep, and, the head wife, often the oldest of the many wives, served as the "captain" or the "over-seer" of the household. This head wife assembled the wives at the end of each month to give them instructions, including specific dates or days on which they would be (or sleep) with the husband.[129]

Invariably, there have been endless debates about African indigenous and traditional institutions and practices as they cross paths with imported or innovative Christian practices. Pouring libation, for example, is mostly done by African traditional rulers, but it is also a traditional practice in Africa for which some Christians and many non-Christians have often found utility. According to Michael Amoah, in his recently published essay, the roots of libation pouring can be "traced back as far as the Bronze Age, an era from which libation pitchers and bowls have been discovered during excavations."[130]

As a traditional religious practice, similar to other practices with controversy surrounding them, Amoah has generously underscored for its readers his implications and importance, and how it is done, in the following words:

> Libation is one of the oldest and, perhaps, least understood of religious rituals. It consists of the sacrificial pouring out of liquid. Its importance seems to lie in the act of pouring, as the liquids that are poured out (wine, milk, honey, water, oil or, in some cases, blood) as well as the places where the ceremony is performed (on the ground, into chasms, upon the altar, over the sacrificial victim, into a sacrificial bowl) vary considerably. . . . The word "libation" is derived from the Latin "libatio" ('sacrificial offering of drink'). The word is connected with the Greek noun "loibe" (libation) and the verb "leib" (to pour out libation), used since Homer. . . . The meaning of libation offering can vary as much as the way in which it is performed.[131]

In spite of the fact that libation is neither highly regarded nor practiced among many African intellectuals, especially those with Christian roots or training, some of the postcolonial leaders, in spite of their religious affiliations, dabbled in it. Although many colonial officials and Christian missionaries did everything to undermine such traditional practices, the first indigenous president of Ghana, Western-educated Nkrumah, allowed some of the practices at public functions.

Back in America, in 1943, Nkrumah got into very serious trouble with his theology professors at Lincoln Theological Seminary in Pennsylvania for traveling to North Carolina to participate in a libation-pouring ceremony that was described by the university officials as "heathen." Nkrumah angered the institution's Christian authorities by visiting the Salisbury, North Carolina grave site of Dr. James Emman Kwegyir Aggrey, one of the pioneers of America-trained African scholars who worked in North Carolina. Dr. Aggrey, a graduate of Livingstone College in Salisbury and of Columbia University in New York, was buried in North Carolina after dying suddenly in New York on July 30, 1927 of pneumococcus meningitis.[132]

Nkrumah had been a student of Dr. Aggrey's back in the former Gold Coast, at Achimota College, where Dr. Aggrey served as a vice-principals. As an ardent admirer of the pioneering African educator and scholar, Nkrumah in 1957 confirmed Aggrey's influence on him in these words, "It was because of my great admiration for Aggrey, both as a man and a scholar, that I first formed the idea of furthering my studies in the United States of America."[133] Therefore, as a student in Pennsylvania, the future Ghanaian president, Nkrumah, and several other African students paid a pilgrimage visit to the grave, where they poured libations to urge "the soul of Aggrey to get out of the grave and go to Africa to rest more peacefully."[134]

Lincoln Seminary Dean George Johnson, an admirer of Nkrumah, often regarded him as being very religious. This time, however, he was very much disappointed when he read from the African students' campus newspaper, *The Interpreter*, that Nkrumah was among those who did the libation pouring in his capacity as the president of the African Students Association of America and Canada. The seminary dean showed his disappointment in a letter to Nkrumah dated April 3, 1943, in which he condemned the libation pouring as part of African funeral rites. Dean Johnson was concerned about Nkrumah as a Christian, spelling out in his letter that to "perform such after taking vows for licensure in our Church passes my understanding."[135]

Dean Johnson, went on to describe libation pouring as being a heathen ceremony, adding:

When we recall the terrific damage to the African that Animism has caused, it is imperative that we who profess ourselves Christians should give no encouragement to it. We should stand fast in the liberty [from superstition] wherewith Christ has made us free, and be not entangled again in the yoke of bondage.[136]

In response to Dean Johnson's very long letter, Nkrumah sent only a terse response dated April 24, 1943, which was also published in *The African Interpreter*:

You seem to have misunderstood me partially and you are right at that if all your reasons are culled from the report in *The Interpreter*. May I say, however, that to meet Christ on the highway of Christian ethics and principles by way of Christian salvation, and turn back is a spiritual impossibility. The burden of my life is to live such a way that I may become a living symbol of all that is best both in Christianity and in the laws, customs and beliefs of my people. I am a Christian and will ever remain so, but never a blind Christian.[137]

As we noticed in our research for this book, there can be a lot of misunderstanding where African customs and traditions are concerned, especially from the perspectives or standpoints of Western scholars and, in colonialized Africa, where colonial authorities with Christian morals were concerned. It is, however, noteworthy that while African customs and traditions were clashing with mainstream Christian activities or values in various areas of the continent and even in overseas nations—when Africans sought to exercise their beliefs, like Nkrumah's case in America—very determined African Christian leaders, based on the continent, invariably used the Christian religion for liberation purposes. An example happened to be the circumstances of the Kitawala and Kimbanguist Churches, which were established in the 1920s in what used to be called the Belgian Congo, mainly to bring socio-Christian and even political awareness to their followers. Indeed, when Simon Kimbangu, an ordained Catechist, established the Kimbanguist Church in 1921 and declared that he was a messenger (or emissary) of God, he also declared publicly that he had been sent by God "to deliver Africans from colonial rule."[138]

Similar to the cases of several other prominent African traditional and religious leaders who were exiled but not imprisoned by colonial administrations and had troops occupy their areas of authority, Kimbangu was arrested in September 1921 and exiled to the Katanga area of the Congo, thus alienated by the colonial leaders. He died there in the early 1950s. Also, King Prempeh I of the Asante people, East Africa's King Kabarega, and several of their royal aides were deported by colonial officials to the Seychelles Islands in early 1900s.[139]

When postcolonial *African* leaders used political detentions without trial to undermine their opponent's popularity and political strength, former *colonial* rulers decried the method. In Ghana, for example, Nana Ofori Atta I, the Okyehene (prominent paramount chief), for political reasons, suffered what is known as internal exile; while in exile, he was succeeded by Nana Ofori Atta II, born in 1898, as Okyehene. The late Kwame Kesse-Adu, a Ghanaian journalist from the chief's area, has catalogued most of these political abuses in his book, *The Politics of Political Detention* (1971), and he was himself a victim of one of Nkrumah's political detentions.[140]

Some Christian religious leaders, including the late Reverend J. Damuah, a radical Ghanaian Catholic priest, suffered under what came to be known as the Preventive Detention Act (PDA) of the Nkrumah regime. Under it an expatriate Anglican Bishop was also deported from Ghana. Apart from Ghanaian critics escaping into exile, foreigners were also deported, including Bankole Timothy, a Sierra Leonean journalist who was among the early biographers of Nkrumah. In Timothy's 1981 book, he wrote extensively about how he worked in Accra, the capital of Ghana, writing for local newspapers as a journalist. He was arrested and deported from Ghana under the new post-independence laws, which allowed newly elected African leaders to arrest and detain their own citizens without trial and also to deport foreigners.[141]

Apart from the Nkrumah regime, the postcolonial administrations of Kenya's President Jomo Kenyatta and then Tanzanian President Julius K. Nyerere used similar measures "to tame their opponents," and that "in fact, what happened in Ghana and Kenya in terms of political detention was more like what Nyerere practiced in Tanzania."[142] However, it is also important to underscore that several of the post-independence African leaders did not waste time in pointing out that the new repressive measures that they adopted were for genuine security reasons, and that such measures had earlier been introduced in India and also in Northern Ireland by the British to suppress terrorist activities.[143]

Above all, it is important to point out that although several studies have amply demonstrated that expatriate religious organizations in Africa meant well in a variety of ways, Africans still had very cogent reasons to suspect their motives both during colonial rule and after independence was attained. As Arizona State University History Professor Andrew E. Barnes points out in a 1997 study, colonial education (interrelated with religion) played a major role in European colonialism to the extent that "scholars, seeking to identify the cultural impact of European colonialism on African societies, have left out relatively unexamined one very important source [cultural education] for understanding European thought and action."[144]

Certainly, Barnes agrees that colonial school systems enrolled only a small portion of the indigenous populace and that only a few of such schools existed to offer any meaningful or coherent programs of study, yet in colonial Africa "the educational policy behind these systems was invariably a blue print for the construction of future society."[145] Furthermore, Barnes demonstrates, with specific examples from Nigeria, how colonial educational policy was not very much different from other colonial policies, although—in his opinion—"a striking example of educational policy serving to give focus to broader schemes of cultural engineering can be seen in colonial Northern Nigeria, where the British government sought to encapsulate in an education program for the region's Muslim elite the social processes perceived to have contributed to the formation of elite values in the graduates of England's public schools."[146]

In colonial Africa, education was, therefore, a crucial issue, hence Professor Barnes—again using the Nigerian example for illustration—added that "officially, the battle over educational policy in Northern Nigeria took the form of a debate over the amalgamation of the Northern and Southern Nigerian Departments of Education under a director who would be answerable to the governor in Lagos."[147] Interestingly, one can today see the roots of the British calculation of creating a leadership class for Nigeria in a small group of educated northern citizens. This a situation has ensured that northern Nigerians would continue to dominate Nigeria in a variety of ways, controlling even the army, which has been used since January 1966 to make political changes through coups d'etat.

Barnes confirms the foregoing situation by reiterating:

The [colonial] government hoped that the students who emerged from the Northern Nigerian school system would provide the leading edge for a modern and aristocratic Anglo-Muslim civilization. The successful creation of an aristocratic civilization would in turn preclude the need for Christian missionaries and their African converts to introduce bourgeois values into the region. In order for the program to mature and produce results, the government proscribed Christian proselytization in the Muslim-dominated portions of the region, while severely limiting the activities of Christian missionaries in other areas.[148]

As has been seen, various Christian missionary organizations, including the Church Missionary Society (CMS) and the Presbyterian, Catholic, and Methodist churches, concentrated in establishing educational institutions in several colonial African nations. This was done to ensure that Christian education was offered as part of the so-called "civilizing mission," as well as to limit the establishment of schools like the Nigeria-based Abinisi Pagan school, whose principal said unequivocally that "the time was not ripe to introduce the boys [of his school] to Christianity, but the goal of the school was, instead, to teach the boys, 'how to play the game'."[149] By game, he meant political and traditional affairs, such as ancestral worship and the pouring of libation.

Indeed, even on the eve of the twenty-first century, many of Africa's intellectuals and some traditional leaders still harbor the feeling that Christian missionaries were not as good for the people in the colonies as have been evaluated from Eurocentric perspectives. For example, Baffour Ankomah, a London-based Ghanaian journalist, in May 1998 wrote dispassionately about colonialism in his "Baffour Beefs" column for the New African Magazine of London, of which he is now the editor. In his opinion, Africans know what price they paid "when the Europeans arrived on our shores 400 years ago with bagfuls of 'good intentions'. We saw their Bible, but sadly we didn't see the sword they had in their other hand. Today, we know what the those 'good intentions' have done to our race, our self-esteem, our culture, our politics, our economies, our nations."[150]

Citing further examples of what colonialism has done to Africa, in particular the circumstances of the Republic of Congo (the former Zaire) after the rule of President Mobutu, Ankomah went on to estimate some of the woes that the Bible-wielding colonialists visited on Africans:

Today we [Africans] have become a begging race. From Africa to Britain, from America to Brazil, from Australia to the Caribbean, Africans and people of African descent are always at the bottom of the pile, down-trodden. While others are landing sophisticated crafts on Mars, Africa (with the largest pool of the world's still unexploited natural resources) has become so poor that we can afford a Mars bar [chocolate bar] only at the mercy of a World Bank and an IMF controlled by people who scarcely know our countries and our way of life. Last year, Chester Crocker, the former U.S. Assistant Secretary of State for African Affairs under President Reagan, arrogantly declared: "We and our friends control the keys to the clubs and the treasuries that Kabila [Congo late leader] will need to tap, if he is going to rebuild the country." Brutal, but it was the truth! The whole truth.[151]

After Africa's Active Colonization: Decolonization, Neocolonization, Freedom, Redemption, or Neoslavery?

The following statement is very helpful as we begin a discussion the subheading above:

> The first and the most important of the economic changes that had occurred in Africa by 1880 was the abolition and suppression of that most inhuman and abominable of all trading activities—namely, the slave trade—and its replacement by trade in natural products, which has become known in typical Eurocentric terms as legitimate trade.[152]

Also, the following pronouncements, culled from two separate sources, offer an elucidation of the definition of slavery:

> At this point we may offer a preliminary definition of slavery on the level of personal relations: slavery is the permanent, violent domination of natally alienated and generally dishonored persons.[153]
>   Perhaps the most frequently cited definition [of slavery] is that given by the League of Nations committee on slavery: "the status or condition of a person over whom any or all the powers attaching to the right of ownership are exercised."[154]

The first quotation is from Professor Adu Boahen's 1987 study, which offers indigenous perspectives on colonialism. It explains the "most inhuman and abominable" nature of the slave trade and how that terrible trade was replaced by trade in natural products. Consequently, it is the conclusion of critics of tyrannical and dictatorial rule in Africa that any attempts by either new leaders of postcolonial Africa or neocolonialists to treat Africans after the dawn of modern independence—specifically, since 1957—with any form of inhumanity and abomination should, indeed, be tantamount to a form of slavery. Indeed, there are ample examples of foreign acts in various post-independence African nations that could be measured by the foregoing definitions.

The follow-up quote, from Harvard sociology Professor Orlando Patterson, citing the erstwhile League of Nations' April 5, 1938 report of its Advisory Committee of Experts on Slavery, also provides definitions of and an expansion on what might constitute enslavement of one person by another. Using these working definitions of slavery, we should be able to assess the plight and overall circumstances of postcolonial Africans to see if there are any lingering elements of slavery. Also, as some observers of modern African independence have opined, it is helpful to use these definitions to ascertain whether or not ordinary citizens of African countries fare better today, when, to a large extent, their own kith and kin are in political control of the ships of state as well as in command of the national economies.

Most certainly, it is not an exaggeration to conclude that almost all nations of Africa tasted either direct or indirect colonial domination. The only limited exceptions are two countries named in University of Wisconsin Professor Crawford Young's contention that "Africa, by the early twentieth century—save Ethiopia and Liberia—was reconfigured into colonial space."[155]

Even so, Ethiopia and Liberia were not seen in any flattering terms, as Dr. Young further added that Ethiopia could easily be described as "a sub-imperial polity," and Liberia as "a precarious polity subsisting by American patronage and Franco-British sufferance, loosely managed by a small *America-Liberian* minority; that, of course, was before the April 1980 coup led by a soldier of the native ethnic stock.[156]

Africans who were very familiar with the internal politics of Ethiopia and Liberia, before their respective coups d'etat, would agree with Young that, certainly, the two nations—which often prided themselves in the 1950–1960 period as having received their freedom charters on silver platters—left much to be desired, especially where true African independence, freedom, and justice were concerned.

It has conclusively been shown that at the 1896 Battle of Adowa, the invading Italian forces were crushed by Ethiopia's poorly armed but motivated and highly-spirited nationalist forces in protection of the ruling imperial dynasty. Yet, after the successful 1935 Italian invasion and the subsequent settlement negotiated by the League of Nations, dynastic Ethiopia never divorced itself completely from Italo-European control throughout the long administration of Emperor Haile Selassie, whose official titles included "His Imperial Majesty" and "The Lion of Judah."

Liberia was not very much different where neocolonialism and continued foreign domination were concerned, yet Nkrumah expressed surprise at seeing non–Blacks in government during and after his state visit to Liberia in January 1953 aboard the late President William V. S. Tubman's presidential yacht, which was named *S.S. President Edward J. Roye* and commanded by an all-Dutch crew. It was, unbelievably, a lifestyle of opulence or sheer luxury when aboard the ship on the high seas. Certainly, it was a lifestyle that a developing nation, without the active support of a major capitalist nation, could hardly afford, a fact Nkrumah expressed to Kojo Botsio, a close aide and a cabinet member in his government who, incidentally, was sharing a cabin with him aboard the luxurious yacht. Botsio died recently in Ghana.[157]

For various reasons, indigenous Liberian men, enlisted in the country's armed forces, and led by a master-sergeant from the Krahn ethnic group, led a bloody uprising in April 1980 to topple the country's Americo-Liberian regime and assassinated its leader, President Tolbert. The angry "natives," as they were contemptuously called in the international news media, did not appreciate their demeaning lot and circumstances, compared to the opulent and extravagant circumstances of the Americo-Liberian leadership. In 1957, however, Nkrumah felt that Tubman, an Americo-Liberian and as a national leader, had made a difference in Liberian politics, as Nkrumah spells out in this account of his official visit to Liberia:

> [As] I looked around, it became increasingly difficult to believe that this was the same city that I had visited in 1947. I said so to President Tubman, who was sitting by my side and congratulated him on the development that had taken place during his term of office. Prior to his election as President [ruling Liberia from 1944 to 1971], Liberia was far from being an encouragement and an incentive to countries aspiring to independence. Even to-day there is much to be done in the Republic to make it a model independent state in West Africa, for the roads are about the worst that I have seen in any country; without good roads the hinterland is cut off from the coastal belt. There is also much evidence of poverty among the masses, even in Monrovia itself.[158]

In contrast of the luxury that Nkrumah experienced on the Liberian presidential yacht and the mass poverty with which he was confronted in Monrovia during his private and official visits, tells an interesting story about Liberia that is echoed in several other African nations. In many African nations since the 1960s, the governed can be taken for granted by the governing authorities, who happen to be the electorate's own elected kith and kin, a situation that has led to some of the violent military coups that toppled several of the elected leaders, including Nkrumah himself in February 1966.

It is on the foregoing basis that many indigenous African and international commentators have concluded that African independence, although necessary, since it ushered in indigenous leadership, was either a farce or an empty exercise. Rene Dumont, a French agronomist and political commentator who is quoted much more extensively elsewhere in this study, concluded in *False Start in Africa* (1966) that African independence was ushered into existence on a false start or premise, and that there was no difference between indigenous leadership and colonial rule when it came to the neglected plight of the common citizenry. Dumont, who would later be declared persona non grata in several independent African nations, was adamantly opposed to what he saw and commented on as hero-*cum*-pecuniary worship in most of the decolonized nations, a situation that would bring about indigenous tyranny and, sadly, the rampant and inevitable military interventions in politics on the continent.[159]

Dumont was not alone in bemoaning tyranny and corrupt practices in many African nations, as several other commentators and analysts have made similar painful calculations, including embittered African writers. Liberia's Wreh was among some of his African compatriots, in critiquing personalized rule and tyranny on the continent, discussing in particular the life and tyrannical rule of President William V. S. Tubman in Liberia.[160] As Wreh recounted in his study, Tubman, as the elected president from 1944 to 1971, ruled Liberia autocratically.

Although he was considered affable, both loved and feared by Liberians, when Tubman died in 1971 at a London Clinic after surgery, many Liberians came out fearlessly to make it clear that he had governed too long. Wreh added:

Under Tubman's rule, there was no countervailing power from the people or from the constitutionally created National Legislature and judiciary, institutions which should provide the checks and balances to the executive branch and mutually between each other. Unchallenged and unfettered, Tubman had everything to himself and ruled as he pleased. The people [of Liberia] escheated their freedom of speech, of conscience and of the press to the great dictator—the like of whom, I devoutly hope, Liberians will never see again.[161]

The foregoing statements could easily be applied to several other postcolonial African leaders at their dictatorial and brutal worst. Just as Nkrumah concluded upon visiting Liberia, Wreh, too, promptly added:

Tubman was a big man, who brought Liberia into the mainstream of twentieth-century development. . . . But to everything positive, there must be a negative, and it is expected as normal that not everyone will want to speak well all the time of a leader. . . . Compared with some of the tyrannies which have arisen in Africa since the end of colonialism, Tubman's must appear mild, yet under his rule power became an end in its self. Those who opposed him legally in his early presidential election campaigns were put down ruthlessly and he had the Constitution altered to enable him to succeed himself indefinitely.[162]

Although for various cogent reasons many foreigners or non-Africans often took it upon themselves to catalogue abuses of power in postcolonial Africa, Wreh—like Nigeria's Professor Wole Soyinka, Kenya's Professor Ngugi, and Ghana's Mr. Kesse-Adu—was surely qualified to perform the task of exposing tyrannical rule where Liberia was concerned. After all, he was someone "who personally suffered maltreatment for a newspaper article he wrote in 1955 criticizing the Tubman administration." Wreh added that he saluted Tubman for his good deeds, "but because he did not know when to bow out with grace and dignity and make way for a new leader, and perpetuated himself in office ruthlessly and tyrannically, I denounce him."[163]

Tubman's reported ruthlessness and tyrannical rule, which lasted for over a quarter of a century, was phenomenal but, as Wreh agreed, not necessarily unheard of in African historical and political parlance. However, the cited Liberian examples—which were very similar to repressive political instances in several other postcolonial African nations, do fit well into the discussions on African dictatorships and tyranny. For, like other known dictatorial situations in postcolonial Africa, the Liberian people had little or no say themselves when their "elected" representatives in the capital of Monrovia decided, as Wreh wrote in his book, to have the Liberian "Constitution altered to enable him [Tubman] to succeed himself indefinitely."[164]

In a nutshell, the pre-1980 sufferings of indigenous Liberians under the Americo-Liberian political apparatus were also very much similar to the prevailing political circumstances of many postcolonial countries on the continent.

The situation showed how men and women could be held hostage by the political leaders that they had elected to lead them to the proverbial promised land of political and economic prosperity. Sadly, instead several postcolonial African countries fell prey to the throes of dictatorial or tyrannical rule.

For example, in a 1995 study of post-coup Gambia (sometimes called The Republic of Gambia), Zaya Yeebo, a London-based writer and political activist, recalled the open-mindedness with which he arrived in the country to work for Action Aid, a humanitarian organization. He promptly added, "I was also aware of the inhumane and predatory nature of some sections of the African ruling class, and so I was wondering if the Gambian ruling class would be different."[165]

As a typical example of a nation with neocolonialist status, the Gambia that Yeebo saw—very much like the Liberia that Nkrumah had seen several decades before—was a so-called independent nation whose "poverty was of unimaginable proportions and unbelievably horrendous."[166] As expected, in the wave of Africa's decolonization debacle, Gambia gained its independence from the British in 1965 with Sir Dawda Jawara, a British knighted politician, as its new leader. His People's Progressive Party (PPP) had swept the pre-independence polls, just as Nkrumah's Convention People's Party (CPP) had done in Ghana before the country's independence in 1957.

Yet, Yeebo attested to the deplorable state of the Gambia; Sir Dawda's indigenous leadership had made no difference and, if anything, conditions were possibly worse than when the country was under colonial rule. The Ghanaian observer, among other disturbing details, wrote:

> It was evident that thirty years of PPP rule had brought about little socio-
> economic development. Apart from two main hospitals, schools and a few
> hundred kilometers of tarred road between the capital Banjul [formerly
> called Bathurst] and a few major towns, the PPP had little to boast of in
> terms of real socio-economic development. The lack of basic welfare facil
> ities, poor roads, rural retardation, are evident.[167]

In writing about Gambia, Yeebo compared a great deal of Gambian politics with those of Ghana. For example, he underscored that Nkrumah and his government were supposed to have failed the Ghanaian people in their quest for political and economic salvation, hence his overthrow in the February 1966 military coup, just like the instances of many "couped" places and of Sir Dawda in Gambia on July 22, 1994. Yeebo deemed it necessary to quote, for illustrative purposes, Nkrumah's 1957 clarion promise to his people: "We shall measure our progress by the improvement in the health of our people; by the number of children in school, and by the quality of their education, by the availability of water and electricity in our towns and villages; by the happiness which our people take in being able to manage their own affairs."[168] For several years, the Ghanaian populace kept on waiting for these developments, until a "liberation force" of the country's armed forces, called the National Liberation Council, seized power from the CPP government of Nkrumah.

Again, the circumstances of Gambia in 1994–95 were very much similar to the situation in Liberia during the True Whig Party rule, whereby in the midst of abject poverty, President Tubman owned a luxurious presidential yacht manned by an entire foreign crew: There was opulence, abundance and relative affluence, as Yeebo saw, in the Banjul area or capital of the country. He wrote: "I was equally amazed to find that in the midst of such abject poverty, the supermarkets, owned by wealthy Lebanese, were overflowing with goods until I realized that only expatriates, tourists and a tiny fraction of the Gambian elite could afford the prices."[169]

Unlike Liberia and other postcolonial tyrannical African situations, Yeebo did underscore that, in the Gambia that he lived as an employee for Action Aid, "there were no obvious political prisoners, even though there were instances of the bad treatment of prisoners and torture by individual policemen."[170] However, it was added that Gambia's democracy, like that of other places on the continent, was an illusion, although the PPP regime exercised a measure of tolerance of its opposition, and, in the words of Yeebo, "like similar tolerant governments, it paid the ultimate price [referring to the eventual 1994 coup d'etat]."[171]

Gambia's leadership problems were very much similar to those of Liberia under Tolbert: before the 1980 coup, Tolbert had earlier been Tubman's vice-president for 19 years until he became President in July 1971. Gambia, like Liberia, was eventually engulfed in multifarious socioeconomic problems that would consume it to bring about the 1994 coup led by the young Captain Yaya Jammeh. The coup event was seen by Yeebo as a subversion "by the neo-colonial reactionary armed forces."[172]

The irony, however, was that the strong expatriate presence in Gambia's economy, spearheaded by Lebanese merchants, as commented on by Yeebo, was very much similar to what prevailed in the Liberian regimes, which had been controlled for almost a century by Americo-Liberians. Interestingly, non-African business presence in many postcolonial African countries was so crucial to economic prosperity that the Lebanese in West Africa and the Asians in East Africa became a fact of life. For example, it is reported that after becoming the nineteenth President of Liberia in 1971, Tolbert allegedly dismissed some leading public officials of his regime in 1974 because of the tough legal actions they had, reportedly, taken against a Lebanese businessman by the name of Ali Ayad, and his son, Emmanuel Ayad. Both Lebanese nationals operated from Liberia's Mano River area.[173]

Reportedly, the dismissed officials included Justice Minister and Attorney-General Clarence Lorenzo Simpson, Jr., Immigration Commissioner and Deputy Attorney-General Peter Amos George, and Deputy Justice Minister (for Litigation) Emmanuel Gbalezeh. The substance of their "crimes" was that these officials had allowed Liberia's Commerce, Industry and Transportation Ministry to "acquire" the power to impose heavy fines on merchants who sold commodities above the Ministry's so-called "regulated commodity prices." In applying the power, the officials of the Commerce Ministry "fined him [Ayad] $2,000 and gave him 24 hours to pay; he refused, and his shop was closed down, and his [sale] licence canceled."[174]

The incident demonstrated two sides of a coin in Americo-Liberian-dominated Liberia. First, to show how highly connected the Lebanese were in Liberia, Mr. Ayad's lawyer took the matter to the Liberian Supreme Court for adjudication, and the Court ruled that the Commerce Ministry had no legal right to impose such fines on arrested merchants, with Associate Supreme Court Justice George Henries—son of the Liberian House of Representatives' Speaker Richard Henries—stating in his written ruling that "the Ministry cannot be the accuser and the judge at the same time."[175] Second, it also showed how cabinet members of the government could flout court orders in spite of the traditional separation of powers borrowed from the American system of democratic governance. Therefore, instead of obeying the Supreme Court's ruling and, subsequently, permitting Mr. Ayad to go back to his business as well as not pay the levied heavy fine of $2,000, Justice Minister Simpson, not pleased with the ruling, "issued a writ for the arrest, detention and the subsequent deportation of the Lebanese merchant."[176]

Reportedly, acting with impunity and in clear violation of a court order, the Justice Minister sent a security officer of his Ministry to Mano River to serve the writ on Mr. Ali Ayad, who was not at home. Therefore, the writ was served on his 22–year-old son, Emmanuel, who was arrested and brought to Monrovia to be detained until his father was found. On the orders of Judge Emma Walser, the young Ayad was ordered freed from further detention, as he was not Ali Ayad, and the Judge, among other critical words, also stated the following in her ruling against the Ministry of Justice in the matter of the detention: "The handling of the matter is fraught with incompetency."[177]

Another interesting scenario also depicts the arrogance of Liberian government officials that would precipitate the 1980 military coup d'etat: the arrest and several hours of detention of editors of both the ruling True Whig Party newspaper, *The Liberian Age,* and the privately-owned *Liberian Star* newspaper of Monrovia. The "crime" was that their newspapers were accused by then Justice Minister Simpson's Ministry of "promoting gambling by publishing football pools results from U.K. and Australia."[178] Since advertising the sporting results for football pool enthusiasts was done in numerous African countries without any repercussions or official sanctions, Liberians wondered if their country, under the tight control of emancipated slaves from America, was treating them as captives and, to an extent, even as modern-day slaves. To assuage this fear; President Tolbert removed all the top officials of his Justice Ministry, although his action was also seen as catering to the rich Lebanese constituency.

On the other hand, since Tolbert was an ordained Baptist minister (or preacher), one felt that he would applaud the arrest of editors whose newspapers were promoting the overseas football pools, which was considered a form of gambling in Liberia. The situation showed the obvious contradictions in African leadership, especially where Tolbert and other Americo-Liberian leaders were concerned. Liberia's native populace had become a captive audience, mere hewers of wood and drawers of water in the nation of their birth. The moaning and loud cry of the indigenous Liberians would be answered in the April 1980 coup d'etat, which turned out to be very deadly for the Americo-Liberian leaders, as many of the top officials were arrested and summarily executed in public.

Examples of Misrule, Neocolonialism, and
Eventual Coups from Northern and Eastern Africa

Apart from Liberia and Ethiopia, which used to boast about being pioneers in the receipt of freedom, independence had also come very early to Libya, on December 24, 1951; to Sudan on January 1, 1956; to Morocco on March 2, 1956; and to Tunisia on March 20, 1956. Yet, there is ample evidence from prevailing local and international reports that citizens of these postcolonial African nations, too, had forfeited freedom and justice under regimes headed by autocratic indigenous leadership. Although most of the leaders of the postindependence tyrannies that Rene Dumont, in *False Start in Africa* (1967), and other writers have catalogued in their published studies have reasons to back their repressive actions, it is still a fact that the political independence for which they fought European colonial authorities with the loyal support of the mass populace withered away.

In fact, situations deteriorated to such a point that several African writers, including the mainstream intellectuals, felt that Blacks in South Africa, under the grip of Apartheid rule before ex-President Nelson Mandela's release from jail, were better off than Blacks in many postindependence African nations, including countries where military regimes had replaced elected regimes, because they knew where their government stood in matters dealing with freedom, justice and, indeed, the lack of both essential elements. Indeed, pre-Mandela South Africa was described by Lewis Nkosi, the celebrated South African writer, as "a situation so fraught with evil that you are brought into collision with it."[179] Yet, Professor Soyinka of Nigeria, a fierce critic of tyranny in Africa, concluded that, at least, South African Blacks, under apartheid, knew exactly their sad, racist and exploited circumstances while, in other so-called independent nations of Africa, violence was the order of the day and, as Professor Dennis Austin reiterated, "violence had lost its way and was running wild."[180]

In retrospect, one wonders if the sum total of the humiliating and repressive circumstances of Africans in postcolonial regimes on the continent could be akin to a form of enslavement. What is sad, however, is the fact that slavery is the same decadent and immoral institution—as culled and quoted above—that Professors Adu Boahen, Orlando Patterson, and the erstwhile League of Nations' Committee on Slavery, among several others, have defined as being (1) "most inhuman and abominable"; (2) a "permanent, violent domination of natally alienated and generally dishonored persons"; and (3) "a person over whom any or all the powers attaching to the right of ownership are exercised." Slavery has, particularly, been deemed so terrible that, recently Pope John Paul II, became first head of the Catholic Church to condemn slavery outright, and the American President Bill Clinton, in his spring 1998 trip to Africa, was quoted as offering a personal apology "for sins from slavery to genocide in Africa."[181]

Yet, several elected leaders of postcolonial Africa have not shied away from treating their own people so terribly that, very often, one could easily compare the plight of many suffering Africans to that which prevailed in slave times. Sadly, however, most of the leaders perpetuating these inhuman political behaviors—the national bourgeoisie and the ruling elite—have often been educated in some of the finest institutions of learning in and outside Africa. Consequently, Nigeria-born Professor Abiola Irele of Ohio State University is very correct in his categorization: "The converse of this state of confusion is the spurious westernization of the national bourgeoisie."[182]

Knowing the abominable nature of the national bourgeoisie, Professor Irele cited several authorities, including Frantz Fanon, the well-known radical psychiatrist-analyst, in offering a "celebrated denunciation of this social category in Africa." He also quotes Ayi Kwei Armah, a Ghanaian writer, as describing the situation of "the cargo cult," or slave mentality.[183] Harvard sociologist Patterson identifies alienation as part of the dilemma of the enslaved community, and Irele expands on this idea in his 1982 University of Ibadan professorial inaugural address in which he discusses the topic of alienation.

In postcolonial Africa, alienation of political opponents, often in isolated prison cells is a daily occurrence. A typical example was what happened to Dr. Joseph Boakye Danquah, who was described by Dr. Nnamdi Azikiwe to be the first African to earn a doctoral degree in law from the University of London.[184] As Nkrumah has confirmed, he was also one of the leading nationalists of the former Gold Coast who played a major role in bringing Nkrumah from Britain to head the United Gold Coast Convention (UGCC) and, subsequently, to participate actively in the decolonization struggle against the British. Yet, Dr. Danquah ended up being accused of plotting to overthrow Nkrumah's regime and was, for several years, jailed without court trial. In the end, he died in chains in political detention in Ghana.[185]

Other African countries have had their share of tyrannical rule, whereby many vocal citizens had their freedoms curtailed. In his prison memoirs, *Detained: A Writer's Prison Diary* (1981), Ngugi wa Thiong'o of Kenya recalled his own sad circumstances in a postindependence Kenyan prison, after his arrest without trial, mainly because of his writings. He was not the only Kenyan so shabbily and humiliatingly treated, as several leading politicians suffered a similar fate, including the first postindependence vice-president, Oginga Odinga. Thiong'o saw a slavish mentality in the way Kenyatta's regime, allegedly in complicity with some foreign powers, treated fellow Kenyans. Among other details, he said:

> I have tried to see it [my arrest and detention without trial] in the context of the historical attempts, from colonial times to the present, by a foreign imperialist bourgeoisie, in alliance with its local Kenyan representatives, to turn Kenyans into slaves, and of the historical struggles of Kenyan people against economic, political and cultural slavery.[186]

In the sphere of genocide in human history and politics, Adolf Hitler and his Nazi cohorts have often led the way in their inhuman treatment of the Jews in and outside of Germany. That was especially so in situations whereby even innocent children and helpless women were grouped with distrusted or envied Jewish businessmen and sent to their deaths at concentration camps. In postcolonial

Africa, tribal or ethnic friction and jealousies have led to cases of outright genocide of countless men and women, in sad cases bordering on ethnic cleansing. In
fact, some of the situations were so intolerable that international commissions of
enquiry and tribunals had to be established to try, convict, and sentence the
guilty ones to terms of imprisonment and, sometimes, to death. All of these
human rights violations were perpetrated once again, because of ethnic or tribal
differences. Indeed, Professor Austin put it well when he wrote that "it can
hardly be said that tribalism was created by colonial rule, but it was certainly
evoked by its passing."[187]

Where balkanization of the African continent is concerned, colonial authorities carved ethnic entities into regional and, sometimes, even district groups.
Again, Austin gave a very useful description, when he further wrote:

> European control put a boundary around culturally disparate entities that
> have now become powerful ingredients of rivalry in almost every aspect of
> the state: in the army, in party politics, in the trade unions, in the universi-
> ties, and in the public service. They are the ethnic solidarities that form the
> slopes of the social pyramid.[188]

In postcolonial Africa, therefore, most of the newly elected indigenous leaders
sought ethnic allegiance in making key or sensitive appointments in all aspects of
national and international development. In Kenya, for example, Kenyatta's
Kikuyu ethnic group held sway where top security and governmental appointments were concerned, although it is to the Mzee's or Kenyatta's credit that his
ethnically diverse vice-presidents, first of Odinga (a Luo) and, later, of Daniel
arap Moi (of the minority Kalenjin ethnic group, who succeeded Kenyatta after
his death in office on August 22, 1978) were not Kikuyus. In Ghana Nkrumah
sought to minimize ethnic or tribal friction by encouraging the learning of
indigenous languages at all levels and by all citizens as well as by encouraging
politicians to run for offices outside their ethnic domains. Some of these actions
later, unfortunately came to haunt him, just as Yeebo said of the unlimited tolerant aspects of the deposed Jawara regime, thus the Gambian regime tolerated too
much criticism.

For the men and women of the various tribal or ethnic groups in the northern part of Ghana to catch up in development and education with others from
elsewhere in Ghana, Nkrumah's government floated a form of "affirmative
action," whereby educational scholarships and other incentives for higher education were made easily available to Ghanaians of the northern regional extraction, such as Hausas, Fulanis, Dagombas. Through these very progressive
measures, many Ghanaians from the northern areas of the country attained
higher education to the extent that one of them, Dr. Hilla Limann, qualified to
lead the nation as the president or the head of state of the Third Republic of
Ghana. Yet, as a diplomat, Limann was suspected of participating in anti-
Nkrumah activities to make sure that the deposed president would not be able
to return to political power in Ghana from his 1966–1972 exile. The activities
included Ghanaian diplomats, allegedly including Limann, reporting on sup-

porters or agents of deposed President Nkrumah in exile. These were part of the reasons that Dr. Limann was labeled a closet Nkrumah opponent, or "a covert anti-Nkrumaist."[189] As a result of the foregoing suspicion, critics felt that if Limann, who died in the spring of 1998, had come from Nkrumah's Nzima ethnic group of the Western Region of Ghana, he would not have, reportedly, done anything undermining to hamper his former benefactor's interests, since it was through Nkrumah's generous educational programs that Limann earned his university education up to the doctoral level in France and Britain, as well as gained employment in the Research Bureau of Ghana's Foreign Ministry (which was similar to the American CIA).[190] Since Dr. Limann was performing his bona fide duties as a diplomat, some Ghanaians often excuse his actions, including the anti-Nkrumah information he allegedly supplied from his diplomatic position.

Certainly, tribal or ethnic convulsions in African political history have caused more harm than good. Also, in Nigeria and other areas, as Professor Austin wrote, they were the underlining reason for some of the reported violence and political problems:

> Competing local interests of many different kinds, more often than not ethnic or "tribal" in character, put forward claims on the central government . . . their leaders arguing the case for a distribution of resources rather different from the constitution of colonial rule by nationalist politicians. The effect was pervasively and continuously disruptive. At different levels of intensity such claims led to civil war in Nigeria, the suppression of local kingdoms in Uganda, Ghana's closing of its frontiers with neighboring states, and the imprisonment of factional leaders, including such notables as Diallo Telli (to give only one example of a great many), who was once a close associate of Sekou Toure and a former Secretary-General of the Organization of African Unity (OAU) but is now in prison in Guinea accused of the double crime of being "a CIA agent and a Fullah secessionist."[191]

Sadly, Mr. Telli, a well-educated Guinean who became the first Secretary-General of OAU and spearheaded its quest for African unity, died miserably in Sekou Toure's political prison. A similar plight befell many other African politicians and diplomats, in most cases because of tribalism or ethnic strife. Where ethnic nuances result in deaths, including public executions of condemned criminals, many Africans from different ethnic groups hardly ever raise fingers of protest. For example, it was reported in April 1998 that Rwandans of the Tutsi ethnic group were jubilating over the public execution of 22 Hutu ethnic men and women who had been found guilty of ethnic violence and murders at a Kigali-based trial. Mr. Froduald Karamira—who was unsuccessfully defended by Attorney Paul Atita—specifically condemned on the argument that "during the Spring of 1994, Mr. Karamira's daily hate broadcasts on the radio encouraged Hutu to take part in mass killings of Tutsi."[192]

Of course, the death of a family member often evokes sadness and deep emotions for the bereaved family. Yet, in Rwanda, the ethnic sentiments were so high that the *New York Times* reported: "After the executions, several people who had watched said they felt a confused and bittersweet sense that justice had been done. Many expressed a hope that the executions would deter Hutu extremists from further massacres. Others said that putting the ringleaders of the 1994 killings to death was the only way to begin rebuilding the divided country."[193]

Genocidal killings stemming from ethnic violence have happened in many other places in Africa, including Somalia, Burundi, and even Nigeria, during the Nigeria-Biafra civil war, the cause of which was the claim by Igbo leaders that Igbo men and women were earmarked for extermination. However, in a 1975 book, Joe Igbokwe, a Nigerian engineer by training, lamented that almost all major ethnic groups in Nigeria—namely Hausa/Fulani, Yoruba, and Igbo[194]—had seen injustice in the country since 1932, adding that "the only viable option open to these oppressed people of Nigeria is to present a common front to save Nigeria from disintegration."[195]

In retrospect, one ponders over the foregoing "Black on Black" murderous situations, arrests, and detentions without trial in several postcolonial nations on the continent, very often perpetrated on the African populace by its own elected indigenous leadership. All one can conjure are the sad descriptions that Africa was given by its critics, including that of the inappropriate description of being a "dark continent." As quoted in Premier Busia's book, *The Challenge of Africa* (1962), the Roman historian Pliny was on target in his description of Africa: "Africa always offers something new."[196] While it is a histo-political truth that many of today's developed nations went through some of these upheavals, it is just sad that the situation in Africa is not abating in any measure. All over the continent, there is turmoil in the midst of genuine nationalist efforts on the part of some dedicated leaders to seek redress for the downtrodden. Nigerian President Obasanjo, who bemoaned these human rights shortcomings on the part of tyrannical rulers of Africa and is the elected leader of his country, is a typical example of a ruler who means well for his people and, hence for Africa.

As Dr. Busia intimated as far back as 1962, it is a fact that precolonial African nationalism demanded racial equality and that colonialism in Africa had been marked by the domination of Africans by Europeans. "Emancipation" came through independence in most of these nations but, as the eminent sociologist saw from his own circumstances, when he had to escape in a hurry from Ghana into exile, "that does not by itself give personal freedom to the individual citizen."[197] Based on the foregoing circumstances, Obasanjo—Nigeria's elected president since February 1999—very well captured the plight of Africa and Africans when he described the decolonization revolution of Africa in this statement: "Yet no sooner had colonial rule ended than our new rulers set about converting the revolution into one of fire and thunder against their own people."[198]

In the context of Pliny's earlier assertion, many situations in Africa have been so much twisted and changed that, very unfortunately, they have become unrecognizable. For example, both indigenous African scholars and foreign leaders threw the challenge to African leaders that there should be individual freedom. However, in observing the trends in independent African states, foreign observers and some patriotic intellectuals of Africa, as stated by a recent writer, "contend that democracy is not suited to Africa and that the peoples of Africa themselves prefer authoritarian rule."[199] Such an abysmal and sad reflection is revealed to be untrue, when one takes a good look at the varied struggles going on throughout the continent for freedom, the very reason for some of the coups d'etat that we plan to discuss in detail in subsequent chapters of this study.

Whether the contention that democracy is not suited to the African continent, and that Africans prefer authoritarian rule is true or not can be seen in the circumstances of Africa and Africans before and after independence. This is especially so in the very exercise that, in a 1992 study of the Middle East, independence was termed "controlled independence" in several places of the Middle East, including Egypt. The colonial powers tended to control certain services, including defense and foreign affairs at the initial stage of independence, and their "control" still seems to be firmly in place many years through neocolonialism and, in some instances, neoimperialism.[200]

As described by Peter Woodward, a senior lecturer in politics at Britain's University of Reading, even the military, which would play a decisive political role in postcolonial Africa through coups d'etat, was an organization that had no democratic basis. That is the reason that, sometimes, one wonders why good-natured men and women opt for enlistment in the armed forces of various African countries. Toward that end, Woodward has wondered and asserted that "it might seem strange that a young student radical [speaking of Nasser] should have been drawn to a career in an authoritarian organization like the army."[201] Maybe critics are correct in thinking that it is because of the authoritarian nature of many of the armed forces of African countries, coupled with the earlier contention that Africans themselves are deemed to "prefer authoritarian rule," that permanent military rule or involvement has been planted in the minds of some of Africa's military dictators and their supporters.

Also, several experts or writers on African military issues have often seen unlimited contradictions in the military setup in postcolonial Africa, which will be discussed in detail elsewhere in this study. Among such writers is Dr. Alaba Ogunsanwo, the Nigerian university professor-turned-diplomat, whose literary canons would be silenced as a diplomat. Known as an expert on Asia, Professor Ogunsanwo, who does not mince words in his criticism of several aspects of military rule, took a foreign service position to serve Nigeria at an ambassadorial level.[202] Additionally, Dennis Austin and Robin Luckham, of the Victoria University and the Institute of Development Studies at Essex, England, respectively, have also drawn interesting conclusions in their 1975 study of Africa's armed forces, often making very enlightened distinctions among several coups d'etat that they studied, including the Ghanaian coups of 1966 and 1972, both of which unseated elected civilian regimes. In their eyes, there was no reason for the military intervention in either instance, no matter how long the Nkrumah regime had succeeded itself in political office.[203]

As will be shown later, some of the rampant military takeovers, or coups d'etat were attributed to the accusation that several of the postindependence African leaders never wanted to leave political office and that they used every means—legal, extralegal, and foul, including outright rigging of electoral processes—to perpetuate their rule. In jest, it was often claimed by political opponents that most of these long-serving leaders did so in order to get official or state burial; if so, they clearly forget that any good nation would honor a deceased former leader, as America did for several of its ex-presidents, including Mr. Richard Nixon, an astute politician who sadly got embroiled in the Watergate political fiasco and had to resign from office.

It is a fact that long-serving African leaders of the postcolonial era had often occupied political offices for decades. As an example, Nkrumah's regime was overthrown in 1966, it had been in power since 1951, the year that the Ghanaian leader first became the "Leader of Government Business" under the British colonial officials. Apart from Nkrumah's instance, others included Kenya's Jomo Kenyatta; Liberia's Tubman; Malawi's Banda, who formalized his rule to become president for life; Toure of Guinea; Modibo Keita of Mali; Hamadou Diori of Niger; H. Boigny of the Ivory Coast; and several others. (Some of them, after several years' rule, decided to retire gracefully, including Cameroon's A. Ahidjo, Senegal's Leopold Senghor, and Tanzania's Julius Nyerere (who died in October 1999 in London). A most recent example of longevity in African political office is 71–year old President Hosni Mubarak of Egypt, who in 1998 became the longest-serving Egyptian leader in the twentieth century. He came to power in 1981, when President Anwar el-Sadat was assassinated at a public function and, in 1998, the Egyptian leader accepted a third four-year term of presidential office, with 67–year old U.S.-educated Atef Obeid, as his new prime minister. As reported, Mr. Obeid, who will predictably succeed Mr. Mubarak when the Egyptian President retires, has famously been credited with guiding his country's privatization program, an essential economic plan to stimulate and ensure economic growth.[204]

Certainly, Africa has had an intriguing political history since 1900 and, as the records portray, it is hoped that its politicians, to an extent, and soldiers will one day allow democratic governance and true human rights to prevail. In that case, coups d'etat may be become outdated and unnecessary when the time comes for a change of leadership. Africans—as was seen in the Ivory Coast in October 2000—are no longer willing to tolerate rigged national elections and leadership arrogance. The fate of the retired General Robert Guei, who had to escape into exile in the Benin Republic, is instructive.[205]

After leading a successful coup to unseat the elected regime in the Ivory Coast, Buei promised to hand power over to democratically elected government later. Instead, he decided to run for the presidential office and tried to rig the presidential election but was chased out of office through street protests by the people of Ivory Coast. He lived in exile briefly but, reportedly, returned a few months later to live a quiet life out of politics. Normally, Guei would have been present to hand over the leadership baton to his successor, but he forfeited that privilege by being in exile when the new Ivory Coast president was sworn in to succeed him.

In the new millennium, Africa's future looks bright where democracy is concerned, as recent encouraging events have shown: in Nigeria, the military leaders allowed presidential elections to go ahead, which led to the installation of the new civilian regime headed by retired General Olusegun Obasanjo; in Senegal, opposition leader Abdoulaye Wade won the presidential elections to wrestle power from President Abdou Diouf, while the fiercely contested presidential elections in Ghana led to the victory of the opposition presidential candidate John Kufuor, who succeeded retiring President John Jerry Rawlings, as the latter had yielded to the constitutional requirement of a two-term presidency. Also, leaders of the Economic Community of West African States (ECOWAS), out of democratic zeal, have used the military wing called ECOMOG to restore to power the temporarily overthrown government of elected Sierra Leonean President Tejan Kabbah. Several other nations on the continent are moving along with democratic successions, including South Africa, where Mr. Thabo Mbeki succeeded President Nelson Mandela as post-apartheid's elected president. Mr. Mbeki is currently advocating the overhaul of the Organization of African Unity (OAU) and the Southern African Developmental Community (SADC) in order to promote the economic and political integration of Africa, a measure that was expected to support the call for continental unity by Libyan President Muammar Gaddafy.

CHAPTER TWO

Africa's Armed Forces in Retrospect:
The History of the Colonial and Postcolonial Forces

> For most of the new leaders of African states the problems of their armed
> forces were both unexpected and unwelcome. Unexpected, because in the
> pursuit of political power they had assumed that after their independence
> neither internal security nor external defense would constitute grave
> threats; and unwelcome because they would have preferred to devote
> resources to social and economic ends. But in some cases the threats
> were soon found to be more serious than foreseen, and moreover
> armed forces became status symbols.
>
> —Sir Robert H. Scott quoting Major-General H. T. Alexander, *African
> Tightrope: My Two Years as Nkrumah's Chief of Staff* (1965).[1]

The foregoing statement sums up a lot about the military aspect of African politics. It applies well to African military leaders who had the armed forces
bequeathed to them by departing colonial officials, especially as regards their
expectations and their perception of the military as a status symbol. Yet, from
time immemorial, militarism has played a crucial role in African affairs, especially
in the historical and political evolutionary processes, which have often been
abbreviated by Eurocentric scholars. Such scholars often only began interpreting
these events from the moment that Europeans set their foot in Africa.

Ian Fowler and David Zeitlyn quote Basil Davidson, the celebrated London-
based scholar on Africa, in their edited volume, *African Crossroads:* "Africans have
been alienated from their own history by Europeans."[2] This chapter will analyze, historically and politically, the emergence of Africa's multifarious armed
forces, and the role that colonial forces, and—to a lesser extent—religion and the
slave trade played in their organizational structure.

It is a fact that Shaka Zulu of South Africa had his own Zulu Kingdom—also

called KwaZulu Natal—which has been described by Professor Carolyn Hamilton of the South Africa-based University of Witwatersrand as an "independent
polity in southeast Africa established by Shaka in the 1810s and ruled by his
descendants until 1879."[3] Though Shaka must have had an army of his own for
him to be able to survive the Anglo-Zulu war as he did,[4] many Eurocentric
scholars have often given the impression that African societies either never had
or were incapable of maintaining armies until the European arrival on the continent. Shaka's army and its military prowess disproves it.

In trying to show the long history of African armies, F. K. Buah, a Ghanaian
historian and author, has written:

> During the eighteenth and the nineteenth centuries there were many
> armed clashes between the *Asante* [or Ashanti] and the states in southern
> Ghana, with the British on the coast becoming increasingly involved in
> these conflicts. These armed confrontations were the result of a complex
> pattern of events and circumstances.[5]

Indeed, it has been shown that some of these early Pan-African military
forces were both well-trained and formidable. It is further stated that in one of
the local wars, "the British rushed men to meet the *Asante* at *Adanse Praso*, but the
heavy rains and the resulting inclement weather helped the *Asante*. Many of the
British troops died of fever and dysentery, and the men who survived retraced
their steps down to the coast in 1864."[6]

These Asante-British wars were taken so seriously that out of desperation even
women sometimes led them, as it happened in the Yaa Asantewaa War, in which
the Asante people were defeated in 1901 by the British, and the colony, now called
Ghana's Ashanti Region, was annexed as a British colony on January 1, 1902. This
war was led by Queen Yaa Asantewaa of Ejisu (then spelled as Edweso), in a town
near Kumasi, the capital of the present-day Ashanti Region. Also annexed was the
area called the Brong-Ahafo region, then called Bono Ahafo. Much earlier, in
1896, the British had arrested and exiled Nana Prempeh I, the militant and much-
feared Asante king (regularly called the Asantehene). Exiled with the king to island
of Seychelles in the Indian Ocean were many of his elders. Nana Prempeh I was
permitted to return to the Ashanti region of the former Gold Coast in 1924, long
after the Asantes had been subdued by the British forces.[7]

Professor Harry A. Gailey, Jr. of San Jose State University, has shown that
there were African armies in empires as early as the eleventh century. At that
time there was especially the need for military forces to fight in civil wars and to
be used to carry out the invasion of other geographic regions. Consequently,
Gailey surmised that Akan migrations that took place during this period were
probably "motivated by population pressure combined with disturbances atten-
dant upon the wars in the Western Sudan in the eleventh and twelfth centuries. . . . *Akan* invaders from the north met other migrants expanding into the
Gold Coast from the east into the Accra plain."[8]

Dahomey—now called the Republic of Benin—in West Africa received its
major military setback after 1730. The greatest threat to Dahomey's peace and

existence was Oyo, a neighboring empire that was situated in present-day Nigeria. Also, as explained by Gailey, "the history of Dahomey in the eighteenth century is inextricably bound to the slave trade."[9]

Since all of the foregoing events required military involvement, most likely all of the old kingdoms, empires, and nation-states of Africa had early standing armies. Such a confirmation disputes the notion that Africa had no military forces of its own until the exploring, "civilizing," and "Christianizing" Europeans arrived on the continent. The precolonial armies were not as organized, nor did they have the equipment or manpower of the armed forces of the colonial and postcolonial times.

Even so, it can be argued that the type of armed forces the Africans created and used from the early centuries to Shaka Zulu's time were very well suited to their military purposes at the time, just as the Europeans' military forces were created within the context of their military exigencies. Early African military forces used what they could manufacture, such as bows, poisoned arrows and other "primitive" weapons, just as the colonial powers and trading Europeans utilized canons, canon balls, guns, and gun powder.[10]

Furthermore, it is a historical and political fact that, as early as the 1600s, European traders, fearing indigenous armed forces and pirates, built forts and castles along the West African coast for protective and trading purposes. Professor Albert van Dantzig of the University of Ghana, Legon, discusses in *Forts and Castles of Ghana* that Fort St. Louis, a wooden French fort, was built in 1698 at Assini in present-day Ivory Coast, near the Ghana–Ivory Coast border, but was abandoned in 1704. He adds that the numerous forts and castles built along Ghana's coastal shores have played important roles in her economic, political, and social history. They are today one of Ghana's most striking postcolonial features and are still well kept and used in the country.[11]

To demonstrate the military aspects of these buildings, Professor van Dantzig wrote:

> The essential purpose of all of these buildings was to serve as store-houses for goods brought from Europe and bought on the Coast, and as living quarters for a permanent commercial and military staff. If the earliest of these buildings were mainly fortified on the land-side against enemies expected from that side, soon the real danger appeared to come rather from the side of the sea, in the form of European competitors. During the sixteenth century a growing number of French and English ships came to trade in what was supposed to be a Portuguese monopoly area. An even more serious threat to Portuguese supremacy on the Coast came from the Dutch, who had arrived in large numbers on the coast by the end of that century. In 1612 they built a fort of their own at Mori after the local chief of *Asebu,* who had for some time been trading with them, had sent two ambassadors on one of their ships to the Netherlands with the report that a fort be built in his state.[12]

Professor van Dantzig, himself a Dutch historian, has shown that before the Assini fort was constructed in 1698, the Dutch had already erected one in 1612 at Mori, this time inside Ghana. However, Professor Gailey has pointed out in *History of Africa, Volume I,* that in southern Africa, forts were in use at an earlier date, adding that "some Bantu [a South African ethnic group] established a series of fortified outcrops in the northern Transvaal area and manned these until the fifteenth century. The major rock fortress of these people was the Mapungubwe."[13]

The military significance of these buildings prompted van Dantzig to offer an explanation of the differences between a castle and a fort, although often the terms become almost interchangeable in usage:

> The appellation *castle* is applied only to the three biggest of these buildings: Elmina castle, Cape Coast Castle and Christianborg Castle, the former headquarters of, respectively, the Portuguese (later of the Dutch), the British and the Danes. *Fort* is applied to the larger fortified buildings, and *lodge* to small trade-factories, sometimes virtually unfortified.[14]

All of the foregoing activities are indications that the people of Africa had military precision and awareness long before the arrival of European traders as well as colonizers. However, it is clear that the Europeans came with their own of military and security purposes, as they introduced fortified forts and castles. Africans, on their own, had a high sense of military needs and security, as the Bantu in southern Africa, and others in the West African subregion of the continent, had well fortified buildings that were similar to forts and castles introduced later by European traders.

Additionally, many scholars have failed to elaborate on the connections between the Islamic religion, African slavery and African military regimes. The history of Islam shows that the religion—founded by the Prophet Muhammad around A.D. 570–632[15]—was the dominant religion in North Africa, and that, as professor G. B. Martin has explained, spread very fast and was "soon deeply rooted, answering to the spiritual and cultural needs of millions of Arabs, Iranians, Turks, and, within a few centuries, large numbers of Africans."[16] It is further noted by Martin that, after A.D. 1000, the coastal settlements of Islam along the shores of Kenya, Tanganyika, and northern Mozambique increased their size and economic stature, and that "for the next four hundred years, they carried on a coastal trade based on commercial links from one city-state to another."[17]

The early trade involved natural and human resources, including the purchasing and shipment of precious metals and slaves, but how early the slave trade started and endured is a historical, political, and sociological conjecture. Interestingly, there is something subtle about the slave trade, hence that many societies have not succeeded in pinpointing the exact dates when the trade reared its ugly head. For example, Peter J. Parish, in *Slavery: History and Historian,* offers the following scenario about North American slavery: "There is nothing clear-cut about the beginnings of slavery on the North American mainland. It is impossible to name one specific date at which slavery began its long history there."[18] However, Harvard University sociology Professor Orlando Patterson has concluded that "the study of slavery dates back to the very beginnings of the modern world and the rebirth of scholarship in the Renaissance."[19] On this basis, one can also postulate that the brutal and inhuman trade in human cargo, which is mildly described as the "slave trade," required armed personnel as slave hunters and buyers, just to ensure that enemies of the traders would not disrupt their trade.

However, Patterson and other modern-day scholars of the trade understandably disagree with the evolutionary origins of the trade theorized by such earlier scholars as H. Spencer, in his 1893 *Principles of Sociology;* L. T. Hobhouse and others in the 1930 treatise, *The Material and Social Institutions of* the Simpler Peoples; and G. Landman in his 1938 study, *The Origin of the Inequality of the Social Classes.* Among points of disagreement between the Patterson camp and the Landman perspective was where, as the former wrote, the latter (Spencer) "hypothesized that slavery was the joint product of warfare and cannibalism."[20]

Patterson further explained the Spencer hypothesis in the following words:

> It was during the critical period of delay between capture and preparation for [the human] sacrifice—which sometimes may have lasted for several months—that the idea presented itself of making the captive at least work for his keep. Under the right socioeconomic circumstances, namely where the condemned person could produce more than he consumed, the conquering group would eventually come to see that more might be gained by making the captive a permanent slave.[21]

Enslavement came into the picture of early military evolution in Africa in the fact that—as Professor Patterson has discussed here and in his 1985 book, *Slavery and Social Death: A Comparative Study*—it required well-armed persons or groups to be able to capture others to send them into slavery. Capturing free persons in civil wars and treating them as "booty of war" for future enslavement necessitated standing or ad hoc military forces. Hence it is a historical and political fact that, since slavery existed very early on,[22] the African societies that served as lucrative conduits or pipelines for the supply of the slaves needed well-developed armies, or temporary ones, to do the fighting, the capturing, the guarding, and the eventual disposal of the "human cargo" as sold slaves.[23]

The various African societies involved in the slave trade did not necessarily have streamlined military forces to capture men and women for enslavement. Therefore, their armies at the time were so weak that they cannot be compared to the modernized and heavily armed forces that we see today in various African nations, most of which have become so politicized that their leaders have deemed it necessary to bypass the democratic machinery of electoral practices and, instead, use their weapons to seize political power through coups d'etat.

Unlike the armed forces that one sees in African nations today, early pockets of military force in several areas of the continent never took into account the possibility that one day the leadership might get involved and be entrenched in politics. Instead, such armed forces were created to maintain national security.

The Evolution of Modern Armed Forces in Africa:
An Example from the British Creation of
West African Military or Frontier Forces

The methods through which Africans were captured for enslavement and the evolution of various armed forces on the continent seem to be interconnected. *The Sierra Leonean Army: A Century of History,* by Fourah Bay College professors E. D. A. Turay and A. Abraham, begins its analysis with the chronicle of how "beginning with the Portuguese in the fifteenth century, Europeans took Africans across the seas to Europe and the New World to serve either as objects of curiosity or as domestic servants."[24] Turay and Abraham went on to catalogue the early history of Sierra Leone, in particular how a group of Englishmen, who received British governmental support to constitute themselves into a committee for the Black Poor, "had many of these [freed] blacks shipped to that section of the West African coast known as Sierra Leone in 1787. In 1791, the original settlers were joined by the Nova Scotia blacks, most of whom had participated in the War for American Independence and were later sent by the British to Nova Scotia."[25] From Nova Scotia, these Blacks were sent to Sierra Leone as part of the new settlers.

Meanwhile, what was uppermost on the minds of the new immigrant leaders of the so-called Province of Freedom (Sierra Leone), with its capital of Freetown, was the concern for welfare and security. As relations between the settlers and their native Temne neighbors, from whom they acquired land for their settlement, were not always cordial. For self-defense, particularly of their settlement, the settlers were reportedly given arms and six cannons but, as the cannon balls lacked carriage and were, therefore, deemed useless, "a militia was raised to guard the settlement."[26]

Furthermore, Professors Turay and Abraham confirm that "the importance of having a strong defense force was the concern driven home to the inhabitants, when the settlement of Freetown was attacked by the French in September 1794. . . . The invaders did not depart until mid-October, leaving damage in the region of $55,000."[27] Zachary Macauley, who was the new governor of Sierra Leone at the time, "established a militia consisting of Nova Scotians and Europeans in the employ of the Sierra Leone Company."[28]

The need for a more formidable armed force in Sierra Leone became apparent when, in October 1800, 45 soldiers of His Majesty's 24th Regiment teamed up with the Nova Scotians to defeat an indigenous Temne armed group in a skirmish. In 1801, with the aid of Temne King Tom, there was a more serious attack by the Temnes in which 12 militia men were killed and several of them, including Governor A. Dawes, were wounded. To ensure stronger security, a new charter for the governance of Sierra Leone included a provision for a detachment of 50 European soldiers of the Royal African Corps to be brought from the island of Goree, a slave dispatching post at the time (which was visited in 1999 by American President Bill Clinton during his African tour). These troops would carry out garrison duties as well as rebuilding the fort at Thornton Hill. However, under Governor William Day, a stronger defense program was instituted, establishing the Corps of Volunteers in 1803, which consisted of Nova Scotians, Maroons, and others from the settlement.[29]

When the British abolished the slave trade in 1807, more Blacks were enlisted in the Royal African Corps, some of whom were aided by the Dutch in rebuilding Fort Thornton and constructing a battery at Falconbridge Point on which their cannons were to be remounted. In May 1890, at the suggestion of Sir Francis de Winton, who led an expeditionary force against the Temnes, newly-appointed Governor James Shaw Hay established the better-armed Frontier Police Force, with Major A. V. Moore as the first Inspector-General; membership was drawn from all of Sierra Leone's ethnic or tribal groups. It was in 1894 that the Frontier Police Force was reorganized by Sir Frederic Cardew, the interim Governor of Sierra Leone and a former British colonel in the Indian Army, as well as a former (1890–94) commissioner in Zululand. As part of the Governor's reorganization plan, the strength of the force was increased from 300 to 500 men, who were divided into five armed companies that were used to demand that local chiefs and their subjects begin to pay taxes.[30]

Meanwhile, the British used the same Frontier Police Force, commanded by Lieutenant Edwards, against the Asante of the Ghana, defeating them and subsequently exiling their king, as earlier discussed. After that, colonial police forces were created for both Nigeria and Ghana. However, several Ghanian citizens were scared to enlist in the newly created force for fear of reprisals from the Asantes, who were defeated by the pro-British force from Sierra Leone. Therefore, the governor of Sierra Leone dispatched several Mende and Temne citizens from the local force to help the British control of the Asantes. Private Adamu of the Frontier Police Force was the first to fight his way to the Asante postkades, or area, and was promptly promoted to the rank of a lieutenant sergeant and decorated with the Distinguished Service Medal (DSM), with his boss, Edwards, earning the Distinguished Service Order (DSO) medallion.[31]

To aid the colonial acquisition of additional land in West Africa, the British created the armed West Africa Frontier Force in 1898, and, by an ordinance, a Sierra Leonean battalion of the West African Frontier Force was established on June 26, 1902. The both frontier forces, coupled with the Constabularies of Nigeria and Ghana "could be regarded in some respects as a military establishment. It undertook drills and was armed and trained in military tactics."[32]

The African Armed Forces versus the Civil Services: Both Created for Similar Interests but to Perform Different Duties

The much-decorated, superb African civil servant and British Commonwealth Secretariat's Deputy Secretary-General, A. L. Adu of Ghana, shows in his study of the Commonwealth's African civil service that there were similar reasons for the creating both the civil service and the armed forces, initially called the Frontier Forces on the continent. He also demonstrates that both the judiciary and the armed forces could not properly be included in the civil service as defined, adding that the definition of the civil service "specifically excluded the Judiciary and also the Armed Forces because employment in them is not in a civil capacity."[33]

In *The Civil Service in Commonwealth Africa: Development and Transition,* Mr. Adu, a Cambridge University–educated bureaucrat, explains that African civil service within the British Commonwealth did have its origins in the creation of a machinery by Britain to consolidate her colonial administration across her various dependent territories in Africa. He added further that the service was founded specifically and essentially to "prosecute the imperial policies in Africa, and its orientation and personnel were, therefore, suited to this purpose."[34]

As the creation of the Sierra Leonean Armed Forces (earlier called the Frontier Force) and other armed forces demonstrated, Mr. Adu also amply showed that the armed forces, in Commonwealth Africa, were created for specific purposes:

> The role of the Armed Forces is to be responsible for the defense of the nation against any external threats and to reinforce the ability of the Government to exert its influence, and act with confidence, in the exercise of its foreign policy. None of the African States [nations] can afford to maintain large Armed Forces since they are in peacetime non-productive in their normal responsibilities. Unless, therefore, there is a real threat to the security of the nation, the size of the Armed Forces should be relatively small.[35]

Interestingly, the threat that Adu and other bureaucratic experts either envisioned or feared in the creation of large and well-stocked armed forces is what African nations seemed to be faced with since the emergence of the wave of coups, counter-coups and armed confrontations on the continent. Mr. Adu writes that the policy regarding the size of a national Army should "be one which is termed by some people [as] the 'hedgehog' policy, that is, that the Armed Forces should not be large enough to be a threat to neighboring States."[36]

Additionally, Mr. Adu writes that although most African nations do not expect to be attacked by other nations, they still "maintain small Armed Forces partly for prestige reasons since—all or nearly all—independent states have them, but mainly for the purposes of assisting the civil power in restoring law and order wherever and whenever they break down."[37] The Ghanaian international diplomat furthermore indicated that it is this role of the armed forces that "is in fact the one to which greater importance is attached in most States even where, as in Ghana, it [the role] is not regarded in principle as other than a minor role."[38]

Organizational Parameters of African Military: Linkages between the Police and the Military

Illuminating thoughts about the men and women who constitute the armed forces in African societies were offered in 1982 by Professor Olatunde Odetola of Nigeria's Obafemi Awolowo University, the institution that was formerly known as the University of Ife. In his opinion, the military is "a puritanical organization, and . . . the training which men receive in this institution and subsequent military experience imbues them with austere attitudes and a high sense of discipline and responsibility."[39] Yet, one wonders if, given the politicized atmosphere in which the African armed forces find themselves today, the foregoing qualities made them any different from their continental civil servants, who are easily labeled corrupt, sloppy, as well as "yes men" and "yes women."

Professor Odetola goes further to state, that in Third World societies, the military "is also believed to possess 'rational' norms far above any other institution."[40] That, probably, was the military of the immediate postcolonial period. For looking at the recent reckless lifestyles and corrupt practices of several military leaders on the continent, the Nigerian scholar Dr. Odetola was correct in adding that while the professionalism of the officer corps of the African military can meet the discipline and austere category of rational norms, the listed qualities "should be applied to Third World militaries only with considerable caution."[41]

After all, it is often after counter-coups and the subsequent removal of military officers from political leadership that citizens of various nations become aware of how much money most of the ex-military leaders have stashed away in foreign, particularly Swiss, banking accounts, because their societies do not offer job security. This is part of the corrupt scenario that prompts many of these military officers to seize power through coups d'etat. Major Chukwuma Nzeogwu's January 15, 1966 announcement of martial law and in his promulgation of ten decrees in Nigeria's then northern region, stated unambiguously that corrupt politicians, tribalists, and other antisocial elements of Nigerian society all were what the new military regime was fighting against:

> Our enemies are the political profiteers, swindlers, the men in the high and low places that seek bribes and demand ten percent, those that seek to keep the country divided permanently so that they can remain in office as ministers and VIPs of waste, the tribalists, the nepotics, those that make the country look big for nothing before international circles, those that have corrupted our society and put the Nigerian political calendar back by their words and deeds.
>
> Like good soldiers, we are not, repeat not, promising you anything miraculous or spectacular, but what we do promise every law-abiding citizen is freedom from fear or other forms of oppression, freedom from general inefficiency, and freedom to live and strive in every field of human endeavor both nationally and internationally. We promise that you will no more be ashamed to say that you are Nigerian.[42]

Nzeogwu, who was widely considered a hero of the short-lived January 1966 coup d'etat in Nigeria, was killed in the Nigerian-Biafran civil war.[43] He was revered as a very disciplined and austere soldier. Yet, he was the exception for a military leader and Africans learned from news stories in the *New York Times* and other publications in mid-1998 about the horrible and immoral last hours of a West African military dictator who allegedly suffered congestive heart failure in the company of two prostitutes and, reportedly, died later. Indeed, many Africans would wonder if that was part of the disciplined and austere living that Professor Odetola described in his useful study, *Military Regimes and Development: A Comparative Analysis in African Societies.* The military and police officers who take arms to remove ostensibly corrupt politicians end up being corrupt themselves.

Invariably, when scholars write about the armed forces in an African context, they often include the police personnel, especially in those countries where the police are armed. However, wherever the police use batons and shocking-gear gadgets instead of loaded rifles or pistols in their day-to-day duties, their units are regarded as service departments; typical examples of such units are the pre–January 15, 1966 Nigerian Police Service and the pre–February 24, 1966 Ghana Police Service.

In Nkrumah's *Dark Days in Ghana,* he reports how he was seen off at the Ghana airport on February 21, 1966—three days before his regime's overthrow— "by most of the leading government and Party officials, and by service chiefs. . . . These men, smiling and ingratiating, had all the time treason and treachery in their minds"[44] Among the "service chiefs"—as Nkrumah describes the police officers—named in the book were the late Inspector-General of Police John Willie Kofi Harlley (promoted from police commissioner on the day of the anti-Nkrumah coup to the rank of an inspector-general), Police Commissioner Anthony Deku, and Police Commissioner B. A. Yakubu, who later became an inspector-general of police.

It is common knowledge that most coups in many African countries would have failed woefully if the police officials and their personnel did not cooperate fully. In fact, the arrests and detentions of political leaders of toppled regimes after coups d'etat are often carried out by policemen and women, if the overthrown leaders haven't already been earmarked to be killed. In those cases, armed military men are sent on an "arrest" mission to storm their target's residence and, later, announce that those killed resisted arrest and died while fighting back.

As an example of doing away with military officers who supported an overthrown civilian government, Nkrumah wrote in *Dark Days in Ghana* about how Major-General Barwah, his army chief, was killed:

> [Brigadier] Hassan was arrested, but [Colonel] Zanerigu, when confronted, escaped through a window of his house and drove to Flagstaff House [Nkrumah's official residence] to warn the Presidential Guard Regiment. [Brigadier] Barwah could not be intimidated. Woken from his sleep in the early hours of the morning of the 24th [February, 1966] by the arrival of [1966 coup leader] Kotoka and some 25 men, he courageously refused either to join the traitors or to surrender. Thereupon, Kotoka shot him dead at point-blank range in cold blood in the presence of his wife and children. The seven security officers who were stationed at Barwah's house were also murdered on the spot on Kotoka's orders. . . . Kotoka subsequently boasted of his killing of Barwah but said because he [Kotoka] was protected by a *juju* he was able to catch the bullets which Barwah fired in his defense and to throw them back at him.[45]

It is simply amazing that the African military forces have become so accustomed to seizing power and entrenching themselves in political offices. In fact, coups seem to breed counter-coups. On April 17, 1967, Lieutenant Samuel Arthur of the Ghana Army and three other officers planned, staged, and announced (for almost four hours) that they had overthrown the military regime that General Kotoka and others had installed in Ghana in February 1966. The counter-coup was thwarted by pro-NLC soldiers and Arthur and his young collaborating officers were overpowered and captured.[46]

Overall, this chapter has made an effort to confirm the creation and the historical role that African military units across the continent have played in the politics of various African countries, regardless of who the colonial power happened to be during active colonial rule. In doing so, the chapter has outlined the roles of colonial forces as well as organizational structures and resources within the military. These structures have continued to this day, when military officers are playing active roles in continental politics through coups d'etat.

How the African Military Was Placed on an Important Keel by Colonial Leaders with Top Cabinet Positions

It became possible for partial self-governance to be given to most of the African colonies under European control after the scramble for Africa at the Berlin Conference. It became apparent that various transitional governments were to be under indigenous African leadership. Typical examples were the limited measure of devolution applied by the British colonial leaders in Ghana and Nigeria. In Ghana the first general elections were held in February 1951, when Nkrumah was still in prison. Nkrumah, although in prison, had succeeded in having his name on the ballot, and received 22,789 out of a possible 23,122 votes. It was upon the victory of his Convention People's Party (CPP) that he was released from prison on February 12, 1951 and asked to form a new government.[47]

Nkrumah's new position would be titled leader of government business, not prime minister, as he and his supporters had hoped. He wrote about it in these terms:

The day after my release from prison, I was invited by the Governor [Sir Charles Arden-Clarke] to meet with him at nine o'clock that morning. When I walked into the courtyard of Christianborg Castle, I suddenly realized that it was the first time I had set eyes on the place. . . . I left the castle with instructions from the Governor to form a government.[48]

Nkrumah had no problem with the new title, but his supporters and followers wanted more, at least for him to become prime minister.

The first indigenous cabinet was very limited in scope like those in other former British colonies before full self-governance was granted. For example, the arrangement was the same situation in Nigeria before the country's October 1960 independence. Then, the victorious political alliance of Alhaji Sir Tafawa Balewa, Dr. Nnamdi Azikiwe, and others was given a similar opportunity to form a transitional government. There also the colonial authorities—before full-fledged independence—made sure that certain important ministerial (or cabinet) positions were reserved for colonial appointees. Among these were the defense, finance, and foreign affairs positions, as demonstrated in figure 2.1 below:

Figure 2.1

Cabinet Portfolios Initially Reserved by Colonial Administrators
Finance
Defense
Foreign Affairs
Interior (Internal Affairs)

Cabinet Portfolios Africans Could Hold
Agriculture
Commerce
Education
Works
Health
Local government (sometimes seen to be similar to Interior)
Housing
Trade
Labor/Works

Source: Ghana Ministry of Information, Accra; 1951–56 Cabinet files.

And, because of financial exigencies or prudence, certain positions had to be merged. Nkrumah's first cabinet, therefore, looked like the following:[49]

Minister of Education and Social Welfare—Mr. Kojo Botsio.
Minister of Health and Labor—Mr. K. A. Gbedemah.
Minister of Agriculture and Natural Resources—Mr. A. Casely-Hayford.
Minister of Commerce, Industry and Mines—T. Hutton-Mills.
Minister of Communications and Works—Dr. Ansah Koi.

Military and police affairs, under the defense portfolio, were considered so important that the colonial authorities in many colonies of Africa at the time—especially where the British were concerned—reserved them for trustworthy appointees. When Nkrumah's political party triumphed at the June 15, 1954 general elections, making him the prime minister, the governor advised all cabinet portfolios, except that of defense, were to be filled by his appointees. As Nkrumah wrote in his 1957 published memoirs: "On 28th July [1954] all members [of the new cabinet] were sworn in at the new Legislative Assembly and the Speaker, Sir Emmanuel Quist, was re-elected. On the following day, the assembly was ceremonially opened by His Excellency the Governor . . ."[50]

Since the 1954 general elections and the transitional government of the Gold Coast were a prelude to full-fledged independence, which came on March 6, 1957, one would expect that the colonial administration would relinquish its hold on the armed forces. Yet, the defense portfolio was invariably reserved for "trusted" colonial appointees, sometimes the governors themselves, thus confirming Sir Robert H. Scott's assertion that "the armed forces of the former colonies became status symbols."[51] To come out of their symbolic status, most of the officers of the armed forces of the postcolonial era have taken on the cloak of political importance. Many of them have used coups d'etat to reach the top of the continent's politics as heads of state and chairmen of provisional military regimes. While they enjoy their temporary political status, the temporary military leaders would often try to use the electoral processes to legitimize their rule, as the unsuccessful October 2000 attempt in the Ivory Coast demonstrated. In the next chapter, we endeavor to rely on extant, primary, and secondary research sources to explore how the context of rampant and pervasive corruption has often invited military intervention and coups, with Professor John Mukum Mbaku's favored phrase of "bureaucratic corruption" seriously in mind.[52]

CHAPTER THREE

Corrupt and Dictatorial Tendencies:
The Tacit Invitation for Military Intervention

The much-respected retired General Olusegun Obasanjo, who became Nigeria's elected civilian head of state in February 1999, made an unequivocal statement in 1991 that is very much similar to conclusions reached in several of the most recent books on African political history, including *African Political Leadership* (1998). Looking at the pathetic nature of African politics, whereby dictators and outright tyrants have held their own people captive, Obasanjo wrote that the anticolonialist struggles in Africa were "waged as much to end foreign rule, racial bigotry, and the associated indignities as to extirpate illiteracy and all manners of backwardness. Yet, no sooner had colonial rule ended than our new [African] rulers set about converting the revolution into one of fire and thunder against their own people."[1]

President Obasanjo's anguish about the corrupt and dictatorial rule in many post-independence African nations he witnessed while in semiretirement from politics, was very much shared by many of postcolonial Africa's writers and experts. Further examples have been provided by Professors John Mukum Mbaku and Julius O. Ihonvbere in their coauthored book, *Multi-Party Democracy and Political Change: Constraints to Democratization in Africa* (1998); and in Dr. Mbaku's *Corruption and the Crisis of Institutional Reforms in Africa* (1998).

Regarded as a distinguished elder statesman with a penchant for public service, President Obasanjo was a former military ruler, who in semiretirement became the respected chairman of the African Leadership Forum (ALF). His political views were still vigorously sought even when he was not in active partisan politics. His 1999 election to the civilian presidency of Africa's most populous nation was reported with fanfare, including a London-based news magazine article that heralded "Soldiers Go, soldiers Come."[2]

Using a multicountry framework, this chapter assesses the role that corruption and dictatorships, coupled with sheer intolerance of political opposition, no matter the opposition's viability and genuineness, have played in the persistent phenomenon of African military interventions.

Sadly, the foregoing words of the Nigerian president most certainly summarize part of the prevailing, and unbelievably limited and undermined social, economic, and political circumstances in which numerous citizens of African nations have found themselves in the post-colonial era. Their desperate, poverty-stricken plight, unabated and ever-growing, prompted many Africans to yell for avenues through which their "new," or indigenous postcolonial leaders—including both those elected to office and those swept into political power through coups d'etat—could be removed from power by any means possible.

To a true believer of democracy, the ballot box should be the only avenue for removal of an elected leader from office. Yet, in many African nations that became impossible as elections were either easily cancelled or rigged to satisfy the political whims and caprices of the incumbent political leaders.

Indeed, the ever-deteriorating postcolonial political and economic situations in various countries of Africa became so unbearable that, as articulated by General Obasanjo, the common dilemma was that of the new, indigenous rulers very simply converting the fierce anticolonialist revolutions or struggles into both personalized rule as well as into "one of fire and thunder against their own people."[3] The private and public lamentations of the retired general and a few other fearless patriotic Africans, some of whom could easily be counted among the elder statesmen of their impoverished continent, have confirmed the reasons for several of the military interventions that are prevalent in Africa. They also give transparency to the reported active roles that Obasanjo was personally forced to play in various military coups d'etat in his native Nigeria. Such participation happened before he succeeded the assassinated and much revered General Murtala Mohammed as Nigeria's head of state, an exceptional circumstance in which a southern-born Nigerian—of the Yoruba ethnic group, for that matter—was unanimously accepted by the northern-dominated military hierarchy to become the head of state of Africa's most populous and powerful nation.

Obasanjo's clean leadership slate as an army officer accounted for his selection to succeed the assassinated leader. Although effective Nigerian leadership had often been inherited by northern-born politicians or military officers, the death of General Mohammed in an abortive "Colonel's coup" led by Colonel Bukar Sukar Dimka (later executed), helped in elevating the southern-born General into the position of one of the most senior and respected military officers. Also, it was felt by the hierarchy of the Nigerian armed forces that Obasanjo could control the near-anarchical situation that the aborted Dimka uprising, which had resulted in the deaths of General Mohammed, Kwara State Governor Colonel Ibrahim Taiwo, and Mohammed's aide de camp, Lieutenant Akinseyinwa, had temporarily created.

As Bernard-Thompson O. Ikegwuoha described in *Nigeria: An Endless Cycle of Coups d'Etat* (1994), it was with military alacrity that, as later reported, "new appointments and postings became inevitable, [and] accordingly, Lt.-General Olusegun Obasanjo became the Head of State of the Federal Republic of Nigeria, an unanimous appointment by the [ruling] Supreme Military Council in succession to the assassinated Head of State."[4] If the leaders of already overthrown and yet-to-be removed regimes of Africa had been as upright as

Obasanjo, the continent might have been spared of the spate of coups d'etat that were led or staged by army officers as corrective measures.

The Evolution of Dictatorial Tactics in Africa

Apart from ascending to African leadership through the barrel of the gun, as many soldiers have done, indigenous leaders of postcolonial Africa often attained their leadership positions through democratically-held elections. This new breed of leaders needed the popular support of the local electorate to convince the departing colonial leaders, whom they had vehemently opposed in their nationalist struggles, to hand power to them. Yet, upon receiving the mantle of national leadership, these new leaders adopted political titles like "president-for-life," the Osagyefo and Mzee or Oga. Enjoying their power, these leaders did not want any measure of political opposition, not even as a token, or public criticism by the very men and women who had elected them to power.

Interestingly, in their strenuous pre-independence quests for political power, the black nationalist leaders and their supporters had made it seem that a viable and constructive political opposition was a prerequisite for good governance in independent Africa. Since Ghana led the way in sub-Saharan Africa's postcolonial leadership in 1957, many of our illustrative examples, fortunately or unfortunately, emanate from there. For example, in his initial position as the Leader of Government Business in the 1951 transitional government of Ghana, Kwame Nkrumah had publicly made it clear that his government needed a viable political opposition that could either keep it on its political toes or serve as a watch-dog over his government's actions. During Nkrumah's first overseas trip as an elected African leader, which began on May 30, 1951 with his arrival in the British imperial capital of London from Accra, he drummed continuously in speeches that there was the need for opposition as a necessary ingredient for true democracy. Also, Nkrumah made the urgent need for democratic governance abundantly clear in his June 1951 commencement speech at his alma mater, Lincoln University in Pennsylvania, an auspicious event for which he was the keynote (or commencement) speaker and at which he received the honorary Doctor of Laws degree from the university president, Dr. Horace Mann Bond.

Among other details about his ascendancy to the leadership of Ghana, Nkrumah said loudly and clearly: "We are aiming to work under democratic principles such as exist in Britain and the United States. What we want is the right to govern ourselves, or even to misgovern ourselves."[5]

Indeed, both opposing an existing government and working within it to achieve one's lofty political aims were deemed good ideas. After all, it is true that most of Africa's nationalist leaders worked within existing governing systems before they achieved their political objectives. As it was spelled out by Professor Yuri Smertin, a Russian writer, in Kwame Nkrumah (1987) even Nkrumah initially had to work within the colonial British system, the very system he had opposed uncompromisingly. As reported, he was indeed an ally of the colonial system, knowing that that would bestow on him the national leadership of the Ghana. Nkrumah reportedly said in 1951 of his unusual political flexibility:

I would like to make it absolutely clear that I am a friend of Britain. I desire for the Gold Coast dominion status within the Commonwealth. We shall remain within the British Commonwealth of Nations. I am not even thinking of a republic.[6]

Consequently, Nkrumah tactically and patiently agreed to serve in the colonial administrative setup in 1951, and, as expected of a cunning political leader, used the opportunity of serving in that nebulous position to get to know many who would later help in his own political ambitions.

From earlier political calculations, it was obvious to Nkrumah that a nationalist leader needed to be able to compromise and be flexible if he were to realize his political ambitions uninhibited. In doing so, Nkrumah also became very popular, to the point that, in June 1948, he would receive massive public support for the launching of his own political party, the Convention People's Party (CPP), through which he would ascend to the country's political leadership. The tantalizing motto of his party was "Forward ever, backward never."[7]

Since Ghana's successful anticolonialist struggle and the independence of the country in 1957 were seen as beacons for subsequent struggles of other colonized African nations, Nkrumah's pronouncements about the need for true democratic principles in all of the emergent African nations were very crucial. Invariably, they also gave hope to his political opponents as well as allowed the departing colonial leadership to harbor the feeling that, in their absence, democracy would thrive, whether just as they knew it or in a varied form. Yet, as Nigerian President Obasanjo eloquently spelled out, no sooner had power been transferred into the hands of the struggling indigenous African leaders than the power was converted "into one of fire and thunder against their own people."[8]

The subversion of democratic norms and human rights in these new nations came with amazing speed, often to the disgust of political opponents of these new leaders of postcolonial Africa. Therefore, the words from General Obasanjo are very unusual coming from an African with political leadership ambitions. After all, he was commenting from such a rich political experience as well as a particular enlightened awareness that the honesty in his expression could be neither underestimated nor ignored by anyone. For, in every geographic region of postcolonial Africa, there have been new black leaders who took very inimical and repressive steps to perpetuate their rule in political office, very often without the requisite electoral processes. In several instances, these leaders have remained in power until their deaths, as happened with most of the first generation of postcolonial African leaders, including Liberia's Tubman, Kenya's Kenyatta, Guinea's Toure, and, to an extent, Malaui's Banda.

At the time that the 1966 coup d'etat unseated Nkrumah, he and his CPP government "had been in office since February 1951."[9] Malawi's Hastings Banda—who lost power to his opposition—was an early Nkrumah protege that declared himself president for life and ruled with unlimited autocracy. It is simply interesting that some of the laws that Malawi, under Banda, used to clip the wings of political opposition and suspected opposition of any type were similar to those of Nkrumah, including the notorious detention laws that most of these postcolonial regimes either instituted or revived from the colonial era. After all, Banda lived in Nkrumah's regime before returning to Malawi.

Indeed, unlike in Great Britain and the United States, there were neither fair electoral practices nor leadership term limits in most of these postcolonial African countries. However, where a handful of African leaders have tried to allow elections and other democratic norms to flourish, they have done so at their own peril. In fact, newly elected leaders from the opposition groups have, very unfortunately, turned around to be more dictatorial than the previous government that they had relentlessly fought hard to defeat at the honestly-contested and, sometimes, foreigners-monitored elections. The Jimmy Carter Presidential Center in Atlanta, Georgia, for example, has made it a regular and admirable business to travel to some of these countries—where they are welcome, of course—to sponsor electioneering monitors to ensure smooth and fair elections, particularly in several Third World nations in and outside of the African continent.

In some instances, former or defeated political leaders have had to flee the very country for which they had fought the colonialists for independence. They then live in self-imposed exile in colonial capitals, often at the financial mercy of the very colonialist governments that they drove away during their uncompromising nationalist struggles. In fact, the plight of former Zambian President Kenneth Kaunda, which is discussed later in detail elsewhere, is a typical example. Kaunda was forced to flee Zambia, a country for which he and his political colleagues fought to achieve independence.

Kaunda's opponents, led by newly-elected President Federick Chiluba, accused him of many things, including involvement in an aborted coup. They went to the extent of trying to deprive the former Zambian leader, defeated at fairly-contested polls, of Zambian citizenship on the pretext that the former president, was not a Zambian citizen because his parents were Malawians, or non-Zambians.

The late Zimbabwean freedom fighter, Mr. Joshua Nkomo, also once had to escape from his country, reportedly disguised as a woman and temporarily live in exile in London because his former nationalist struggle ally, President Robert Mugabe, suspected him of an involvement in a coup plot. In many countries of Africa, similar stories and circumstances prevailed, a sad situation that made political events in several places of the continent resemble the contents of George Orlwell's prophetic books *Animal Farm* and *Nineteen Eighty-Four.*[10]

Anti-Opposition Measures: Political Arrests, Intolerance, Detentions, Executions, Exiles, and the Struggles of Exiled African Opposition Leaders

Political intolerance and sheer repression of fellow Africans by many governing authorities have, sadly, marked the lot of many citizens in postcolonial Africa. Some of the oppressed citizens would resort to varied measures—both deemed legal, like the ballot box, and illegal, like subversion and outright coups d'etat— to help bring about either temporary relief or outright change in leadership.

Interestingly, the various 1951–1966 regimes that Ghana's late President Kwame Nkrumah headed did not necessarily seem to inherit, not even from the departing colonial leadership, many of the repressive measures that his opponents loudly decried and that Obasanjo would later characterize as "fire and thunder."

In several postcolonial countries, like Ghana, Nigeria, and Kenya, laws were resurrected from the colonial era, including the restraining order laws that were used by the departing British colonial officials to deal with the much-feared events and movements like the Mau Mau rebellion, led by some of Kenya's nationalists to oppose the colonialists. For example, in Sub-Saharan Africa, Nkrumah's leadership was among the earliest examples of postcolonial indigenous rule, but its subsequent intolerance of vibrant political opposition paved the way for the institution of various draconian political measures. While some of these were introduced for lofty reasons, they did not necessarily satisfy the democratic principles and governance loudly promised by the newly-elected nationalist leaders.

Also, it is a historical as well as a political truth that, under the various colonial regimes of Africa, the ruling authorities often resorted to internal exiles to curb indigenous political opposition. With that measure, any citizen deemed "undesirable" or an agitator was "deported" to a faraway area of the colony in order to ensure peace and tranquility. In fact, some politically important agitators were treated in the same manner that the British colonial officials treated the King of the Asantes, the Asantehene, King Agyeman Prempeh I. He and a retinue of his royal supporters were arrested and exiled to the Seychelles Islands. When he returned to Ghana in humiliation, the former King was no longer received as the powerful Asantehene, but merely as the chief of the city Kumasi (with the indigenous title of Kumasihene, or Chief of Kumasi). In Kenya, Zambia, Uganda, Ivory Coast, Mozambique, Angola, and many other African nations, the colonial authorities mostly used the internal exile mechanism (not external deportation) to control rebellious agitators, local chieftains, and their supporters.

Indeed, as the citizenry judged the prevailing political situation in postcolonial Africa, these measures—often cloaked in legislative terms—were strictly intended either to curb clear acts of violence or to undermine the strength of the political opposition to the prevailing political leadership. Very sadly, Nkrumah's political colleagues in other parts of Africa emulated some of his examples of tough and, indeed, undemocratic legislative measures to curb growing political opposition and unrest in their own nations.

Sometimes, the measures were meant to stifle free speech, as confirmed by the distinguished Ghanaian writer Professor Paul A. V. Ansah of the University of Ghana in his 1993 study, "Kwame Nkrumah and the Mass Media." Ansah, then head of the Graduate School of Journalism at the university, stated that "the political atmosphere created after the passing of the Preventive Detention Act in 1958 and other laws [that were] specifically designed to limit the freedom of expression and of the press, adversely affected the development of the press."[11] As a trained journalist, scholar, and prolific writer, Professor Ansah saw how such a law put fear in many of the local journalists, as they did not want to offend the political rulers for fear of being arrested and jailed without trial.

To dress up undemocratic measures in democratic clothing, many of Africa's repressive regimes would argue that, indeed, the adopted measures were debated and democratically approved by the "representatives" of the people (the electorate). However, if the elected officers happened to have been elected through rigged or bankrupt electoral practices, then how could one count on such "elected" men and women to do what is in the supreme interests of the people? After all, it is also known that some parliamentary or congressional leaders in various parts of Africa often harped on the comical assertion that a parliament in Africa (similar to the U.S. Congress, with legislative powers) could be so powerful that it could do anything, with the exception of changing a man into a woman and vice versa. Some politicians even stood on political campaign platforms to blurt out such ridiculous assertions. "Mind you, vote for me so that I can protect you, as parliament can do and undo anything," some of them announced boastfully and with fanfare.

However, a sad situation in postcolonial Africa was that while the colonial leaders, mostly Europeans and their selective indigenous leadership (called "stooges" by radical politicians), minimally tolerated political opposition, the new or emerging postcolonial Black leadership in African nations had no tolerance for similar opposition. Again, to use the case of Ghana as a typical example, it is recorded that as far back as the late 1940s, Nkrumah and his band of fierce nationalists and anticolonialist were locked in bitter anticolonial struggles, mainly against British colonial rule. Toward that end, in 1949, the Western-educated Nkrumah stepped up his struggle against what he saw as the yoke of European—indeed British—colonialism and imperialism. To ensure widespread success of his struggle, he used political speeches and editorial opinions in politically-controlled newspapers, including his own Accra Evening News, as he urged his supporters and other compatriots to become well organized for what he regarded to be the anticolonial war.[12] In Nigeria, Dr. Azikiwe and other nationalist leaders used newspaper columns to start their own agitation.

For example, at worst, the colonial leaders in various parts of Africa merely tried to muzzle or undermine political opposition of the indigenous anticolonial nationalist struggling groups, which included the various liberation movements of the then Gold Coast, Kenya's Mau-Mau movement, and several others in other parts of the continent. The main weapons of the colonialists (known in Kenya and other places as "settlers") were political arrests, farcical public court trials, resulting in manipulated guilty verdicts calling for jail terms for convicted nationalist leaders. In the opinions of the colonial officials, such arrested nationalists were indigenous anarchists who wanted to wreak havoc through both demonstrations and guerrilla-type bush warfare.

After the widespread defeat of the colonial leadership in indigenous African nationalist struggles, things changed. New Black leaders of post-independence African nations met political opposition with treasonable felony laws and other repressive measures, some of which even called for unlimited political detentions without. Some of the convicted opposition members were publicly hanged or executed by firing squads. Most such horrible postcolonial measures were meted out to citizens of the newly-independent nations by their own elected leaders, often merely to deter future opposition to the status quo.

It is unfortunate that some of the opposition leaders languished or died in political detentions or prisons in various post-independence African countries. They could have been politically and intellectually astute citizens and served as the main alternatives to the repressive post-independence ruling elite. Instead, their lives were easily wasted. In the West African nation of Guinea, under President Ahmed Sekou Toure, for example, the first Organization for African Unity (OAU) Secretary-General Diallo Telli died in political detention under mysterious circumstances. Some of these early African bureaucrats and international civil servants were eventually suspected of foreign intelligence connections and, as a result, were dealt with ruthlessly. Mr. Telli had served Guinea at the United Nations and in cabinet positions.

As a matter of fact, many of the postcolonial black leaders were so anxious to perpetuate their rule that they overlooked both traditional and customary norms in dealing with their political opponents, using repressive behaviors that could only be curbed by military (or military-cum-police) interventions through coups d'etat, instead of via elections (which were, in any case, being rigged in most of these countries).

For example, the prevailing repressive situation in Guinea under Toure's leadership stated in 1958, when Guineans voted their famous "non" to end French colonial rule and to reject membership in the French Union, until Toure died, after decades of autocratic rule. Guinea and Mali, under Modibo Keita, were former French colonies that shared a lot of similarities in their style of governance; it was, therefore, interesting that their leaders teamed up with Ghana's Nkrumah to form the Ghana-Guinea-Mali Union, which was seen by many as the nucleus of African political unity.

Among the various opposition groups in Ghana, the main political leader struggling against the Nkrumah regime was Dr. Joseph Boakye (J. B.) Danquah, first of the political party called the National Liberation Movement (NLM) and later of the United Party (UP), which came into existence as a result of the merger of most of the splinter opposition groups. Born in December 1895, Dr. Danquah, a lawyer by profession, had played a vital leadership role in bringing Nkrumah back to Ghana from his academic sojourn in Great Britain (preceded by a stint of about a dozen years in America as a student).

The main aim of Danquah and other leaders of the early nationalist movement, called the United Gold Coast Convention (UGCC), was to get Nkrumah to coordinate the activities of the movement on a full-time basis, so the other leaders could concentrate on their professions and careers, mostly in law. There is the prevailing claim that Nkrumah was so financially despondent that he was unable to purchase his own boat fare to return to Ghana, and that Dr. Danquah and the other UGCC officials, on the recommendation of Mr. Ako Adjei, had to help him. Attorney Adjei was a contemporary of Nkrumah's at Lincoln University and had arranged for funds to be collected and sent to the future Ghanaian leader. Subsequently, on November 14, 1947, Nkrumah left for the Gold Coast from the British seaport of Liverpool, accompanied by Mr. Kojo Botsio, a close friend who was educated at Cambridge University. Mr. Botsio would later become a member of Nkrumah's cabinet, holding various important positions.

In the end, Dr. Danquah disagreed with Nkrumah, spoke out openly against his dictatorship, and, as a result, ended up in Nkrumah's Nsawam political detention center, where on February 4, 1965, he reportedly died of a heart attack. His death was cloaked in suspicion, as a heart attack or congestive heart failure was the popular excuse given for the death of political opponents in many places in Africa. About 70 years old at the time he died, Dr. Danquah had been first arrested on October 3, 1961 and detained at the notorious Nsawam political prison, allegedly for hosting his United Party's meeting that month at his law office to discuss "the demonstration by the [Ghana] Railway and other workers against certain aspects of the 1961–62 [Nkrumah] Budget, together with the general financial policy of the Government."[13]

Apart from Dr. Danquah, several other known and suspected Ghanaian political opponents of Nkrumah were arrested and clamped into political detention both during the same period and later in Ghanaian politics. The most prominent citizens to be detained included Ako Adjei, a lawyer and one of those who had given Nkrumah financial means to return to Ghana; Tawia Adamafio, a former cabinet member in Nkrumah's government; Kwame Kesse-Adu, a professional journalist; and the lawyer Obetsebi Lamptey, who also died, reportedly, as a result of a political detention that prevented him from getting needed medical attention. When the Ghana armed forces and the police, led by Colonel Emmanuel K. Kotoka, overthrew the Nkrumah regime on February 24, 1966 in a coup d'etat, among the publicly-announced grounds for the action were the detention-without-trial punishment of the Nkrumah regime; such detentions were carried out under the Preventive Detention Act (PDA) of July 1958, a repressive law that was passed a year after Ghana's independence to "tame" political opponents of Nkrumah.

There were often similarities in the content, style, and reasons for the coups d'etat that unseated many of the postcolonial African leaders. For example, often leaders of the political opposition group would benefit from the overthrow, since they would be seen as viable allies and supporters of the incoming military leadership. Logically, the military leaders would confidently have trust in the opponents of the overthrown regime. Again, an example was what happened in Ghana, whereby Dr. Danquah's successor as the opposition leader, sociology Professor K. A. Busia, played a very active anti-Nkrumah role while in self-imposed exile in Europe.

Early in his opposition leadership role, Professor Busia had seen the "handwriting" of dictatorship on the walls of Ghanaian politics and spoken out forcefully against what he saw as *Animal Farm* and *Nineteen Eighty-Four* Orwellian-type politics in Nkrumah's Ghana. In debating one of Nkrumah's favorable bills, the so-called "Avoidance of Discrimination Bill" in the Ghanaian parliament, Busia, *inter alia,* said: "Our problem is one of nation-building, and you do not do it by repressive legislation but by education and the growth of cooperation and leaving parties and policies to the choice of the people (Opposition cheers)."[14]

In addition to his political stature, Dr. Busia was a force to reckon with as a scholar. Among his published books was a 1967 publication, *Africa in Search of Democracy,* in which he spelled out his anguish over "the contemporary African political scene, with its bewildering upheavals and revolutions."[15] He also offered an explanation for reasons behind his desire to offer his hopes for democracy in Africa, as well as his opposition to corruption, inefficiency, and oppression in his native Ghana. He wrote:

> This book is a humble contribution to Africa's search for political wisdom whereby to avoid destruction. If any of my readers should think I have pitched my hopes for democracy in Africa too high, I can only say that I have not written as one who is a stranger to political life in Africa. I took an active part in political life in my own country in Ghana, where I was leader of the Parliamentary Opposition and of the United Party, which opposed the tyrannical rule of Nkrumah and his Convention People's Party. I have written this book while in voluntary exile, still continuing to oppose and expose the corruption, inefficiency and oppression of the Nkrumah regime; constantly bearing in my heart a harrowing distress at the sufferings of my former colleagues and countrymen imprisoned without trial, denied justice, ignominiously humiliated, some even maltreated to death; and painfully conscious of the reckless waste of our country's rich human and material resources.[16]

Given Busia's strong opposition to Nkrumah's regime, even when in voluntary political exile, it is not surprising that in the 1969 political elections, Ghanaians deemed it fit to elect into power his Progress Party (PP) candidates. He himself was sworn into office on October 1, 1969, as Ghana's new prime minister and, in effect, head of state with executive powers, different from Nkrumah's presidential title. When in exile, before the 1966 Ghana coup Dr. Busia served for many years as a don at St. Antony's College, Oxford, as well as a roving scholarly lecturer in Europe, Asia, and other places. Back in Ghana, he led his post-1966 political party to defeat the combined political forces of other political parties, including Nkrumah's supporters in a newly-created political party (since the CPP and all of the old other pre-1966 political parties were proscribed after the 1966 coup).[17]

Apart from the tyrannical tendencies of various postcolonial African regimes, which made military interventions very attractive, other factors included outright corruption and an overwhelming mismanagement of human, natural, and material resources, very much similar to those that prevailed in Nigeria and Ghana and prompted the military-cum-police forces to stage their coups. Several scholars on African politics and history, including coauthor Assensoh, have used specific examples to illustrate this point very clearly, including the fact that, under Nkrumah's rule, corruption had become so intolerable that the armed forces were compelled to act in 1966. Also, Professor J. D. Esseks of the University of Northern Illinois, in his book *Politicians and Soldiers in Ghana* (1995) effectively discussed the moribund nature of Ghanaian politics at the beginning of 1966, on the eve of the February coup.[18]

Indeed, several economic and political experts also see economic mismanagement as a serious problem in various African countries, especially in postcolonial regimes of Africa. Some economic analysts point out that some of the new indigenous leaders betrayed their ignorance of economic matters to the point of embarrassing their nations, their citizens, and, of course, themselves.

However, the forceful condemnation of many of Africa's postcolonial leaders and their shortcomings by overseas-based African scholars have often been seen by many non-Africans as being either too conservative or favoring Western nations. Some of these critics—mostly very radical Blacks in the diaspora—wish that the Africa-born critics would go to Africa to make their grievances known, instead of berating the continent and its leadership from foreign soil. However, many of the critics have understandably underscored publicly that they would either be imprisoned or even killed, if they preached the "gospel" of discontent on African soil.

Instead, most of these African writers have remained in self-imposed exile in order to have the luxury and flexibility of writing scores of very critical newspaper as well as journal columns about African problems, and, in several cases, some of them have even come out with very critical books about specific leaders on the continent. Unfortunately, however, these authors sometimes misapplied or took out of context quotations by colleagues still in Africa. Those being quoted seemed to be in support of the critical items being published against African nations and their leaders. Such actions alone can make both the main authors and those being quoted either hated or persona non grata entities back in Africa.

We, the coauthors of this book, are active members of International P.E.N., the England-based international writers' association for Poets, Playwrights, Essayists, and Novelists; we believe in its major obligation of championing freedom of literary and verbal expressions throughout the world. P.E.N., Amnesty International, Freedom Watch, and other international watchdog groups have helped in both monitoring human rights violations and in getting political prisoners released in Third World countries. Therefore, as always, we felt very honored when we sat among very distinguished writers and members of P.E.N. at the 1997 Mexico P.E.N. annual congress to read a coauthored research paper, which did a comparative study of the output, circumstances, and accolades of Black writers from Africa and those in the diaspora, specifically comparing African-American authors with their African compatriots, most of whom have suffered untold hardships, arrests, detentions without trial, and, in some cases, even murderous acts at the hands of intolerant African dictators. A revised version of the study was published in the April–June 1997 (volumes 4–6) issue of *Indian P.E.N.,* which is published by the Bombay chapter of International P.E.N.[19]

As already pointed out, many of the scholars from Africa would selflessly take it upon themselves to loudly drum out political corruption and dictatorial tendencies on the part of many of the known corrupt leaders of the continent. That is where Nigeria's current leader, President Obasanjo, is lauded immeasurably for his boldness and democratic ideals, which prompted him to condemn what he saw to be wrong in the aftermath of the anticolonial revolution. As quoted at the beginning of this chapter and elsewhere, the general's words recall what has been harped on for years by many exasperated writers from Africa and elsewhere, including some angry experts on Africa, who have indefatigably tried to call attention to the plight of African nations and their "captive" citizens. An example of expert criticism of a politically corrupt situation in an African nation is found in the article, "A Test for France," that the influential London-based journal, the *Economist,* published about postcolonial Togo in July 1998. The journal's editorial writers felt that France, as the colonial master of the West African nation, still had a responsibility toward its former colony, because, as the journal underscored boldly, "in practice, French interests have until recently still taken precedence over democracy and human rights."[20]

The *Economist* story on Togo, condemning what the journal saw as transparent political corruption in the country, described the results of the June 21, 1998 Togolese general elections in the following terms:

This was daylight robbery. Many elections suffer from a few irregularities—impersonation, double-voting, a bit of ballot-stuffing, people in uniform trying to make sure you vote the right way. But the election in Togo on June 21st went far beyond irregularities. It was blatantly stolen by the government [of Mr. Gnassingbe Eyadema].[21]

The journal went on to stress that Togo, with about four million people in total population, had been ruled by President Gnassingbe Eyadema "for the past 31 years. He is no democrat."[22] Indeed, Eyadema had ruled Togo with an iron fist for most of those years under a one-party decree, mainly as a former military leader, until 1991, when—as the *Economist* reported—an uprising "forced him to allow a national conference to discuss the country's future. When the conference tried to examine the shortcomings of his dictatorship, he sent the army to close it down."[23] Like several other politically corrupt African nations, Mr. Eyadema relied heavily on ethnic or tribal support from his own Kabaye ethnic group from central Togo who, according to the *Economist,* backed "the army, the police and the bureaucracy, fiddled the electoral lists, denied the opposition access to the state-run media and intimidated opposition politicians."[24]

The journal further revealed:

When the votes began to be counted, it was clear that Gilchrist Olympio, the chief opposition candidate and son of the country's first president, was going to win. Whereupon, the paramilitary police stepped in and stopped the count in Lome: ballot boxes, it is reported, were seized and burnt. The head of the electoral commission and four of its members resigned. The interior minister declared President Eyadema the winner anyway.[25]

This is similar to a situation in Ghana in the mid-1970s, when electoral commissioner Abban, under the visibly corrupt National Redemption Council military regime of Ignatius Acheampong, reportedly had to go into hiding to save his life from progovernment forces when he was unwilling to announce the tainted results of the so-called union government ("unigov") elections. As reported, the elections were openly rigged to give Acheampong and his supporters' victory. This was to signal that Ghana needed a unitary form of government in which Acheampong and his military cohorts would play leading roles, particularly those in the political leadership. In the case of the Togolese electoral fiasco, the electoral commissioner and his leading officials were able to resign.

While Great Britain has not seen the need to meddle in the affairs of its former mineral-rich colony, Ghana, France is known to have done the exact opposite in its former colonies in Africa. The *Economist* writer on the Togolese elections of June 1998 had cause to reflect this in the following words:

> The question applies particularly to France, which once ruled Togo. In the past France has supported its allies in Africa, democratic or not, and Mr. Eyadema has been a faithful and enduring friend. In return France provides Togo with almost a third of its aid, about $60m a year. But loyalty to its local allies has put France on the losing side in many recent conflicts in Africa—most notably in Rwanda, where it helped those responsible for genocide, and in Zaire, where it backed Mobutu Sese Seko long after it was clear that he was losing control of the country. Officially, the government in Paris wants to end the cozy relationship between France and French-speaking African rulers. It talks of moving from paternalism to fraternalism.[26]

While President Eyadema's security forces—reportedly led by top officers from his Kabaye ethnic group—are still able to ensure that his regime is insulated from Africa's wave of military-cum-police coups d'etat, Acheampong is not that blessed. Instead, his deputy in leadership command, General Fred W. Akuffo, unseated him in a palace coup, and, later, both of the leaders were swept out of office in the June 4, 1979 coup, led by a young air force officer, Flt.-Lieutenant Jerry John Rawlings, who retired from his two-term Ghanaian presidency, after having retired from the Ghana Air Force and having won civilian elections.

However, some anti-Rawlings writers and political opponents have often claimed that, like many other African military regimes, some of the regimes that Flt.-Lieutenant Rawlings headed were corrupt and brutal. In fact, there have been three such separate regimes since June 4, 1979, including the two in which he was elected and re-elected as the Ghanaian president. To an extent, the coauthors of this book, who visited Ghana for research and other purposes, have their own opinions.

During their research visit to Ghana in 1994, both authors saw matters differently—particularly Dr. Alex-Assensoh, who, as an American citizen, had heard so much about nondemocratic norms in African governance. They saw a different picture of the leadership of President Rawlings. The opposition newspapers of Ghana were having a field day with the publication of very critical articles about misdeeds in high places, including a report that a cabinet member in the first elected Rawlings regime had fathered a child out of wedlock with a Canadian diplomat, in what was described as an adulterous relationship. Therefore, we found it very hard to accept sweeping allegations that the Rawlings civilian leadership in Ghana, did not allow press freedom, although it was not impossible. Since military regimes often use excessive force in dealing with crime, suspects, and opponents, the AFRC and PNDC regimes that Rawlings earlier headed could have done likewise. After all, even several democratically-elected regimes in Africa were known to have exceeded their electoral mandates and become both capricious and utterly undemocratic.

However, several incidents in other parts of Africa confirm some matters discussed earlier. For example, a sad situation was what became of General Obasanjo's plight in his native Nigeria. First, while in retirement, he was falsely accused of having knowledge of a coup plot, tried by a kangaroo court, and sentenced to death. Due to international outcries, he was reprieved and spent three years in jail, from 1995 to 1998. His suffering resulted from the allegation that he and several other military officers, including his deputy head of state, General Shehu Musa Yaradua (or Ya'Aradua), merely failed to report an alleged coup plot. Ya'Aradua unfortunately died in one of the notorious prisons of Nigerian military leader Sanni Abacha.[27] What would befall General Obasanjo's fate inside Nigeria, as a former head of state of the country, on the basis of a mere allegation was an example ironically of what prompted him earlier to make the comment that many African leaders had eventually converted the liberation struggle into one of fire and thunder against their own people.

Being highly respected in and outside of Nigeria for his leadership and intellectual abilities, Obasanjo's arrest and subsequent imprisonment were not appreciated by many world leaders. In the words of Roger Cohen of the *New York Times,* the retired general, aged 63 in 1998, "gained lasting esteem through the rare act of handing over power to a civilian government."[28] His willingness, as a military ruler, to relinquish political power voluntarily had prompted many world leaders to doubt that the retired General Obasanjo would do anything undemocratic to unseat a government, military or otherwise, in order to attain power. According to Cohen, Obasanjo was "widely viewed as one bulwark, an elder statesman for a disoriented nation."[29] Yet, it was a reality that Obasanjo was arrested and jailed with his former deputy and Chief of Army Staff, Yaradua, who would die in jail, as reported, "under suspicious circumstances. Officially, cardiac arrest killed him."[30]

The sad circumstances of Obasanjo, Yaradua and others in the alleged 1995 coup plot were not the end of the matter. To make the allegations appear to be credible, on April 28, 1997, several other Nigerians, mainly military officers, were sentenced to death and various prison terms for their reported involvement in the aborted coup d'etat plot. Those sentenced to death by firing squad were: Lieutenant-General D. O. Diya, Abacha's deputy; Major-Generals A. T. Olanrewaju and A. K. Adisa; Lt.-Colonel Olu Akiyode; Major O. Fadipe; and Engineer A. A. Adebanjo. Those who received jail terms for their alleged roles included Colonel E. I. Jando; Colonel Y. Bako; Lt.-Col. I. A. Yakassai; Major B. M. Mohammed; and Lance-Corporal G. Tanko. With the death of Abacha, most of the 1995 accused and jailed military officers and civilians, who were arrested or "tried" under specific military decrees—including the infamous anti-rumors decree and the so-called Failed Banks Decree No. 18—have been pardoned. Many of them are sighing relief that, unlike Yaradua, their lives were not cut short by the usual "heart attacks" from which jailed political opponents die.

Indeed, "heart attack" deaths in African political prisons have a long history, as Ghana's late doyen of national politics, Dr. Danquah, and several others were among the early casualties in post-independence Africa. It is ironic that these noble lives were not terminated or wasted when the colonialists were in control of the colonies, as all of the nationalists that were arrested, tried, and imprisoned during colonial rule, including Nkrumah, Kenyatta, and others, came out of jail alive, later to become heroes and national leaders.

The most recent incidents of "heart attack" deaths have included the sudden death of the much-hated but feared Nigerian dictator, Abacha. His death—celebrated with gleeful measures in and outside Nigeria—invited the headline, "Nigeria Dictator Dies after 5 Years of Ruthless Rule: Key Aide Sworn in . . . Heart Attack Said to Be Cause of Death."[31] Although Abacha was swiftly replaced by the moderate General Abdulsalam Abubakar as Nigeria's new military ruler, and it was reported that exiled Nigerians "in Washington, London, Paris and other [world] capitals, said the general's death heralded an opportunity for Nigeria to release hundreds of political prisoners, cancel executions set by kangaroo courts and restore civilian government."[32]

Among prominent and well-meaning Nigerians who promptly wanted to see change in the giant West African nation was Professor Wole Soyinka, the 1986 Nobel Prize in Literature laureate. Soyinka, who had fled Nigeria into exile in 1994, was charged in absentia in March 1997 with treason by the Abacha regime. At the time of Abacha's death by "heart attack," Professor Soyinka was visiting Jerusalem, from where he said that the dictator's death was an "incredible opportunity" for his native Nigeria to resurrect democracy.[33]

Just like several other brutal regimes in Africa that prompted exiles and critics to call for a change of governance and leadership by any means possible—including coups d'etat—the Abacha regime had, reportedly, caused the deaths and imprisonment of numerous Nigerians who stood in Abacha's ambitious way of becoming an elected leader of his country. Elsewhere in Africa, several military rulers had taken democratic measures seeking the electoral mandate to become civilian presidents. Therefore, sycophantic supporters saw nothing wrong with a serving military ruler deciding to submit himself to the electoral test.

In fact, fellow Economic Community of West African States (ECOWAS) member Ghana witnessed a similar transformation when Air Force Flt.-Lieutenant Jerry John Rawlings led Ghana for almost a decade, from 1981, through some of its economically prosperous years. Rawlings sought the electoral mandate, and he was elected twice for the limited two-term presidency of Ghana. The difference between President Rawlings and General Abacha was that the Ghanaian leader, although also militarily trained, used a lot of tact and deft diplomacy to woo the Ghanaian electorate, although his opponents in the official opposition, led by the famous historian Professor Albert Adu Boahen, "have consistently cried foul at the [Ghanaian] polls."[34]

As an example of how democratic Ghana had become in the 1990s, even if on a limited score, Dr. Adu Boahen and his allies of the Ghanaian opposition were consistently able to register their suspicions of and displeasure with the

November 3, 1992 presidential elections. Apart from his public complaints inside Ghana, the retired history professor wrote an analysis of what he considered to be the "stolen ballot" in Ghana for publication in the London-based *African Affairs* journal.

Utilizing his well-known scholarly prowess, Adu Boahen, *inter alia,* pointed out that his opposition group would not accept the results of the 1992 Ghanaian presidential elections for various reasons. These included the fact that he and his allies "believed and still do [believe] that the presidential election was . . . rigged."[35] Comparatively, observers of the Ghanaian political scene still commend the fact that, when compared to the leadership of Nkrumah, which ended in the February 1966 coup d'etat, at least "the Ghanaian electorate has opted for a multi-partism."[36] What has been interesting is the fact that earlier Ghanaian elections, especially those in colonial Gold Coast, in which Nkrumah and his CPP followers scored stunning electoral victories were both fairly and honestly contested.

However, many Nigerians, in their political astuteness and enlightenment, knew that Abacha wanted to use brutal force, instead of persuasion and diplomacy, to become an elected president of their nation. That was part of the reason for the public jubilation over his death, despite it being very un-African to display joy publicly over another person's death. Several Nigerian families whose loved ones had died under Abacha's leadership felt the need to celebrate. However, after Abacha's death in June 1998, executed writer and environmentalist Ken Saro Wiwa's son, Ken Wiwa, had cause to say that in spite of the jubilation, "Abacha's death is not going to bring my father back."[37] Ken Wiwa's father and his eight other Ogoni compatriots were "publicly hanged for 'treason' in 1995 while a worldwide outpouring of appeals for mercy was icily ignored."[38]

The Abola Factor in African Politics

When Abacha died suddenly in 1998, Chief Moshood K. O. Abiola, the presumed winner of the 1993 annulled Nigerian presidential elections, had been in jail for over three years for daring to pronounce himself the elected president of Nigeria. His daughter, 23–year-old Harvard-educated Hafsat Abiola, called on the Nigerian military rulers to step down and, also, related Abacha's death in the following words, "It's the end of an era, and I hope, the end of military rule." Calling for the release of her father from Nigerian prison, Hafsat said that she was "very concerned about his safety."[39]

In an earlier *Time* magazine article, titled "Nigeria's Orphan," Hafsat was interviewed by Farai Chideya, the celebrated author of *Don't Believe the Hype,* an excellent book that is used as a standard text in an urban politics course at Indiana University by coauthor Alex-Assensoh. In the interview, she disclosed to Chideya that she was working hard for her father's freedom; in contrast to the title of the *Time* article, Hafsat did not want to become an orphan. Her mother, who was the senior wife of Chief Abiola (Mrs. Kudirat Abiola) had been expected to attend Hasfat's 1996 Harvard graduation, but she had been brutally murdered in Nigeria. As the story went, Hasfat got a phone call demanding that she fly to Washington to meet with family friends. When she arrived, they sat her down and told her that her mother had been gunned down in Lagos."[40]

Less than a month after the June 1998 interview with Chideya, Ms. Abiola, who lived in suburban Maryland with 5 of her 18 siblings, would truly become an orphan: Her father, Chief Abiola, a hard-working and very generous African politician, had died from an alleged "heart attack" while still in the custody of the Nigerian military leaders. Before an international panel of medical experts could travel to Nigeria to perform an autopsy to confirm the true cause of the chief's death, speculations about foul play were rife, especially since many Africans and their foreign friends had limited trust or confidence in military governance.

Coauthor Assensoh, who knew the late Chief Abiola personally and had experienced his warm Pan-African spirit, had two feature articles published about Chief Abiola's death, one in *Indiana Daily Student* (*IDS*), the main Indiana University daily newspaper, and the other in the *Herald Times,* the major city newspaper in Bloomington, Indiana. Written to offer local readers an insight into what could have happened, several theories were offered in both articles. The international medical team later carried out an autopsy and announced their preliminary medical conclusions to the effect that, given the circumstances, cardiac arrest could have been the cause of Chief Abiola's death. To help explain why Abiola supporters and others suspected foul play in the chief's sudden death, the *Herald Times'* version of Assensoh's two closely-related published articles is culled with permission and offered below. Styled as a guest column, it here reads in full:

The Herald-Times reported that 17 demonstrators died in Nigerian riots "triggered by the death of Nigeria's best-known political prisoner," Chief Moshood Kashimawoo Olawale (M. K. O.) Abiola (July 9). Reportedly, the 60–year old Chief died on Tuesday, July 7, from an apparent heart attack. He was meeting with former U.S. Ambassador to Nigeria and current Under-Secretary of State Thomas Pickering's delegation and, since then, the discussion of past "political murders" in African politics has created a web of suspicion around the detained Chief's death.

To compound the problems for the Nigerian leadership, led by General Abdulsalam Abubakar, the family and supporters of Chief Abiola still suspect a foul play, pending the results of an autopsy to be performed by Nigerian and international experts, including Dr. John E. Pless, an IU pathologist whose trip to Nigeria is being sponsored by the Boston-based Physicians for Human Rights. Chief Abiola's 23–year old Harvard-educated daughter, Hafsat Abiola, has openly blamed the Nigerian military leaders for her father's death and, as quoted in the *New York Times,* added: "My position is simple. My father was in their custody. Anything that happened to him while he was in their custody is their responsibility. I can't believe they did this." President Clinton's special envoy to Africa, Rev. Jesse L. Jackson, also said of Abiola's death: "The way he died arouses real suspicion." In 1996, Hafsat's mother, Mrs. Kudirat Abiola, was mysteriously murdered on a Lagos street.

Many Africans and non-Africans hold views similar to those of Hafsat Abiola and Rev. Jackson on the death of Chief Abiola, especially as the history of "accidental" and "political" deaths in African politics are promptly recalled. Some of these deaths happened when the victims, often arch critics of the ruling elite of some African countries, were either in detention (also called "protective custody") or in exile.

In fact, it has been alleged on several occasions that some of the methods used in murdering many political opponents in some African nations are beyond western medical or intelligence detention. For example, there has reportedly been the use of "dried and powdered bile" of the crocodile, a potent poison that could cause instant death when mixed with the food of the earmarked victim; this type of poison is hard to detect in a dead person. Indeed, there have also been sad cases whereby political opponents have been kidnapped and brutally killed, including that of prominent Kenyan politician J. M. Kariuki, whose mutilated body was found on Ngong Hills, near Nairobi, during the presidency of the late Jomo Kenyatta. Also, dying suspiciously in a "car accident" was Ronald Ngala, the president of the then Kenyan opposition party, Kenya African Democratic Union (KADU). On July 3, 1969, Tom Mboya, a popular Luo tribesman in the Kenyatta cabinet, was gunned down outside the Channi Pharmacy in Nairobi, Kenya, allegedly by a hired assassin from the Kikuyu tribe, reportedly, to prevent him from becoming Kenyatta's presidential heir-apparent; Kenyan foreign minister Okoh, with presidential ambitions, disappeared from his home and his badly burned corpse was later discovered.

In Ghana, the most prominent political opposition leader and University of London-educated lawyer, Danquah, also died of a suspicious "heart attack" when in the detention camp of then President Kwame Nkrumah. Sadly, in 1982, three Ghanaian high court judges and a retired army officer, suspected to be anti-government, were murdered, allegedly, on official orders. Uganda's Buganda King Mustapha (or Kabaka) died, under mysterious circumstances, during his exile years in Britain. Although he did not die from the "usual" heart attack, it was rumored over the years that he might have been poisoned by political enemies.

Certainly, most of these "political" deaths—called, "liquidations by any means"—form part of the basis for Africa's military and police officers taking up arms in the rampant coups d'etat to remove unpopular regimes that in turn, tend to outlive their usefulness. Those tainted politicians who had to be removed by the force of arms and rebellion will always be seen as players of a dirty game, and only those who play it well will come out looking clean—a very sad way of seeing the vehicle through which most of human society is governed.

Yet, many Africans have never believed that the assassinations or political murders of their beloved leaders, meant the end of either the revolutions that those leaders led or the cherished ideas that they propagated. A typical example is the assassination of Dr. Eduardo Mondlane, the early leader of the Front for the Liberation of Mozambique (FRELIMO), which was founded in 1962. His death was likened to the demise of Cuba's Che Guevara, who died in Bolivia but, as is pointed out by the author of *Eduardo Mondlane* (1972), still "lives through his ideas and heroic example, meaning much more to the youth of the world than [when] he was alive."[41]

The circumstances of Dr. Mondlane's death support the foregoing suspicions of authority, as it was alleged that he was marked down for liquidation, reportedly, by colonial Portuguese agents on February 3, 1969. He "was going through his normal daily routine; he collected a parcel supposedly containing a book sent from Germany about an early Russian revolutionary. The parcel instead concealed a bomb which, on opening the parcel, exploded in Mondlane's face, killing him instantly."[42]

Just like the popular "dream" of America's Rev. Dr. Martin Luther King, Jr.—who was martyred in April 1968, a year before Mondlane's death in 1969—FRELIMO's quest for a revolutionary solution to the Portuguese occupation of Mozambique was not stopped by Mondlane's death. Samora Moises Machel continued the struggle to its successful end until he, too, died in a mysterious plane crash over apartheid South Africa, then in support of Portuguese colonial designs in Africa.

After Dr. Mondlane's death, many messages were sent to his family and FRELIMO. One particular message, which highlighted the fact that his death would not dim the light of his revolutionary struggle, came from FLN leader Kaid Ahmed: "The physical disappearance of Eduardo Mondlane does not mean the death of the movement he led with courage and wisdom."[43]

It is the same with men and women maimed or killed in Africa's march toward meaningful freedom in the twenty-first century. Historically, their deaths would not be in vain. Instead, the overly ambitious and often corrupt politicians who have been suspected of instigating these deaths, would not live forever. Therefore, as the research in this chapter has demonstrated, military coups d'etat do not necessarily emerge because of the military; many of them are the result of both perceived and real frustrations regarding deteriorating social, economic, and political factors.

As a complement to the discussion in this section, the next chapter discusses military leaders who emerge from coups d'etat and transform themselves into civilian political leaders, which has happened in several countries on the continent.

CHAPTER FOUR

Military Leaders Turned Civilian Rulers

It is a popular historical, as well as political saying, often attributed to Lord Acton, that power corrupts but absolute power corrupts absolutely. Both African citizens and scholars of African or Third World studies have often wondered if the initial taste of political power by African military officers, after leading successful coups d'etat and ruling their countries for periods of time, accounts for their subsequent power-hungry behaviors. Among these behaviors is the ultimate desire of such coup leaders to perpetuate their hold on power as military rulers. Even if they did "voluntarily" hand over power and return to civilian life, they later return in civilian garb to seek political power through the ballot box.[1]

For many decades, many of African military leaders have been repeatedly brought out of their retirement from military and political services to the forefront of the continent's politics, an action that supports the theory that history often repeats itself and, also, that power corrupts. After all, this is verified by a close look at the historical and political paradigms, such as those we saw in the late British Commonwealth Secretariat Deputy Secretary-General A. L. Adu's earlier contentions about the military and the judiciary: that both had been trained to eschew partisan or active politics. Yet, in many African countries, military leaders have been able to transform themselves into civilian leaders, sometimes overnight. While some of them did well as civilian leaders, others did very poorly in new civilian roles.

While historians and political analysts have taken time to describe this phenomenon, there is little scholarship on the specific factors that are responsible for the noted transformation from military office to a head of state or commander-in-chief position in a country. Using several African countries as the focus of this discussion, and a few specific examples from places outside Africa, chapter 4 of our study provides some initial thoughts on several of the issues that bring about the transformations.

In a few instances, including that of Ghana's retired Flt.-Lieutenant Jerry John Rawlings, some very shrewd army or air force officers have succeeded in using the barrel of the gun to remove the very political leaders that they installed in political power through national elections, and replacing them as rulers. In doing so, such officers return to the center stage of their national politics, some-times with much more popularity than when they first seized power in coups d'etat and served as temporary or interim rulers, often because of the misdeeds or corruption of the elected rulers.

Very often, however, there are cogent reasons that the national interest and security are being put at stake, all of which have been advanced to explain the need for the successive African military interventions. As briefly discussed in the preceding chapter, the well-respected news magazine the *Economist* was among the numerous influential voices that locally and internationally clamored for immediate change in Nigeria, when the body politic of Africa's most populous nation seemed to be sliding toward economic and political chaos. In a rare three-page showcase of the "new" Nigeria, after retired General Olusegun Obasanjo cruised to political victory in the spring 1999 presidential elections, the *Economist* made it abundantly clear that, sadly, Nigeria had come to a near-death politically and economically under Abacha, when allegedly all sorts of fraudulent practices held sway.

It claimed further that Nigeria's public and private institutions, coupled with even locally-based foreign companies, were being "eaten away by corruption,"[2] adding:

> Roads, hospitals and schools [in Nigeria] disintegrated as funds for mainte-nance are pocketed. Daily power [electricity] cuts in the cities force facto-ries to close. Drug smuggling, money laundering and all sorts of frauds have made Nigeria synonymous with international crime. American drug officials speak almost in awe of the inventiveness and audacity of Nigerian crime syndicates.[3]

In fairness, it should be pointed out promptly that Nigeria is not the only developing or African nation that finds itself in such deplorable fraudulent situa-tions: there are many others in similar straits in several places in Africa and in other Third World places. However, this quote illustrates a scenario that in the past would have invited young Nigerian military officers to connive and take power in a palace coup, but which did not happen here. In some instances, an African or a Third World situation becomes so hopeless politically and militarily that any type of military person, including noncommissioned or dismissed offi-cers, can be prompted to take action, just as Master-Sergeant Samuel K. Doe succeeded in doing in Liberia after many decades of Americo-Liberian grip on the nation's political and economic life. In the end, he ruined Liberia in a vari-ety of ways, making it worse than it had been found it before his April 1980 coup d'etat, as discussed in much detail elsewhere in this study.

Comparatively, a recent military incursion into national politics in Pakistan offers another example of a Third World nation coup. In a cover story titled "Oh, Pakistan," the *Economist* points out that military coups are rarities these days, but that "there was something rather nostalgic about the events in Pakistan

1999

on October 12th."[4] That was the day that "dismissed" General Pervez Musharraf became Pakistan's new military leader, saying that he led the military coup
d'etat against the elected regime of Prime Minister Nawaz Sharif for the good of
his country. That was, as the *Economist* put it, "after Mr. Sharif had tried to
secure General Musharraf's departure."[5]

The *New York Times'* Celia W. Dugger put it in explicit terms in an October
13, 1999 dispatch, which read, in part, just like a script for a screenplay: "The
Prime Minister of Pakistan fired the powerful army chief Tuesday afternoon, and
hours later the army struck back with a swift, apparently bloodless coup. Troops
surrounded the Prime Minister's home, closed all the major airports and shut
down the state-run television and radio stations for several hours."[6] Apart from
pinpointing corruption and economic mismanagement as part of the reason for
the coup, General Musharraf decried how the Pakistani regime of Sharif had
tried to politicize the army, claiming that he seized power "to stop any further
politicization or de-stabilization of the military . . . the last remaining viable
institution in which all of you take so much pride and look up to at all times for
stability, unity and integrity of our beloved country."[7]

Similar to African situations, the sad economic and self-serving political situation in Pakistan made it possible for an officer who had earlier been removed
from his position by his Prime Minister to succeed in getting popular support
from the Pakistani army and in seizing power from an elected government.
That, of course, was among the reasons that prompted the *Economist* to indicate,
among other details, the following statement in its editorial:

> The instinct to support democrats and condemn military *coups* is correct,
> yet it is worth remembering that not all elected leaders are democrats and
> not all generals are villains. It is regrettable that the army should be the
> instrument of change in Pakistan, but the departure of the government of
> Nawaz Sharif . . . may well bring an improvement to the country's for-
> tunes. Whether in fact it turns out that way depends entirely on what
> General Musharraf does now. He has the power to make his country a
> better place, or to destroy it.[8]

The brief statements above spell out matters that are similar to events that
have led to the spate of coups d'etat in African countries. Indeed, the sordid
details of the Pakistani scenario seem to be a replay of events of an African country that has "suffered" several coups, as Pakistan has been familiar with military
rule in the past. As part of a former British colony, Pakistan's armed forces had
been seasoned along the lines of many former colonial armies in Africa, whereby
soldiers, as we quote the former Commonwealth Deputy Secretary-General
Adu as stating in chapter 3, were expected to be apolitical.

For example, apart from being described as an unlikely coup-maker and
appearing to be an apolitical officer, then 58–year-old General Musharraf of
Pakistan, a military officer for 35 years, was supposed to have "replaced a man
who had political ideas and who was pushed aside largely because he did."[9]
Instead of doing anything to undermine the coup in their country, Pakistanis,

just like Africans of political sophistication and otherwise, turned out in large numbers in Islamabad streets to watch the military drama: "Late-model cars lined the road leading to Prime Minister Nawaz Sharif's official residence, as citizens, hearing that a military coup was in progress, drove in to watch."[10]

However, it is a fact that some Africans became so disillusioned by coups and counter-coups that they were able to rise up against some military interventions and make sure that they were unsuccessful. Such civilian influence was successful in situations where it was deemed that the ensuing coup was neither called for nor necessary. A typical example was what happened to Major Dimka of the Nigerian Army. The major's expertise was reported to be in physical education and not in public administration, but he was bold enough to lead the unsuccessful counter-coup against General Murtala Muhammed's military regime in Nigeria. The General, regarded as comparatively an upright and progressive leader, was assassinated. Nigerians in large numbers came out to demonstrate openly in their country's streets against both the coup and what they saw as a mere opportunistic military insurrection by junior officers. Also, they felt that the leadership of Muhammed and Obasanjo had been very seriously tackling Nigerian problems. In fact, the Muhammed-Obasanjo regime's greatly-admired achievements included the fact that it had very "explicitly recognized the importance of crosscutting cleavages in creating a total of 19 States in Nigeria [seven States more than what deposed General Gowon's regime had created], and in writing into the 1979 constitution provisions requiring that political parties demonstrate a broad national presence, [and] that the winning presidential candidate show trans-ethnic support."[11] Nigerians have cynically claimed that Dimka's coup failed even before the civilians began their street protests, ended by loyal soldiers.

There had been no indication that General Muhammed, a fiercely religious man and disciplined military officer, would have transformed himself into the leader of a civilian regime. To confirm that, his successor, Obasanjo, honorably handed power over to an elected regime. In later years in Nigeria, a saving grace for democracy was the sudden death of General Abacha, who had positioned himself to retire from the Nigerian army and to run for the civilian presidency, irrespective of the fact that his fellow countrymen, en masse and through their exiled political opposition groups, made it amply clear that they were not interested in his leadership. Like other similar military regimes, Abacha would have done everything imaginable, including rigging elections, to have himself elected as a chieftain of Nigeria, if he had not died suddenly of a heart attack.[12]

General Abubakar, who succeeded Abacha, made it clear from the beginning that he was not interested in becoming a civilian leader of Nigeria. Hence he impartially and promptly spearheaded the fall 1998 arrangements that would turn Nigeria into a civilian regime in May 1999. The qualities of efficiency, impartiality and, sometimes, transparent honesty are among the crucial ingredients of leadership that all military leaders of Africa need but that some woefully lack. The main reason for lacking impartiality, of course, is that these military stalwarts are themselves interested in either turning their "coup" regimes into a semblance of civilian governance or simply stepping out of their military garbs, dropping their commander's batons, and assuming civilian suits. In the case of Nigerian and Ghanaian military leaders, it would be a matter of putting on some of the colorful *dahyiki, agbada, batakari* or kente cloth—popular national and public ceremonial attires—and jumping on a political platform to announce a program for seeking civilian status. This does not necessarily mean that President Rawlings, who genuinely shed his military status to compete seriously for the Ghanaian presidency, did any of the foregoing to attain power, although his opponents have made several unfortunate claims.

Impressively, along with seeing the political electoral process through a successful path, Nigeria's General Abubakar, reportedly reached a January 1999 tentative agreement with officials of the International Monetary Fund (IMF). Per the agreement, the staff was expected to monitor Nigeria's basic economic policy until May 1999, when the new regime of General Obasanjo—not expected to be like that of Chief Moshood Abiola—was sworn into office. After that case, Obasanjo, as Nigeria's new head of state, was expected to negotiate an economic reform program to revive his country's moribund economy. So far, Nigeria, which reported oil revenues of $15.2 billion in 1997, is expected to take several bitter economic measures, including efforts to "renegotiate its debt [the amount is disputed: $28 billion says the IMF, $31 billion, says the World Bank, $26 billion, says Nigeria]."[13]

In trying to play the role of political chameleon, whereby retired General Obasanjo shed his military image in order to run successfully for Nigeria's civilian presidency, a lot of juggling had to take place, even within the context of the military leadership. For example, there were unconfirmed reports that the soon-to-retire General Abubakar had "trumpeted the discovery of $800 m[illion], stolen by Abacha."[14] As alleged, to make the retiring members of the ruling PRC happy and, ostensibly, willing to retire, diplomats claimed that "the stolen money [had] been distributed to members of the PRC, as their final pay-off before leaving office." This may sound strange to people outside developing societies, but it seemed to be necessary to make sure that, there would be no dissatisfaction among the departing officer corps and the PRC leadership at relinquishing power to an elected leader.

In observing 38 years of Nigerian independence, General Abubakar made it abundantly clear that his regime had learned and benefited from lessons of Nigeria's past errors and, as a result, was prepared to prevent a repetition of those errors, adding: "While we celebrate the triumph of our continued existence as one great country, we must acknowledge the political frustration that we have to go through in our efforts to forge a great nation."[15] In the midst of the arrangements for a civilian leadership, which had been scheduled to take place in May 1999, General Abubakar also assured his fellow Nigerians: "We are committed to giving our fellow citizens the political environment of their choice within the context of one Nigeria. We are also committed to handing over [political power] to a democratically elected government on May 29, 1999. This is our solemn pledge."[16]

The Nigerian transition to civilian rule had hurdles that needed to be overcome, including the reported suit of President-elect Obsanjo's challenger, former Finance Minister Olu Falae. These events made some Nigerians feel that one could, somewhat, understand why many African military dictators have very often decided to either stay on for years or merely appoint an admixture of civilian and service officers to their cabinet positions to help with the governance of the nation and give a semblance of civilian rule. "With 7m [million] more votes than Mr. Falae," wrote the *Economist,* "Mr. Obasanjo has a comfortable-sounding margin."[17] Yet, Mr. Falae cried foul about the results of the February Nigerian presidential elections, and it was reported that he filed court papers to challenge the election results, claiming that voting was rigged and ballot boxes were stuffed. However, as reported, "international monitors agree up to a point, but say that any rigging was done by the [various] contesting political parties, not by the [Abubakar] government, and that anyway it was not on a big enough scale to affect the results."[18]

Also, in spite of the fact that Obasanjo would be an elected leader with a military past, Western nations were simply happy that democracy, through the ballot box, was being given a chance in Nigeria. As reported, election monitors from overseas suspected minimal electoral irregularities in General Obasanjo's presidential victory on 27 February but they also saw the election in a good light: "The result was not 'free and fair' but 'generally reflects the will of the [Nigerian] people.' That is the verdict of the European Union and the United Nations."[19]

Former President Jimmy Carter and his team of American monitors, reportedly, "questioned the wide disparity between the number of voters observed at the polling stations and the final result that [had] been reported from many States."[20] However, the seemingly vigilant Nigerian Transition Monitoring Group (NTMG), reportedly with 10,700 observers across the country, "judged that the 'incidence of electoral fraud was not great enough to completely distort the election result.'"[21] As expected, Obasanjo's main presidential challenger, Mr. Falae "declared the election to be 'a farce and a charade,' while his spokesman Yusuf Mamman, a former Ambassador to Madrid, said it amounted to a 'coup d'etat' against democracy."[22]

Western observers and governments were very excited by the fact that a military regime in Nigeria was giving up power voluntarily, and for the second time in the country's long experience with military dictatorships, since Obasanjo did so. For, the military leaders "nobly handed over to an elected civilian government."[23] Former President Carter concluded that "it is not possible for us to make an accurate judgment about the outcome of the [Nigerian] presidential election."[24] Yet, the U.S. government was said to be "right behind Obsanjo," especially as Washington "ended all sanctions against Abuja on the eve of voting, and [could] now support World Bank and International Monetary Fund loans [for Nigeria]."[25]

Also, Britain, and France "endorsed Obasanjo's victory under the cautious EU 'will of the people' formula, so Europe will almost certainly unblock aid funds of some 365 million Euroes [US$401 million] after Obasanjo's civilians take over on 29 May. Officials from Brussels and Abuja are already discussing how to apportion that money between anti-poverty programmes and mutually lucrative 'strategic energy' projects."[26]

In neighboring Ghana, President Rawlings was due to step down as Ghana's elected civilian leader after successfully serving two presidential terms. He is another West African subregional example of a military leader, who retired from his military duties and, subsequently, came through the political front door to lead a major African nation. He had already been reelected once, and his second four-year mandate was due to expire in December of 2000. Indeed, President Rawlings' performance in Ghana has been so much admired by Western leaders that, in stepping down as the elected Ghanaian leader, he has been received with open arms by Western leaders, who normally shun leaders with tainted military pasts. As the *Economist* put it, "the instinct to support democrats and condemn military coups is correct, yet it is worth remembering that not all elected leaders are democrats and not all generals are villains."[27] The most recent Western welcome was evident in President Rawlings's triumphant February 1999 visit to the American White House, his second as a Ghanaian leader; President Clinton showed a lot of warmth toward him, as demonstrated at their joint press conference.

As things such as multiparty politics have prevailed in Ghana since the reintroduction of democracy, one can easily see how only a few military leaders would give up political power, if they feel that they have a good hold on it. For example, President Rawlings endeavored to achieve many important strides for Ghana on many fronts, including the area of international diplomacy, which paved the way for Washington and other major countries of the world to support Mr. Kofi Annan's election to the U.N. secretary-general position. Yet, some press men and women often hid behind the new air of openness and democracy in the country to question various actions of the Rawlings regime, and even the First Lady of the country, Nana Konadu Agyeman Rawlings. Although many Ghanaians agreed that the presidential jet that Rawlings used on official trips was too old and, essentially, a "death trap," the National Democratic Congress (NDC) regime was forced to refute reports that a better presidential jet was being purchased for use by President Rawlings. And in a libel court trial of Ghana's Free-Press newspaper and its publishers, the First Lady spiritedly had to defend her honor in varied ways, including refuting allegations that she "had peddled drugs on her trips overseas."[28]

As part of her court cross-examination, Nana Agyeman Rawlings denied that she owned any property and operated a bank account in Switzerland, saying that "although she had visited Switzerland on several occasions, she had done so in an official capacity, attending UN meetings as head of a non-governmental organization."[29] Also, since the Ghanaian presidential jet reportedly developed an engine problem during Mr. Rawlings' Spring 1999 visits to the U.S. and Cuba, respectively, the Ghanaian government was listening to public opinion, as all democratically-elected regimes do, including the exhortations of many Ghanaians that their leader (President Rawlings) should not fly again on the jet that they considered to be a "death trap," as in the last two years, it had developed engine trouble while the President was on board, adding: "In the latest incident, the plane was abandoned in Miami in the U.S. When the president returned home on a commercial flight, he was met by placard-bearing support-

ers. One of the banners read: 'Change the flying coffin'."[30] All of these incidents, accusations, counter-accusations and elucidations show that a former military leader could still allow democracy to thrive in his country, thus Ghana.

As further reported, the Fokker 28 plane was meant for traveling along the
West African coast, not for cross-Atlantic flights. Ghanaian deputy Minister
(Secretary) for Roads and Transportation, Mr. Mike Hammah, in trying to
explain the government's side of the rumpus over the possibility of purchasing a
new plane to serve as a presidential jet, told the local press:

> The truth of the matter is that the presidential jet is old and no matter the
> level of maintenance it goes through, it is not advisable to use the jet for
> long distances. We cannot, however, wait for a calamity to befall the nation
> before we think of going for a new jet. Mind you, the president does not
> travel alone. The jet is for the nation and we will not be sending it away
> after his [Rawlings'] term of office.[31] Indeed, the air of democratic discus-
> sions in Ghana was so good that Ghanaian opposition parliamentary
> leader, the former finance minister J. H. Mensah, reportedly, did not agree
> with the Ghanaian deputy roads and transportation boss, as he felt that
> Ghana could not afford a new presidential jet at the moment because there
> were other areas [of Ghana] with more pressing needs.[32]

Indeed, a new day was dawning in West African politics for an elected government to be responsive to public opinion. Also, judging further from the
reported Nigerian electoral problems and the seemingly charged Ghanaian
political atmosphere, it is not impossible for proponents of military interventions
in African political affairs to point accusing fingers at efforts to resurrect democracy after a military take-over of the reigns of governance. This is particularly so,
if a specific African leader, upon seizing power, entrenches himself and shows the
relative toughness that helps in bringing about a semblance of national stability
at any cost. The situation in neighboring Togo is a typical example.

After several years of instability in Togo's early civilian regimes, army boss
Gnassingbe Eyadema took power in a popular coup and, for almost 32 years
now, has ruled Togo's population of about four (4) million. As the *Economist*
reported and quoted elsewhere in this study, out of over three decades of his
leadership—which began with his coup of 1967—President Eyadema has led
Togo with an iron fist as a one-party dictator, agreeing to multi-party elections
only in 1991 after a national uprising, which clamored for democratic reforms
and, as a result, almost cost him his job. Sadly, Mr. Eyadema's opponents termed
the result of Togo's June 21, 1998 general elections as "daylight robbery," and
that "was blatantly stolen by the government [of Mr. Eyadema]."[33]

What has baffled many Togolese citizens and experts on the country's politics
is that President Eyadema , just like many postcolonial African leaders, had
openly endorsed the idea of a vibrant opposition. In fact, when the local press,
led by Togo-Presse, mooted the idea in 1969 that there was the immediate need
for a new opposition party that would eschew "hatred, division, strife and personal interest,"[34] Mr. Eyadema reportedly made an official pronouncement wel-

coming it, hence the formation of his new Rassemblement du Peuples Togolai (RPT), with former Organization for African Unity (OAU) secretary-general Edem Kojo as the political party's secretary-general. In order to appease the Togolese military, the pro-Eyadema congress, at which Kojo was chosen as one of the leaders of the RPT, felt the need to applaud the national armed forces and even to emphasize that a military presence in the national affairs of Togo was tolerable because of the fact of "the army's immense contributions to national unification [of Togo]."[35] Indeed, it was in 1991 that Eyadema was transforming himself from a full-fledged military leader of Togo into a semicivilian leader at the head of a newly-installed political party.

In spite of the RPT congress extolling the Togolese army and publicly giving it a mandate to be involved in national politics, there have still been charges of what Samuel Decalo has described in his study as "petty corruption in the Togolese Army [as in other African armies]."[36] Decalo added that the corrupt practices "stood out prominently, especially embarrassing to a military regime seeking popular endorsement."[37] That was in spite of the fact that the Eyadema regime had made it clear on February 10, 1970 that commercial activities by army personnel were not compatible with military service and, as a result, "guilty" officers had a month to repent, or they would face the proverbial music. The regime was so serious that, at the end of the deadline, even Major Robert Adewui, a stalwart officer of Eyadema's 1963 coup d'etat, had to forfeit his Second Motorized Battalion commander's position because of his alleged trucking business interests.[38] What was unique was that Togo was doing something drastic about its "rotten" political eggs, a measure that other military-led regimes could never embark upon for fear of prompting a palace coup. His astute way of doing politics probably accounts for Mr. Eyadema's survival of past treasonous plots, including one in which he almost died in a plane crash in the interior part of Togo.

Next to Togo, is the former Republic of Dahomey, which changed its name to the Republic of Benin (or Benin Republic). A cynical friend from that West African country joked that the political leaders did so to see if the country's problems would disappear with the old name—if new fortunes appear with the new names.[39] Describing the successive military interventions there as being in a "praetorian State," Decalo further wrote that until 1985, Benin "held the unenviable African record of the most coups since independence, a record only matched in that year by Nigeria. Six times in ten years (1963–1972) the army, or factions of it, successfully seized power."[40] Apart from successful military political interventions, the country was "also intermittently rocked by military mutinies, attempted coups, and internal army strife."[41]

Benin's coup-mania created such an economic and political instability that many citizens, experts on Africa, and other people from countries of the subregion sighed relief when a serious young officer by the name of Mathieu Kerekou finally decided in 1972 to seize power, sweeping away forever what Decalo has described "the old political and military establishment."[42] He then stayed in power for a while in order to bring about stability. Before then, there had been what the citizens of Benin saw as the thorny but sad political fracas of leading politicians, as each positioned himself to wrestle power after the overthrow of the regime in 1963. By December of 1965, the situation had deteriorated, and, as General Christophe Soglo claimed, the nation's instability had arisen from the frailty of the nation's economy, which had brought about widespread dissatisfaction. Therefore, on December 22, Soglo staged his own coup, and assumed executive power.[43] He was succeeded by Emil Zinsou as the head of state.

Yet, there was also the Kouandete-led takeover of power in 1969 from Emil Zinsou's regime, although the former's bid to become a provisional president of Benin was thwarted. Instead, a so-called Supreme Council of the Benin armed forces—made up of the top officers—was set up, but was still directed by three people: Kouandete, as army chief; Colonel Sinzogan, the head of the much-feared Gendarmarie; and Paul-Emile de Souza, who had served as deposed President Zinsou's cabinet chief (or chef du cabinet).[44] Indeed, Kerekou's takeover of power in 1972 and its aftermath, coupled with his ability to transform himself into an acceptable civilian leader, are part of the intriguing nuances for this study.

The London-based *West Africa Magazine* quoted the Kerekou group of young radical officers as saying that they were not staging a coup in the October 26, 1972 takeover of the regime. Instead, the officers claimed that they were merely receiving power back from the civilian leadership. The military circumstances in Benin, as claimed by Kerekou and other young officers, were similar to what had happened in Ghana in December 1981, when Rawlings and his group of young officers removed the President, Dr. Hilla Limann, from his elected office, in what Mike Adjei, the prolific Ghanaian journalist, has described as seizing "power from a democratically elected government on 31 December, 1981."[45] Maybe, since they installed the Limann government, the leaders of the PNDC were merely receiving power back from the civilian leadership, as Kerekou and others said in their takeover in Benin.

In the end, the Kerekou group—similar to the suspected socialist and pro-Libyan nationalist ideological inclinations of Rawlings's earlier, June 4, 1979, coup d'etat—introduced Marxism-Leninism as their guiding ideological principle, although they also claimed to be following a so-called Dahomean socialism, maybe similar to President Nyerere's African socialism in Tanzania. As part of the morphosis and idle claim of turning Benin into a semicivilian entity, with military leaders at the top, Kerekou and the other young officers introduced the Parti Revolutionnaire du Peuple Beninois, which would enforce a radical nationalization policy in the country. Among early items to suffer nationalization were petroleum networks, which happened to be made up of only 19 distribution outlets, and then missionary education, mostly Catholic-owned.[46] In Benin, just like the instances of other African nations during and after colonial rule, missionary education of all types—Protestant, Catholic, and Islamic—was very fashionable, as discussed in detail in the first chapter of this book.

Unlike the Kerekou scenario of nationalization, Rawlings's PNDC in Ghana, with its suspected earlier socialist inclinations, did not go far. Instead, it renegotiated certain allegedly tainted contracts that Ghana-based foreign companies had signed with previous regimes, including those dating back to the deposed Nkrumah regime.[47] For the PNDC regime, what seemed to be important to the

military rulers was not ideology, but public accountability of the military officials. Many of them were to be dealt with severely, some of them to the point of
being hurriedly tried and publicly executed. To cite the example of the state of
affairs under the late General Acheampong's regime, Decalo confirmed, "Ultimately, Acheampong's interregnum became one where allegations of 'systematic' corruption appeared almost daily in the press."[48] Reportedly, Acheampong
and several Ghanaian military officers would pay dearly for alleged corrupt practices, as some of them were publicly shot to death.

In fact, to show that Rawlings and his AFRC leadership were serious about
matters involving corruption, charges of corruption were promptly leveled
against several public and military officials, including Acheampong and, indeed,
his family.[49] Accused Ghanaians who could be arrested were dealt with severely
and several former Ghanaian heads of state and top officials retired; some still-
serving military officers also suffered all forms of humiliation for their parts in
the alleged corrupt practices. Locally, corruption was known in a local language
as *Kalabuleism*, as Adjei in his 1993 book, Death and Pain: Rawlings' Ghana, the
Inside Story, narrated in a pictorial caption: "A parade of alleged economic saboteurs in Accra. Some were given long prison terms."[50] Indeed, as Decalo confirmed, major charges were prescribed against Acheampong, "for which he was
executed when Rawlings came to power."[51] As reported elsewhere, another
prominent ex-Ghanaian leader who suffered a similar executionary fate was the
retired General Afrifa, whose death by firing squad was described in these terms:
"A few weeks later [after Afrifa had met the Asantehene, King of the Asanetes
people of Ghana], General Afrifa was shot at the firing range by the AFRC.
How much of the reasons for his death could be attributed to the meeting with
the reported *Asantehene,* to his own character, and how much to fate as well as to
scheming political enemies remains to be seen."[52]

Other accused Ghanaians—including former military intelligence head,
Colonel Annor Odjidja, former police special branch officer Francis Opoku, and
People's National Party (PNP) publicity director Kofi Batsa, who later died in
London—were publicly declared wanted persons, and Ghanaians were urged "to
cooperate with the police and military authorities to effect the arrest of the
three."[53] As reported widely, even company managers and other officials were
treated with scorn by their Workers Defense Committees (AC). Also, AC officials, as an arm of the ruling PNDC in Ghana, were often avenging years of neglect and abject poverty. For example, the following top officials of Ghana Motor
Company (Ghamot), formerly Fattah Motors, were arrested for sale of imported
tires from China: managing director Steve Albert Donkor, a trained engineer and
reportedly former classmate of deposed and executed General Fred Akuffo; chief
internal auditor Agyei Mantey; senior checker Nannor; and spare parts manager
Fred Asante. Reportedly, nothing was proven against the three suspects, but
Judge George Agyekum of the People's Tribunal Court convicted anyway, as
Mike Adjei reported:

On judgement day the tribunal announced it could not find any evidence
of financial impropriety against the accused. Neither had the state lost any

money, but since they could not have sold the tyres without benefitting financially, they had to be jailed. Asante was released because he did not handle the sale of the tyres. Francis [S.A.] Donkor and Agyei Mantey were sentenced to five years imprisonment and Mr. Nannor was given 18 months. All of them served their terms at the Nsawam prison. In March 1983, I took Mrs. Mantey to visit her husband at Nsawam, my first time of setting foot there, but unknown to me then that four months later I [as a journalist] would be going there in my own right. On 14 November 1984 the leaders of the AC, who took over the Ghamot administration, were suspended from office for [alleged] corruption involving millions of tax-payers' money. In July 1985 the culprits . . . had their appointments termi-nated. But they were not jailed like their predecessors.[54]

Both Ghana's Rawlings and Benin's Kerekou, as military leaders, showed toughness and could boast of many successes that would help with their return to active politics as civilian leaders. Hence, both of them—in spite of a few set-backs—would ride high in popularity. They were, therefore, elected in their respective presidential bids to lead their respective nations as civilian presidents. Rawlings's civilian political ambitions, after leading the dissolved PNDC, became known publicly after the ban on Ghanaian politics was lifted on May 12, 1992, and he was selected to lead the NDC. He had as many as a dozen opposing polit-ical parties to contend with, but his most formidable opponent came from the leadership ranks of the National People's Party (NPP), which was being led by the historian Boahen. After Rawlings's first victory as a civilian president, the NPP leaders contested the results of the election in a booklet titled *The Stolen Ballot* listing several of what they saw as anomalies. In the booklet the NDC lead-ers, their supporters, and the leading officials of the Interim National Electoral Commission (INEC) were accused of many things, including intimidation, impersonation, manipulation and reorganization, stuffed ballot boxes, defective electoral register, use of ineligible voters, and other fraudulent INEC practices.[55] As a credible scholar in his own right, Dr. Boahen was believed by many people who knew him, although not necessarily by international observers.

Furthermore, while the visiting foreign electoral monitors, including officials from the Atlanta-based Carter Presidential Center and Library and the Common-wealth Secretariat, now headed by a very competent Nigerian, Chief Emeka Anyaoku, declared Rawlings and his NDC party the winners, the Ghanaian opposition and some commentators felt otherwise. Adjei, among other details, wrote: "For over 10 years the people of Ghana demanded general elections and a return to constitutional government. What they ended up with was one of the most blatantly rigged elections in its [Ghana's] electoral history. The NPP lead-ers narrowly avoided plunging the country into total chaos like Liberia."[56]

The Liberian situation, as briefly mentioned elsewhere, was one of real chaos, and a measure of the wanton destruction that makes the Ghanaian situation seem tame. However, it did provide an interesting scenario in the politics of both the West Africa subregion and in the corridors of the Economic Community of West African States (ECOWAS). Interestingly, the so-called warlords of Liberia started out as civilian operatives, but, in the end, most of them were clad in military clothes and were being referred to as commanders and generals. In fact, after his July 1997 victory at the polls, President Charles Taylor, described as a leading warlord, wasn't reportedly able to make the transition to civilian politics from his military leadership.[57] That, of course, is not strange, as most of these former civil war operatives and leaders were still, after the elections, armed to the teeth and ready to do battle at any given moment.

Also, opponents of Taylor's victorious National Patriotic Front (NPF) happened to be civilians, but several of them were later clothed in military mufti or camouflages, including NPFL leader Prince Yormie Johnson; Ulimo-J leader Roosevelt Johnson; United People's Party leader Ellen Johnson Sirleaf, a superb international civil servant; and Alhaji Kromah, a former top official of Liberia's Information Ministry. Reportedly, many of them left Liberia after the election, allegedly in order to regroup and offer a united opposing front. According to *Africa Confidential,* "Nearly all Taylor's other vocal critics—civilian and military—are now in exile."[58] At the time of the completion of this study, many of these Taylor opponents had returned to Liberia to accept top posts in the Taylor regime, which is a good sign of the genuine reconciliation for which President Taylor had appealed.

Unfortunately, President Taylor was, for some time, accused by America and other Western nations of arming Sierra Leone's Revolutionary United Front (RUF) rebel group. The group, headed by imprisoned Foday Sankoh, allegedly has been battling the elected regime of President Tejan Kabbah. The accusation prompted, reportedly, Mr. Taylor to threaten "to expel all the foreign aid agencies [for Sierra Leone] (many funded by the U.S. Agency for International Development) that provide basic services."[59]

It has recently been explained that the Liberian warlords started out as civilians, but, when plunged into heated battle in the country's civil war, started in December 1989 by Taylor, most of them began to dress like military officers. Hence it is not very surprising that the Taylor regime, although elected, was still seen as an ally of the RUF, which was accused by the international press of various heinous crimes after its troops invaded Freetown in the spring of 1999. Mrs. Aminata Saccoh, the wife of London-based *New African's* Freetown correspondent Sheku Saccoh, was reportedly "shot dead by the [RUF] rebels who raided her home when searching for him. Her body was thrown in the street and the family home was burnt."[60]

For Liberians to keep their conscience clear, Senator Charles Brunskine, who is a deputy speaker of the Liberian House of Representatives and a leading member of President Taylor's ruling NPP, has deemed it necessary to seek an investigation of Liberia's involvement with the RUF. He has, subsequently, "helped draft a law making it a felony for Liberians to fight in Sierra Leone."[61] Brunskine and others, very much pro-America, want to be positively viewed by Washington, D.C., and other Western capitals the way Ghana's Rawlings and a few other pragmatic regional leaders are. In view of Liberia's many economic and social problems, Senator Brunskine's action is commended, as his nation needs all of its resources to rebuild its economic infrastructure.

Liberia also needed international exposure; hence for a November 2000 interview, *West Africa Magazine* editor Adam Gaye went to Liberia, where, as he reported, he "met [Taylor], on October 30, in his huge Malikie Farm, located three miles from his former rebel headquarters of Gbarnga."[62]

As *New African* deputy editor Baffour Ankomah reported in March 1999, Canada was "not known for its political advocacy in Africa." However, the country has "waded in. On 12 February, Canada's foreign affairs minister Lloyd Axworthy formally asked the U.N. to intervene in Sierra Leone. Canada held the rotating presidency of the Security Council for the month of February."[63] That shows how seriously the unfortunate Sierra Leonean situation was being viewed. The good news from Sierra Leone, as this book was being completed, is that President Ahmed Tejan Kabbah, who was temporarily removed from office and then reinstated by an ECOWAS military contingent led by Nigeria, appointed four leading rebel leaders to his cabinet under the July 7, 1999 peace accord, including formerly imprisoned Sankoh of the RUF.[64] President Kabbah's reinstatement signaled a triumph for democracy. After al, he was the legally elected leader of the Sierra Leonean people.

It is not strange that Sankoh and others in Sierra Leone were, for a period, being embraced by the general populace of the country, in spite of their military past or seeming insurrection. After all, in Ghana, Rawlings's leadership has been hailed by the international community, including the IMF and the World Bank, in spite of his military background and his involvement in two coups in his country. Western leaders have also praised his leadership and economic programs, and President Clinton chose Ghana as the first nation to visit on his 1998 African tour, making him the first ruling American president to visit Ghana. Consequently, the reciprocal official visit of President Rawlings and the Ghanaian first lady, Nana Agyeman Rawlings, gave Mr. Clinton and the American first lady, Hillary Rodham Clinton, an opportunity to express their appreciation for the reported wonderful reception they received in Ghana during their tour. Mr. Nixon was the first sitting American vice-president to visit Ghana, as the leader of the Eisenhower administration's official delegation to Ghana's 1957 independence celebrations in Accra. It was, in fact, at the independence event that Mr. Nixon and Dr. Martin Luther King, Jr., had their first momentous face-to-face meeting, as recorded in the book *African Political Leadership* [1998].[65]

President Clinton's fondness for the Ghanaian leader, as shown during their spring 1999 White House joint press conference, did indicate that, certainly, a military leader can transform himself politically and become acceptable to the leader of the world's most powerful democracy. It amazed many people—including Americans, Africans, and others—that Mr. Clinton went to the extent of saying at their joint press conference that the first family's first stop of Ghana allowed them to highlight, for all of their fellow citizens, the vast progress that Africa—led by Ghana's example—has made. At a gala state dinner, hosted by the Clintons for the Rawlingses in the historic state dining room of the White House with not less than 200 invited guests, the two leaders exchanged gifts: President Rawlings received a hand-crafted sterling silver cache pot, while President Clinton was given a traditional Ashanti stool, a symbol of a true Ghanaian welcome.

Back in Ghana, the members of parliament commended President Rawlings on the successful U.S. visit. As reported by *Ghana Review International* of March 13, 1999, both majority and minority members of Parliament on Thursday, March 11, 1999, deemed it necessary to commend President Jerry John Rawlings openly on his recent very successful U.S. visit:

> The five-day visit, from Tuesday, February 23, to Saturday, February 27, at the invitation of President Bill Clinton, was reciprocal to the one he made to Ghana last year as part of a six–nation African tour. In a statement to Parliament on the visit, Mr. Kofi Attor, Chairman of the Committee on Foreign Affairs and member of Parliament for Ho Central, said the President, his wife, and the 14–member delegation were treated to a memorable welcome ceremony on the lawns of the White House. This type of welcome is reserved for treasured visitors to the United States, and President Rawlings is the second African Head of Statem after President Nelson Mandela of South Africa, to be accorded it in the past ten years. The Chairman of the [Ghana] foreign relations committee said it is gratifying to note that President Rawlings chose not to speak for Ghana, but to play the role of a spokesman for Africa. "One thing that has come out clearly from this visit is that Africa has a credible, sincere and acceptable spokesman in the person of the President of the Republic of Ghana." . . . Mr. Attor described the visit as "an overwhelming success in all respects . . ."[66]

To many observers, President Rawlings's presence in the American White House was one of his "good-bye" visits to world leaders, as he plans to step down after two terms of presidency, as the Ghanaian constitution requires of all elected presidents. From 1992 to the year 2000, eight consecutive years, Mr. Rawlings ruled Ghana as an elected civilian President. Added to about a decade of military leadership of Ghana, he has ruled Ghana longer than any other indigenous national leader in Ghanaian history, including the late President Nkrumah, who started out as Leader of Government Business after his political party, the Convention People's Party (CPP), won the February 1951 general elections.[67] From then until his overthrow in the February 24, 1966 coup d'etat, for 15 years he was Ghana's leader. Even so, he couldn't match President Rawlings' 18 years, which surprisingly brought much-needed political and economic stability to Ghana, which in turn prompted major world leaders to laud the Rawlings phenomenon.

Certainly, there have been other military leaders of Africa who could not leave their military uniforms behind and run for elective presidential office as Rawlings and a few others did. Also, in the spring of 1999, retired Nigerian General Olusegun Obasanjo also ran for office, which confirmed the philosophical thought that Ghana and Nigeria are like twin nations: Whatever goes on in one country will also happen, sooner or later, in the other. Yet, many leaders seized political power in coups d'etat, and decided to hang on to it for a while. An example is President Mobutu Sese Seko of the former Zaire Republic (now the Republic of the Congo), who was overthrown by assassinated President

Laurent-Desire Kabila. Mobutu, as army chief, had himself overthrown the regime of Prime Minister Patrice Lumumba, his former boss, who was subsequently assassinated. Mobutu's own removal from power, and his subsequent death in a brief exile shortly after, did not help the former Zaire very much. Sadly, his successor, Kabila, has been embroiled in a civil war against a faction of his forces that broke away to form a rebel group. Although assisted heavily by such southern African presidents as Robert Mugabe (Zimbabwe), Sam Nujoma (Namibia), and Jose Eduarddo dos Santos (Angola), Kabila was, in the spring of 1999, urged by his allies "to seek peace with the rebels . . . as [his] . . . forces are on the run, with his foreign allies threatening to pull out."[68]

In retrospect, there was Idi Amin's leadership in Uganda; Amin had overthrown President Milton Obote's regime in 1971. Also, in 1965, Bokassa had overthrown the ruling leaders of the Central African Republic and, later, lavishly crowned himself an emperor. Modibo Keita's government in Mali, which had formed political alliances with Nkrumah and Guinea's Sekou Toure, as reported earlier, in a futile Ghana–Guine–Mali political union, was overthrown by Moussa Traore. Niger was ruled by Hamani Diori from 1960 to 1974, and his administration in what has been described as resting "upon an intricate and comprehensive alliance of chiefs from all ethnic groups and regions."[69] As reports from postcolonial Niger showed, by 1970 the Diori regime was becoming very unpopular, as it was "in open conflict with the country's student population and urban labor."[70]

Although propped up by France, Niger under Diori had, by 1974, become so unpopular that when the Nigerian leader asked for a revision and strengthening of the France-Niger treaty of friendship, the regime of French Prime Minister Georges Pompidou refused to do so. Therefore, when Pompidou visited Niger, he was confronted with a huge anti-France demonstration in Niamey, the capital. Subsequently, French assistance for Niger was either reduced or, as Decalo reported, frozen in the country that had, hitherto, been labeled as the most loyal client-state. France showed complete neutrality when Colonel Seyni Kountche's coup d'etat took place on April 14, 1974, against what was termed as Diori's "dictatorship", as reported by *West Africa Magazine*.[71]

North Africa's Place in Africa's Coups d'Etat Configuration

Apart from West and Central African nations tasting military upheavals, there were attempted insurrections in various East African nations. Tanzania, under the leadership of President Julius Nyerere, who died in London in October 1999, was once threatened by an internal army mutiny on January 20, 1964, which was quelled by the British Commander of the Tanganyika Rifles Company (army), Brigadier Patrick S. Douglas. Hoping for a lasting peace, Nyerere held discussions, offered to meet with the aggrieved soldiers, and, with his peaceful nature, settled the grievances of the mutineers amicably. Also, a 1964 coup d'etat ended the reign of the Sultanate in the island of Zanzibar (which would later be annexed to Tanganyika to form the Republic of Tanzania). While Kenya's Kenyatta, out of his own revolutionary zeal, recognized the new military leaders of

Zanzibar, Nyerere did not do so, as he had plans to discuss the future unification of the island and mainland Tanganyika, which he achieved with Zanzibar's Sheik A. Karume. Nyerere succeeded in becoming unified Tanzania's first president.[72]

However, Tanzania's most serious threat was posed by Uganda, under Amin. In the words of Decalo, "[Amin] consistently threatened to invade Tanzania because of Obote's presence there, [and] tried to bully Kenya."[73] Kenya, too, suffered an unsuccessful coup attempt, led by Lieutenant Oyoga, a Luo military officer. There has also been the Guinean military intervention, as part of what Samuel Finer and Decalo have termed "Man on the Horseback" syndrome,[74] whereby the author saw the military presence as a perpetual, or recurring, phenomenon.

Historically, the West Africa subregion experienced its first coup d'etat in the Republic of Togo on January 13, 1963, in which the first Togo president Sylvanus Olympio was assassinated. A subsequent civilian regime, backed by the Togolese Army, was overthrown on January 13, 1967, by the Eyadema group, as explained in detail above. Before then, North Africa had seen numerous coups d'etat, some of which would linger in power for so long that they would become indistinguishable from civilian regimes. Henry Bienen once aptly described this aspect of African coups, stressing that "military regimes cannot easily be distinguished from civilian regimes by their economic and social policies or abilities, [and that] an examination of the evidence does not reveal very sharp distinctions between civilian and military leadership in African countries."[75]

However, it is an undeniable fact that without a political mandate to seek and fulfill, some military regimes in Africa have, initially, performed well on several fronts, particularly where the economy was concerned. Where there has, however, been an abysmal performance record is in the area of human rights, in which military leaders often had zero-tolerance for anything that threatened their power base. In fact, whenever Western leaders and their press point to a particular African leader, military or not, whose country is doing well economically, there is invariably an accusing finger pointed at the leader's human rights record. President Rawlings is a typical example. Although nobody has succeeded in tying him personally to some of the horrible murders that were committed in Ghana while he was the military ruler, sad dastardly events abated when he succeeded himself as an elected civilian leader. At that time, as his critics would say, he needed the mandate of the Ghanaian electorate and, therefore, was less likely to abuse his power.

As already detailed elsewhere in this publication, the most terrible murders in Ghana during the leadership of President Rawlings were those of 1982, when three legal luminaries—including a female judge and nursing mother, Mrs. Justice Cecilia Koranteng-Addow—and a retired army officer were kidnapped and murdered in cold blood. Joachim Amartey-Kwei, a cabinet member in Ghana's ruling People's National Defence Council (PNDC), was apprehended and, with the approval of PNDC Chairman Rawlings, was tried, convicted, and "executed for his role in the murder of the judges [and the retired army officer]."[76] The fact that Rawlings sanctioned the execution of his own ruling colleague still did not help in persuading his fellow Ghanaians that he was not party to whatever plot that was hatched to kill the four people.

Some of these excesses in military regimes make it imperative—as many postcolonial African leaders often said—for new military leaders to hand power back to elected leaders as soon as possible. Otherwise, they should put down the military khaki and put on civilian clothes to slug it out at the electoral polls. In that case, a soldier, just like any citizen of a nation, would have the benefit of submitting himself for electoral certification, and could then garner the accolade of soldier-turned-civilian leaders, as Rawlings has done in Ghana, Mubarak has done in Egypt, and, most recently, Obasanjo has done. In doing so, the electorate, too, would have the chance to either stand by or reject such soldiers.

Chapter 5 deals with the subject of how a military presence in Africa affects political stability, both positively and negatively. Even the editors of the reputable *Economist* have made a distinction between bad politicians and soldiers with good intentions. They wrote that the instinct to support democrats and condemn military coups was correct sometimes, yet they wanted their readers to remember that "not all elected leaders are democrats and not all generals are villains."[77] Also discussed in the next chapter is the very sensitive issue of ethnicity, or tribalism, in African political and military matters.

CHAPTER FIVE

Military Presence in African Politics: Stability or Instability?

... the African military has broken down exactly at those points at which
the rest of society has signs of stress. ... The sensitivity of military
institutions to political and class [and ethnic] cleavages makes
them as much part of the problem as the solution.

—J. M. Lee, 1969

On balance, however, the very fact that the military broke down in many
African countries exactly at the same ethnic lines as the rest of the society
reveals that the military organization is not exempt from tribal influences.
At a conceptual level other than the ethnic, the military has often
intervened as arbiters between two warring elite sectors:
the "politician" and the "bureaucrats."

—T.O. Odetola, 1982

The two authors who have captured the essential aspect of the armed forces in
African nations in the foregoing statements are sociology Professor T. O.
Odetola of Obafemi Awolowo University (the former University of Ife) at Ife,
Nigeria, and J. M. Lee, a specialist on African affairs. For many years, the erro-
neous assumption, as Odetola has pointed out, was that "membership in a het-
erogeneous army necessarily fosters a 'national outlook,' [but] evidence shows
that recruitment to African armies is so skewed that it becomes difficult to see
the military as diminishing ethnic rivalry."[1]

Historically, African countries have been affected by interethnic (or inter-
tribal) strife and torturous conflict. The query, therefore, is: What role does the
African military play in facilitating or undermining ethnic and tribal divisions?

Moreover, how does the length of time a coup leader rules affect stability in an African country? These and other questions are addressed in this chapter.

As an ongoing practice, it is also true that very often in Africa, the political leadership of a particular nation can easily determine who gets into the armed forces. This is especially so among the forces' elite officer corps, which, as originally designed, used to be the main segment capable of moving troops to effect a military exercise or takeover of power. That situation has, however, changed as master-sergeants, lieutenants, captains, and other officers in lower ranks have been popular enough to lead many of the postcolonial African coups d'etat.

The composition of the armed forces, the police, and the security services of an African country is determined by the political leadership; one sees a crucial example of this in a study of Kenya by Professors C. Rosberg and C. Nottingham. In the East African nation, where politicization has taken its toll, the political ruling class has been led for over two decades, since Jomo Kenyatta's death in 1978, by President Daniel arap Moi, of the minority Kalenjin ethnic group. The Kalenjin group has other minor subethnic compositions, as shown in figure 5.1 below. In their 1966 study, Rosberg and Nottingham have shown that, despite a minority population of 9–11 percent of the total Kenyan citizenry, not less than 34 percent of the total membership of the country's armed forces— including the police and security agencies since 1961—have been from this Kalenjin ethnic or tribal group.[2]

In a brief interview with Kenyan doctoral student Hannington Ochwada, of the History Department of the University of Florida at Gainesville,[3] it was very instructive to learn that, under the Kenyatta presidency, ethnic feelings within the Kenyan armed forces were under serious check. For example, in military matters Kenyatta, the Kenyan president behaved like Ghana's President Kwame Nkrumah where ethnic sentiments were concerned: both leaders did not tolerate ethnic differences. Although by ethnic description, Kenyatta was a Kikuyu (or Gikuyu, as he described it in his published University of London anthropological study, *Facing Mount Kenya,* 1965), the ethnic group that held dominant sway in the Kenyan armed forces was the Akamba. Similarly, Nkrumah was from

Figure 5.1   Kenyan Example of Ethnic/Tribal Control in Armed Forces

Ethnic Group(s)* %	in Kenyan Population	% in Kenyan Armed Forces
1. Kalenjin (with sub-ethnic groups as Tugen, Nandi, Kipsigis, Terik, Marakwet and Elgeyo)	9–11	34
2. Kikuyu, Luo, Abakuria or Kuria, Maasai, Akamba or Kamba, Giriama, Tarta	89	66

*When evenly distributed, each of the dozen or more remaining ethnic groups (tribes)—apart from the dominant Kikuyu ethnic group from which Kenyatta originated—have no more than 10 percent of their people in the armed forces of Kenya. Thus, the Moi regime and its officials make sure that there is no cohesive ethnic force to pose a threat to their existence since the 1982 abortive coup d'etat led by a noncommissioned officer of the Kenyan airforce. This table is constructed from the available data on the Kenyan armed forces, as of 1990, indeed 12 years after Kenyatta died in 1978.

the Nzema (or Nzima) ethnic (tribal) group of the Western Region of Ghana, but the ethnic groups that dominated in recruitment into the Ghanaian armed forces were from the then northern regions because, as every Ghanaian would agree at the time, they could be trusted by the rulers. The police service, however, had Ewes in the majority, especially in the top echelons. Hence the first ever inspector-general of police, Mr. Harlley, was an Ewe and he played a very decisive role in the success of the 1966 overthrow of the Nkrumah regime and the subsequent arrest and roundup of Nkrumah's cabinet members and political party functionaries. (Mr. Harlley's top police tenure was followed by Mr. B. A. Yakubu as the inspector-general of the Ghanian police, who was from the then northern area of the country.)

In fact, it was not only the Ghanaian military that relied heavily on the citizens of the former northern regions (which have now been split into several regional groups), for recruitment, as affluent Ghanaians also used Ghanaians from that part of the country for security and night guard duties. For after-hours security, the rich Ghanaians trusted Hausa, Fulani or Dagomba security guards at the gates, as it was often said that such security guards would simply tell a visitor to wait outside while they checked with the master to see if he (the master or his spouse) was expecting a particular visitor. In Kenya, as Mr. Ochwada explained to us, special security forces like the General Services Unit (GSU)—similar to Nkrumah's well-armed Special Presidential Guard—did employ, for example, many Kikuyu's from President Kenyatta's area of birth, but the Army did not, as explained above.

Also, even Mr. Moi, who in 1978 succeeded Kenyatta as the second post-independence President of Kenya, tried to follow the Kenyatta tradition until August 1982, the day that airforce noncommissioned officers, led by Hezekiah Ochuka, tried to overthrow the Moi regime. For several hours, Mr. Moi reportedly had to hide in a military barracks at Edoret, his home. It has been explained that the composition of the membership and officer corps of the barracks was made up largely of Mr. Moi's Kalenjin ethnic group. Reportedly, he was so well-protected by his fellow Kalenjins there that immediately after the insurrection was put down, and after coming into power, Mr. Moi overhauled the membership as well as the officer corps of the Kenyan armed forces to the point of disbanding the Kenyan airforce as it was known in 1982. In fact, today, a Kalenjin from the subethnic group of Tugen is the Kenyan army chief reflecting whom Mr. Moi would trust to lead the armed forces during his term in office. (His current term of presidential office is said to be his last.)

Ethnicity and the Composition of the African Military

In Ghana, as it has been amply shown during the research stage of our study, the composition of the armed forces used to be dominated by the ethnic group that held sway over recruitment, including that of the police and the security services. In fact, for many years, membership of the Ghana armed forces and the police was made up of what used to be non-university-bound citizens. In most cases, they were mainly from the ethnic groups of northern and upper regions of the country. Also, entering the armed forces or the police service in pre-1966 Ghana—before the coup d'etat that toppled Nkrumah's regime that year—was not a fashionable event.[4]

Indeed, among the Akan ethnic group of Ashantis, Fantis, Akims, Akwapims, and, to an extent, Nzimas, to enlist in the forces was often considered a silent curse of sorts. Consequently, citizens from areas of Ghana without arable land for farming or from areas without naturally-endowed mineral resources often joined the armed forces. Hence 62 percent of Ghana's so-called "other rank" recruitment came from the northern and upper regions, which are inhabited by the Hausa, Fulani, Dagomba, Basare, among other ethnic groups. Also, in Nigeria in 1961, according to Odetola, of a total of 81 officer corps, about 60 were Igbos from the former eastern region.

However, in Nigeria, the general composition of the army was a different matter, as it has been shown that men and women from the various northern regions mostly populated that structure.[5] The following figures, without ethnic factors, help to explain some details about the Nigerian armed forces, with its four branches:

Figure 5.2

Nigeria's Military Composition as of 1999:
Branches: Army, Navy, Air Force, Police Force
Military Manpower (age for entering the military): 18 years old.
Age of male entrants and total number: 15–49 years old; 25,967,281.
Military expenditure (in dollars) and % GDP: $236 million; 0.7 percent.

(Source: 1999 edition of *CIA World Fact Book*)

In fact, based on factors of ethnicity, which is sometimes crudely called "tribalism" internally, it is not strange that, for reasons of trust, most of the leaders of Nigeria's first coup d'etat, which included the late Major Chukwuma Kaduna Nzeogwu, were of the Igbo ethnic extraction. Nzeogwu had been trained at Britain's elite military academy Sandhurst (together with one of Ghana's military leaders, General Akwasi A. Afrifa). At Sandhurst, Nzeogwu, Afrifa, and the other trainees were instructed to become very competent officers who would, in the future, eschew partisan politics upon their return to their respective armed forces. Yet, Major Adewale Ademoyega, a Yoruba officer, who authored a 1981 book on Nigeria's first military coup of which he was one of the chief architects, had a different story to tell about Nzeogwu, an Igbo officer. He disclosed in his publication that, throughout 1965, Nzeogwu "spoke freely and openly to some young officers [Igbos and non-Igbos] about his intention to stage a revolution which would bring Nigeria to the path of greatness."[6]

The Nigerian coup d'etat was different from that of Ghana, as the Ghanaian coup leaders were a mixture of officers from various ethnic groups, including Akans, Ewes, and the predominantly northern/upper regional ethnic groups of Hausas, Dagbanis, Fulanis, and the like. Therefore, the composition of Ghana's ruling National Liberation Council (NLC) membership, after the first coup d'etat in the former British colony, was made up of the following:

Figure 5.3

Name	Ghana's 1966 Military Rulers of the NLC	
	Ethnic group	Regional affiliation
1. J. A. Ankrah (NLC Chairman)	Ga	Greater-Accra
2. John Willie K. Harlley (NLC Vice-Chairman)	Ewe	Volta region
3. E. K. Kotoka (coup leader)	Ewe	Volta region
4. A. A. Afrifa (deputy coup leader)	Ashanti	Ashanti region
5. B. A. Yakubu (deputy police chief)	Dagomba/Hausa	Northern region
6. J. E. Nunoo	Ga	Greater-Accra
7. A. K. Ocran	Fanti (Fante)	Central region
8. A. K. Deku (internal security chief)	Ewe	Volta region

(Source: Ghana Information Services, Accra, Ghana, 1966)

For ethnic advantage, as shown in the above figure 5.3, three of the eight members of Ghana's February 1966 ruling military council were from the Ewe ethnic group of the Volta Region. Most importantly, the coup leader, General Kotoka, who was from that area of the country, needed to ensure that he had adequate ethnic support on the day of the coup. In addition, Mr. Harlley and Mr. Deku were among the top police officers of Ghana at the time, with the latter having been in charge of the Criminal Investigations Department, or CID; there were two indigenous Ga-speaking members, including retired General Ankrah, who was "resurrected" from military retirement and made chairman of the ruling NLC. Indeed, there was only one person representing each other ethnic group, which, in itself, confirmed the prevailing argument that, depending on who is at the top of military matters, enlistment can often and easily swing to the ethnic group of the leader or leaders in control, as they enlist more of their own ethnic kind.

It is true that General Kotoka and police boss Harlley, who were from the Ghana army and police, respectively, and constituted an influential part of the 1966 coup d'etat leadership, were from the Ewe ethnic group of the Volta region of Ghana. Historically, however, one could not fault the predominance of the Ewe officers in the plotting and implementation of the coup against the Nkrumah regime (as Professor John M. Mbaku and others have done in recent books, including one that Praeger publishing company issued not long ago).[7] For, as intricate matters have shown in coup plots, the ringleader would obviously surround himself with officers that he could totally trust. In General Kotoka's case, he could utilize the support of his fellow Ewes but—as a shrewd officer who wanted a balance in ethnic support for his coup d'etat—he did trust an Ashanti officer, General Afrifa. As was shown in the early days of the coup, Afrifa, as Kotoka's brigade commander, was the closest and most supportive military ally, even on the early February 24, 1966 morning when troops had to be moved from Kumasi area, where both officers were stationed to Accra, the capital, to effect the military change of government. This was done while Nkrumah was en route to Hanoi, North Vietnam, to play an elder statesman role in trying to end the war there.

Certainly, if one learns from the histo-political circumstances of Ethiopia's first successful military coup and the subsequent counter-coup, led by Mengistu Haile Mariam, the Ghanaian coup leader, General Kotoka, cannot be blamed for surrounding himself with additional Ewe officers from the police and security services. As now known, it was during the ruling military council meeting that Mengistu shot his way into power by killing most of the top leadership of the ruling council (the so-called *Derg*). In the words of Professor John Mukum Mbaku of the Utah-based Weber State University, "few governments [have been] faced with a fight for their very survival." Therefore, it has become common practice for several of a coup leader's ethnic people to be placed in the top echelons of the security apparatus, if not directly in the ruling council. Ghana's President Rawlings did that in his two coups d'etat, the AFRC of 1974 and the PNDC of 1981, as well as in his civilian regimes, when the top security job went to retired Army Captain Kojo Tsikata, a fellow Ewe. Also, legal affairs, where court and tribunal prosecutions were crucial, were for many years headed by lawyer Dr. Obed Asamoah, a fellow Ewe.

Hence ethnicity often played a major role in military affairs, and, as Odetola explained, recruitment to African armies can be described as being so skewed that, indeed, "it becomes difficult to see the military as diminishing ethnic rivalry."[8] That, of course, did not bode well for stability, where military rule was concerned. Also, the length of rule that an incoming military dictatorship or regime abrogates to itself can be a factor in determining its stability in a nation's political affairs.

Certainly, many African political leaders, including Ghana's Nkrumah, seemed to be speaking in self-interest when they vehemently opposed military involvement in politics, as, of course, they feared being overthrown in coups. For example, Nkrumah indicated in a 1961 speech and later in early 1966, that the army had no place in politics. Speaking to the cadets of Ghana Military Academy on May 18, 1961, Nkrumah made it clear that it was not the duty of a soldier "to criticize or endeavor to interfere in any way with the political affairs of the country; he must leave that to the politicians, whose business it is. The government expects you, under all circumstances, to serve it and the people of Ghana loyally."[9]

Subsequently, in a February 1, 1966 admonition, barely three weeks before his own overthrow by the Ghana armed forces, Nkrumah touched on the idea that instability and contradictions could be brought about if military leaders seized power from politicians and military rulers. Speaking at Ghana's National Assembly on February 1, 1966, Nkrumah told the Ghanaian Army, police and naval authorities:

It is not the duty of the army to rule or govern, because it has no political mandate and its duty is not to seek a political mandate. The army only operates under the mandate of the civil government. If the national interest compels the armed forces to intervene, then immediately after the intervention the army must hand over [power] to a new civil government elected by the people and enjoying the people's mandate under a constitution accepted by them. If the army does not do this then the position of the army becomes dubious and anomalous and involves a betrayal of the people and the national interest.[10]

Surely, Nkrumah seemed to be protecting his partisan political interest in 1961 and, especially, in 1966, since the Nigerian Armed Forces had, in January of 1966, overthrown the civilian regime of northern-born Alhaji Sir Tafawa Balewa in a very brutal coup d'etat, led by southern-born officers, mostly Igbo-speaking officers of Nigeria's former eastern region. Being the leader of the nation that had lit the torch of colonial liberation in Sub-Saharan Africa in modern times, Nkrumah's supporters felt that he could speak boldly for himself and other African leaders. From what he said in the 1966 parliamentary speech, he seemed to think that, having entrenched his leadership in Ghanaian politics, it would be possible for his supporters to reelect a government that would be very favorable to his interests. He recommended that a replacement government be immediately elected after the intervention by the army, as he feared a coup could take place. However, experiences from several military-ruled African nations have shown that if military authorities stay too long in power, there tend to be counter-coups d'etat, especially since the army, unlike elected politicians, lack the electoral mandate to rule, and petty disagreements often emerge among the ruling military classes.

Indeed, without a political mandate, military officials wielding political power would often go back on their words, instead of fulfilling them to seek victorious or favorable reelection bids. The rule of General Muhammadu Buhari may serve as an example of a partly repressive but popular regime, given the Adiagbon factor, that sought to rule with little or no civilian interests in mind. As Professor Pita O. Agbese of Northern Iowa University has stated clearly in his study of human rights and nation-building, in spite of its popularity the Buhari regime's 1984 decree "made it criminal for anyone to publish anything embarrassing to the government."[11]

Additionally, thousands of Nigerians were, reportedly, held in arbitrary detentions without trial for years, and it took a succeeding military regime to redress several of the publicly announced wrongs. Headed by General Ibrahim Babangida, the new military regime promised to depart from the obvious autocratic manner in which its predecessor ruled Nigeria, as Babangida,

> vowed that he would not preside over "a country where individuals are under the fear of expressing themselves." As part of the new crusade for human rights, some of the more repressive and obnoxious decrees promulgated by the ousted Buhari regime were immediately repealed. . . . Two journalists, Nduka Irabor and Tunde Thompson, who had been convicted and jailed for contravening the decree [Decree No. 4], were set free.[12]

Again, to the surprise of many Nigerians and observers of the West African political scene, the new Babangida government, although a military one like many others, was behaving like an elected regime. It was aiming to win a popularity contest that it needed to "earn" reelection kudos. Toward that end, as Dr. Agbese chronicles, the following surprisingly laudable measures were taken:

In addition, the Babangida regime attempted to provide speedy trials for Nigerians against whom *prima facie* cases of wrong doing had been established by setting up three judicial panels. Two of these panels, the Justice Aguda panel and the Justice Bello panel, reviewed the cases of hundreds of Nigerians who had been found guilty of drug trafficking, economic sabotage, corruption, and the like. They had been convicted by numerous special military tribunals set up by the Buhari regime. The third panel, the Justice Uwaifo panel, was set up to try those who were arrested by the Buhari regime on allegations of corruption and official malfeasance. Most of them had been detained since Buhari came to power in January 1984 [by the time of the coup], but their cases had not been heard. The first two panels speedily reviewed coup cases, and several convictions were quashed and defendants set free. . . . For its part, the Justice Uwaifo panel declared that no case of wrongdoing could be established against many of the detained suspects, including the former president, Shehu Shagari, and the former vice-president, Alex Ekwueme. These measures won [for] the Babangida regime instant legitimacy.[13]

Where stability was concerned, the Nigerian military regime of retired General Babangida was embarking on measures that, in the words of Dr. Agbese, had won for the regime "instant legitimacy." Yet, as a leopard can not change its spots overnight, the new military regime later tended to behave like many other regimes of its kind elsewhere on the African continent, often following measures that would make it unpopular and subsequently require it to take both drastic and autocratic avenues to stay in power. Dr. Agbese confirms this in these words:

The flirtation with respect for fundamental human rights did not last long. After a brief period of political tolerance, the Babangida regime began to detain its critics, close down newspapers, proscribe popular trade union organizations, and sack [terminate] government employees who disagreed with its economic and political policies. Universities whose students demonstrated against the regime's economic and political policies were closed down for months. The Babangida regime has closed down more newspapers than any other government in Nigeria. Its security forces have killed more demonstrators than had all other Nigerian governments. The regime has also banned more popular organizations [than other governments] in Nigeria's postcolonial history. While it repealed some repressive decrees enacted by the Buhari regime, it retained some of Buhari's most notorious decrees. In addition, it enacted its own repressive laws.[14]

Without any surprise Dr. Agbese, as a no-nonsense scholar, further queries, *inter alia:*

Why has repression become the hallmark of a regime that came to power proclaiming respect for fundamental human rights? How could a government that professed an abiding commitment to upholding fundamental human rights and described itself as a "human rights" government use repressive measures against the people of Nigeria?"[15]

Characteristically, Dr. Agbese does not leave his query unanswered, as he writes lucidly:

> Despite its professed respect for human rights, the Babangida regime, due to its commitment to implementing a harsh economic structural adjustment program (SAP), could not realistically have upheld fundamental human rights of Nigerian citizens . . . that respect for fundamental human rights and the SAPs that many African governments are implementing are incompatible goals. The SAP can only be implemented behind the walls of massive human rights abuses.[16]

Being a coauthor from the United States—where individual freedoms are to a large extent guaranteed in the existing constitution and in its amendments—Dr. Alex-Assensoh wondered, while we worked on this book, why bitter and unpopular SAP economic policies were introduced in African nations at all costs—often with iron hands of the rulers—if the citizens whom they were meant to benefit did not want them? She learned later that some of the policies benefitted many of the military rulers directly, especially when such policies needed to be followed before the International Monetary Fund (IMF), the World Bank, and aid-donor organizations would dole out funds to their cash-starved regimes.

Professor George Klay Kieh, Jr., the Liberian-born director of Morehouse College's Center for International Studies and political science professor, states unequivocally where aid money ended up and was used. His position, enshrined in his-well researched study of Liberia for the Transafrica Forum Policy Institute book, is titled *Ending the Liberian Civil War: Implications For United States Policy towards West Africa* (1996). Discussing America's massive assistance, in the form of foreign aid, to the notoriously repressive regime of Samuel K. Doe of Liberia, in spite of its nondemocratic features for governance, Dr. Kieh, *inter alia,* wrote:

> Significantly, the Liberian ruling class was supported by the government of the United States politically, economically, and militarily. For example, under the Doe junta, the United States provided more than $500 million in aid to the Liberian ruling class. The money was used primarily to build up the foreign banking accounts of the members of the Liberian ruling class and to purchase weapons to cow the Liberian people into submission through the use of force and coercion. Interestingly, having provided the oxygen that kept dictatorship alive and well in Liberia, the government of the United States "packed its bags and went on vacation," after the actions of its clients precipitated a cataclysmic raging fire that engulfed all of Liberia. In the parlance of fire-fighters, the behavior of the United States government was analogous to that of a collaborator, who supplies a group of arsonists with matches and gasoline and then pretends to be innocent, after the fire is set and subsequently destroys lives and property.[17]

Assaults on Press Freedom as a Permanent Feature in African Politics: The General Plight of the African Press

There is an important area of African politics that can be a source of unofficial opposition in African civilian or military governance, especially when it becomes clear that all official forms of opposition have been stamped out completely—that is the African press! The muzzling of this crucial segment of Africa's democratic process has contributed to the instability of both military and civilian regimes.

Retired University of Ghana history professor Adu Boahen in writing about the press emphasizes: "The Ghana Press is one of the most important institutions of the land and one of the oldest presses in Africa."[18] Often, new leaders in African countries paid lip service to and commended the press for its vibrant role, but the applauding politicians later behaved like bad quarterbacks in an American football game: they receive the ball, run very hard with it, and come very close to the scoring lines, but, instead of making a touch-down when expected, they often fumble and drop the ball. Most of these post-independence leaders often reneged on their promises to the press. They, instead, saw the press as enemy number one that had to be crushed by every available means, irrespective of the wide denunciations by such credible watchdog organizations as Amnesty International, Media Watch, International P.E.N., and several other press groups throughout the world.

Indeed, as expected, many of the latter actions of General Babangida's repressive military regime, in spite of its honeymoon tolerance of press criticisms, simply confirmed that only a few military governments in Africa can boast of upholding on democratic and human rights policies with the same consistency as democratically-elected regimes. Therefore, the assault on press freedom by African military dictatorships has become a daily occurrence, which can also happen under elected regimes. It is only incredible that not only the press houses but also human lives are often destroyed. According to Dr. Abgese, "the Babangida regime has closed down more newspapers than any other government in Nigeria."[19]

What is most regrettable, of course, is that in the absence of viable opposition under an African military dictatorship, a free press is often one of the only remaining avenues through which the rulers can be kept in check. Yet, one of the most severely hit institutions after an African military coup is the press, so that, in most cases, editors are forced to either close shop or simply to toe the official line by practicing self-censorship, if they want their newspapers and journals to remain in circulation.

A typical example was Gambia after the July 22, 1994 overthrow of the 30–year-old government of Sir Dawda Kairaba Jawara, which was briefly mentioned earlier in this publication. The junior officers who came to power and were led by Captain Yaya Jammeh (now the elected president of Gambia), claimed that they staged their coup d'etat, like everywhere else in African military takeovers, to end several abuses of the Jawara regime. Although some of the claims had been disputed by some writers, many observers agreed that deposed

President Jawara's regime had, after 30 years of governance—and similar to many of the deposed regimes in postcolonial Africa stayed too long in power. The London-based Ghanaian writer, Zaya Yeebo, who lived in Gambia from 1992 to 1994 while working for Action Aid, gave varied seasoned accounts of the Gambian situation, including the following:

> In Sir Dawda's Gambia, there were no obvious political prisoners, even though there were instances of the maltreatment of prisoners and torture by individual policemen. . . . Coming from Ghana, where Rawlings had used prison and torture as his video games, I was most surprised. By African standards, the Sir Dawda government was very tolerant. Like similar other tolerant governments, it paid the ultimate price."[20]

However, the minor difference between the Gambian regime of Sir Dawda and the Rawlings regime in Ghana, as compared by Yeebo, a very serious and fine scholar, is that the former was an elected government with a lot of accountability to the electorate while the latter, in which Yeebo was once a cabinet minister (or secretary), was a military dictatorship that came into power through the barrel of the gun and, indeed, through what the author belatedly saw as sheer brutal force. The Armed Forces Provisional Ruling Council (AFPRC) of Gambia, which replaced Sir Dawda's regime, just like other African military regimes, publicly told the Gambia press: "You are free to criticize us anytime you want and to contribute where you can."[21] Yeebo writes that "to Gambians who were not used to military double standards, this was welcome news. But like other promises a military junta makes on the day it assumes power, the Yaha Jammeh dictatorship had no intention of keeping its promise to the press."[22]

Sadly, the new Gambian military regime (which has now been replaced by an elected government) took several steps to destroy the country's newly-found press freedom and stability, which were not a regular occurrence in a country where—in the words of Yeebo—the press was relatively new itself, adding:

> Newspapers [in Gambia] emerge and disappear without ceremony. But the emergence of *Daily Observer*, owned by Kenneth Best, a Liberian journalist and publisher, revived the dormant newspaper industry and gave it a sense of purpose and credibility. Relying on his several years of experience [in press work] gained in Liberia and Kenya, Kenneth Best built the *Daily Observer* into one of the most reputable daily newspapers in West Africa. None of the other newspapers in The Gambia could be compared to the *Daily Observer* in terms of quality of writing, presentation, layout and news sense. One glaring weakness of the *Daily Observer* was its ownership: the fact that Kenneth Best was a non-Gambian. When the political class cannot attack someone on the basis of principles, they always resort to the question of nationality. That was what happened to Kenneth Best. But more than that, people in power have a love-hate relationship with the press. Politicians are quick to use the media to promote themselves and court public favor. Yet if journalists . . . [see] instances of wrong doing or

corruption, the same people [politicians] have no qualms in attacking the media and journalists.[23]

Initially, the attitude of the ruling AFPRC toward the Gambian press was, reportedly, patronizing because, as Yeebo writes, "Gambian journalism is dominated by ill-trained amateurs without much exposure. Operating in the hostile and uncertain atmosphere generated by the coup made things worse for journalists."[24] However, the problems of the *Daily Observer* newspaper did not begin overnight, as Yeebo also makes it known that even under Sir Dawda's deposed PPP regime External Affairs Minister Omar Sey had launched a fierce attack on the *Observer* in Parliament. A Gambian journalist, Swaebou Conateh, who was in Parliament that day carried a graphic description of the minister's shameful attack on press freedom: Two of the papers in particular, the *Point* and the *Daily Observer* had, by that time, come out with various stories about embezzlements, frauds, and misuse of public funds in some cases, as in the Cooperatives Union for example."[25]

The problems of the *Daily Observer*'s publisher, Best, magnified, as reported, after his newspaper began to document that Gambian businesses were in decline after Jammeh's military coup d'etat and that there were implications for Gambian national security and stability. In a state of either panic or uncertainty, Captain Sadibhou Hydara, as Interior Minister (Secretary) and AFPRC Vice-Chairman Sana Sabally reportedly met with Best to make their government's frustration known to him. Apart from warning Mr. Best—one of Africa's finest and most dedicated journalists—Hydara also showed the *Observer* publisher a report from an America-based publication that quoted Mr. Best as underscoring, *inter alia,* that "the military in Africa do not have a tract record of fulfilling their promises. They make grandiose promises when they come to power, but nothing is achieved."[26]

In his usual cool and very thoughtful manner, Best told the two AFPRC members: "in as much as I have made some negative comments about the nature of the military in Africa, I also said some positive things about the AFPRC, but unfortunately the journalist did not use them."[27] The AFPRC interviewers promised to report their meeting to their leader, Chairman Jammeh; subsequently, on October 21, 1994, Best, who had also written for *Focus on Africa*'s broadcasting program about the Gambian military takeover, was arrested by the Gambian police, after which he was detained for almost 24 hours. A detailed report of the events appeared in an article in the *Daily Observer* by reporter Ebraima Ceesay, including the accusation that the newspaper did not report a presidential event about communal work (or *set-settal*) on the front page of the *Daily Observer,* Yeebo wrote about Best's predicament:

> On 21st October 1994, he [Best] was picked up again by the police, and spent 21 hours in detention. After this incident, Best and his family were subjected to weeks of crude and humiliating harassment symptomatic of a repressive and totally obsessed regime. The style was reminiscent of the defunct and disgraced apartheid regime in South Africa, the US-backed

Pinochet dictatorship in Chile and the CIA-backed Rawlings dictatorship in Ghana.[28]

Mr. Best was to be deported from Gambia because the Jammeh regime did not tolerate his journalistic views; this from a regime that, upon gaining power, immediately urged the press to be bold, to write freely and to help where possible! In fact, on October 30, 1994, Best was arrested at his home by Gambian immigration officers, and he was later served with deportation orders. As reported, Best was "driven straight to the airport and put on a flight to Monrovia [Liberia] without being allowed to pack or even take money. . . . Attempts by Robert Collingwood, the European Union delegate, other well-meaning citizens, and Nana K. A. Busia, a reputable African and international human rights lawyer, to have the deportation order revoked were spurned by the dictatorship bent on ridding the Gambia of one of the most experienced journalists in Africa today."[29]

As later explained by impartial observers, it became known that "Best was the victim of a ploy to silence Gambian journalists, and being a foreigner, could easily be used as a scapegoat. . . . The deportation of Kenneth Best had another twist to it. It appears that the erstwhile AFPRC had wanted to start a daily paper of their own, but were hampered by the dominating role of the *Daily Observer* in the country."[30] Best's departure from Gambia, a result of the foregoing intimidation and threats at the hands of the military regime of army strongman Jammeh, deprived Gambia of the services of an excellent African journalist who took his job very seriously.

After many years of journalistic service in the Liberian Ministry of Information and Cultural Affairs—during the years of E. Reginald Townsend and under the presidential years of Dr. Tubman—Mr. Best had a lot to share with any society as a journalist. In Liberia, he served in a variety of official capacities, rising through the journalistic ranks to become director of publications and assistant minister of information. Apart from doing an excellent journalistic job in Liberia and, later, Gambia, Best is remembered as the brilliant press and communications expert for the Nairobi-based All-Africa Conference of Churches, headed in the 1970s by Liberia's Reverend Burgess Carr, who served for several years as an associate professor at the Yale Divinity School.[31]

Also, several other military regimes treated African journalists shabbily as individual professional men and women, and either banned or suspended their publications. Such actions, on the part of military regimes throughout the continent, undermined the remaining shade of both democratic norms and opposition. The plight of Mike Adjei, also an excellent African journalist from Ghana, is an example that is similar to the sad circumstances of Best of Liberia. Currently living in self-imposed exile in London, it is today a lot easier for him to speak out, hence his 317–page 1993 memoirs, *Death and Pain in Rawlings' Ghana: The Inside Story.* A brief biographical sketch demonstrates amply that, unlike some of Africa's ill-prepared but well-intentioned journalists, Adjei's excellent journalistic preparatory background is similar to that of Best. Yet, he—like Best—could not escape the wrath of a military regime in Ghana, despite the fact that the common man in the streets of Ghana often appreciated his work.

Born at Larteh in eastern Ghana, Mr. Adjei was initially educated at one of Ghana's leading schools, Mfantsipim Secondary School at Cape Coast, from the geographic area of the country known as the central region. It is in this region that quality education began, an area which also had a lot of historical basis in the slave trade. Mfantsipim, as it is simply and popularly called, has educated some of Ghana's best political leaders, including the late Prime Minister Busia and Joe Appiah, a leading lawyer and politician who died a couple of years ago (he was also the father of Harvard-based prolific writer and philosophy professor Kwame Anthony Appiah). The secondary school that Adjei attended as part of his early education before entering the university was established through the collaboration of Fante nationalists and the Methodist Church.[32]

After studying at Mfantsipim Secondary School, Adjei earned a bachelor's degree from the University of Ghana at Legon in 1966, studying economics, sociology, and history. Upon graduating from Legon, he decided to pursue journalism as a career and, therefore, became a reporter for one of Ghana's premier newspapers, *Daily Graphic,* a government-owned newspaper based in the capital, Accra. It was while working for the newspaper that, in 1967, Mr. Adjei received an American Fulbright scholarship to study at the Graduate School of Journalism, Columbia University. From Columbia, Adjei he earned a master's degree in journalism in 1968 by specializing in international affairs reporting. "He returned to Ghana the same year. He worked for the *Graphic* until 1970, when he joined the State Hotels Corporation as a Public Relations Officer. Four years later he joined the Ghana Oil Company [GOIL]. While in these positions, he continued writing for local and international newspapers and magazines."[33]

Mike Adjei suffered like other distinguished African journalists in military and civilian regimes, both of which did not tolerate press freedom or the work of professional journalists. On June 21, 1983, he was reportedly picked up by Ghana's security forces under the PNDC regime of then Flt.-Lieutenant Rawlings and, as his publishers wrote, he

> was held at the Nsawam Medium Security Prison until July the following year. [After his release], he traveled to Nigeria to attend [a job] interview in 1986 [from where he heard that] he was declared wanted and therefore could not return to Ghana. He arrived in the United Kingdom in October 1987, where he was promptly given political asylum. Mike Adjei was declared a "Prisoner of Conscience" by Amnesty International in 1984. He is an Associate Member of the English Center of P.E.N., . . . which is a leading organization for Playwrights, Poets, Essayists, and Novelists (P.E.N.) and, also, a member of the institute of Journalism, London.[34]

An interesting exchange between Adjei and his readers displays how the journalist was a hero to many Africans. Adjei, on hearing about an unsuccessful coup d'etat attempt in Ghana in 1983, wrote:

> I decided to see a friend in the estate [residential area] to ascertain what had taken place that morning. There was a festive mood in the house.

They were having a birthday party for a son who had just returned from the United States. Immediately the party goers saw me enter the gate, almost everybody began shouting my name. I felt like a celebrity, but the meaning was difficult to find. Total strangers wanted to shake hands with me.[35]

[. . .]

"I enjoy your articles in *The Free Press,*" an elderly man said as he stretched out his hand. "Thank you, Sir," I beamed at him. Another said, "I thought you had been detained long ago." "They haven't come for me yet," I replied. "I'm honored to meet you, Mr. Adjei. At least you people have proved there are still men in this country," said a woman in her mid-thirties. "Most Ghanaian men think the only place to prove their manhood is in the bedroom. At a time like this when a rascal is riding roughshod over us, all the men seem to have tucked their tails between their legs and ran under their beds. Then safe in their bedrooms the tail in from of them comes up." The other women with her laughed heartily.[36]

Then, as if a coup d'etat is an act of deliverance in an African country, Adjei, added, "With [the announcement of a coup d'etat], the whole congregation at a Presbyterian Church at Accra's Dansoman Estates started singing songs, praising God for delivering them from the 'evil' PNDC. You should have been there."[37] The coup attempt did not succeed. Being a writer at the time of a failed coup d'etat could lead to one's arrest, especially if the writer was considered to be an opponent of the government that was almost overthrown. Hence Mr. Adjei was reportedly detained in 1983; it is like the biblical phrase: "woe unto the scribes." He later ended up in Great Britain as an African under self-imposed exiled. In *Power and the Press* (1997), Tunde Thompson, the Nigerian writer, dedicated his book: "To all martyrs and marching advocates of Press Freedom world-wide, that through their light, mankind may better appreciate the Word."[38]

When discussing freedom of the press in the 1988 book, Thompson, who is also a veteran Nigerian journalist, devoted an entire chapter to the nature and obstacles of press freedom (chapter 5) and another on how press freedom is undermined in African societies (chapter 6). Here, the author captures the familiar circumstances of various journalists in Africa, whether in a military regime or a civilian government. He writes:

Two of the developments in chapters I to IV now deserve some closer attention. First what does the action of picking someone up from his office, home or anywhere else for that matter, taking him to a publicly inaccessible destination for days on end without being given a right to speak to members of his family, a lawyer or colleagues, amount to? If such a person is thus limited in his movement and communication with other members of his society and profession, what can be said to have [been] lost thereby?[39]

Mr. Thompson goes on to question Decree No. 4 in Nigeria—which, as described elsewhere in the journalist's 1988 book—"turned the Press into a 'toothless tiger' by providing for the conviction and/or fine of journalists and/or their employers who published any reports true or false that embarrassed the government or any of its officials." Subsequently, he quibbled that there is trouble " . . . when journalists in any country are told in advance what they may or may not publish as news, features, editorials, cartoons and pictures . . . ?"[40]

As Professor Agbese discussed earlier, the Babangida regime repealed Decree No. 4 in August 1985, when it seized power from the Buhari military government in a palace coup d'etat. Thompson saw that the press, in these new circumstances, had entered such a new era that he wondered "if Babangida will allow it to return to its old boisterous self."[41] Under pressure, even elected governments in Africa have taken steps to curtail "boisterous press," steps that have included the intimidation of journalists and practitioners of the crucial Fourth Estate, in spite of the right for the public to know, which Thompson quotes from a 1975 roundtable discussion sponsored by the American Enterprise Institute.[42]

To demonstrate that these inimical situations facing the African press are prevalent in developed societies as well, Thompson cited an Indiana case involving the American Broadcasting Corporation (ABC):

> There was a case out in Indiana last year [1974] in which ABC was barred by a prior restraint court injunction, for over 200 days from doing a show demonstrating [and] proving that plastic cribs burned more quickly than wooden cribs. I think the public had a right to know precisely what ABC wanted to tell them, and that the injunction was a most offensive interference with the public's right and the Press's right.[43]

Appropriately, Mr. Thompson went on to lament the fact that, as happened in the Indiana case involving ABC, the courts had since then been "increasingly involved in preventing the dissemination of news and general information through the imposition of injunctions."[44] Yet, Thompson did not explain further that, at least in Indiana—and, indeed, in other parts of America—the courts examine the press events on a case-by-case basis to issue injunctions, unlike the blanket manner in which a mere decree or an edict, issued by a dictator in Africa, could silent the press for countless years.

Other places in Africa have also had their share of similar repression against the press and its practitioners. In Francis P. Kasoma's study of the Zambian press, for example, he discussed in the section on "Critical Role of the Press," how press freedom was closely "connected with State ownership of the press."[45] Significantly, the Zambian journalist pointed out that, both in the colonial and post-independence era, the officers of the ruling class did tend to dictate to newspapermen what they should or should not publish. Where press freedom was concerned, he felt this way:

> Freedom of the press clearly means newsmen alone should decide what they should publish. A press where journalists have surrendered this responsibility to some other people outside their profession is not free. It is censored. The Zambian State press has constantly resisted unofficial cen-

sorship from politicians and civil servants. The struggle is likely to continue until (if the time will ever come) the State introduces official press censorship.[46]

While the Zambian press seemed to be blessed in its efforts to play the role of the unofficial opposition in the absence of multiparty politics, other journalists elsewhere were not that fortunate. This state of affairs, affecting the African press generally, prompted coauthor Assensoh to make the following statement in an earlier previously published article:

> In many areas of the Third World, journalists are faced with various occupational hazards which include arrests and detentions without being formally charged with any offence, outright beatings or torture by State security agents while being held incommunicado in prisons and the curtailment of the journalists' freedom of movement through the seizure of their travel documents or passports. Unfortunately, African journalists have not been spared of such intimidating circumstances simply because they have, invariably, dared to express their candid views in the columns of local and international newspapers, and on radio and television networks.[47]

As shown earlier, Liberia's Kenneth Best suffered similarly in Gambia, after he was accused of having given an unflattering interview to an American journalist. Many other African journalists would suffer similarly, and, in fact, some of them would pay dearly with their very lives simply because the post-independence rulers did not want to see or even sense any shade of opposition: press or political opposition! It is sad that the press, an essential tool in the development of various nations, has had a seriously undermined, even hidden, historical past in Africa. Professor Adu Boahen was on target when he made several memorable assertions, including the fact that "the Ghana Press is one of the most important institutions of the land and one of the oldest presses in Africa, and yet its history is also one of the least researched and documented in anything like a systematic way. Until June 1974 there was not a single comprehensive study of this history published in English."[48]

Professor K. A. B. Jones-Quarter, for whose book on the press Professor Adu Boahen wrote a foreword, did stress, however, that there was a known publication about the Ghanaian press—indeed, done specifically about the vibrant Gold Coast press—which was not a book but a 1971 Wisconsin doctoral dissertation written by Sylvanus A. Ekwelie of Nigeria and titled "The Press in Gold Coast Nationalism, 1890–1957." Also cited was Hans U. Behn's 1968 study, in German, of the West African Press, published in Hamburg.[49] While these publications have been admirably completed, it is still a fact that there are limited studies of how the African press, in trying to play the role of unofficial opposition, has been tamed by circumstances beyond its control, including the intimidation and even outright murder of its practitioners. The dangerous circumstances of many of these journalists have "driven many of them into voluntary exile in various parts of the world; they include such distinguished journalists as Peter Enahoro

[Nigerian], Raph Uwechue [Nigerian], Cameron Duodu [Ghanaian], [and] Elizabeth Ohene [Ghanaian]."[50]

There is a catalogue of numerous examples of pressmen paying with their lives for daring to either expose ills of various regimes or playing the role of unofficial opposition to many of the dictatorial regimes of postcolonial Africa. Often, the erstwhile apartheid regime in South Africa was so strict in its treatment of journalists that it systematically crippled anti-apartheid newspapers. Wiseman Khuzwayo, a London-based South African journalist lamented in the following words the closure of the *Rand Daily Mail* in his native South Africa: "Here lies the *Rand Daily Mail,* 1902–1985." The paper was known to have fought the apartheid leadership squarely, especially, in the 1960s, when Laurence Gander was its editor.[51]

For example, because of his public, unabashed opposition to the apartheid regime, Joe Thloloe, of the newspaper called the *Sowetan* was to suffer imprisonment. He was arrested, tried, convicted, and sentenced to a jail term in the notorious Robben Island prison, where Nelson Mandela spent most of his over two decades of imprisonment. Mr. Thloloe's "crime" was merely possessing a leaflet distributed by the then-banned Pan-African Congress (PAC). There was also the case of Mr. Edgar Mothuba of Lesotho, a newspaper editor who was abducted from his home together with two visiting friends; their bullet-riddled bodies were found on March 8, 1983, but the murderers could not be found. In Zambia, under the regime of President Kaunda, the *Zambian Times* editor-in-chief Naphy Nyalugwe had his appointment terminated suddenly; it was speculated that he was dismissed because he was too critical in his editorial writings about local issues.[52]

Most certainly, the plight of African journalists mimics that of the continent's major authors, all of whom tried to play roles in the unofficial saga opposing one-party dictatorships. Among the many crusading writers who suffered were Nigeria's famous writer and Nobel literature laureate Wole Soyinka; Kenya's Ngugi wa Thing'o, a distinguished author; Ghana's Kwame Kesse-Adu, well-known for his book *The Politics of Political Detention;* Malawi's Jack Mapanje, who went to jail under President-for-Life Kamuzu Banda for writing a poem about vultures; Ghana's distinguished poet-*cum*-diplomat, Professor Kofi Awoonor; and many other writers from central and northern African nations.

Apart from the foregoing instances of military and political leaders taking extraordinary steps to muzzle the press in various African nations, there have often been instances whereby trumped-up charges have been made against writers so that they can be clamped into jail. As recently as April 1999, 12 Zambian journalists of the independent *Post* newspaper had been hauled to a local high court. The journalists were "charged with espionage over a report suggesting that Zambia was ill-equipped to defend itself against neighboring Angola. The charges carry a minimum jail term of 20 years."[53] One would say in advanced nations—as Tunde Thompson underscored with respect to the Indiana case—that the Zambian journalists were working under the "right of the public to know" theory. Yet, it is not so in Africa. Therefore, many societies in Africa lack even such basic elements of opposition from the press. In the absence of formal political opposition the only way to change an unstable government is through undemocratic means, no matter who is in power, the military or civilians. That is why many well-meaning Africans are correct in calling many elected African leaders and military strongmen—no military strong-women yet—dictators.

Among leading Africans, who are very critical of the continent's leadership—whether elected or installed by coups d'etat—is Professor Soyinka, whose critical words about Western leaders are not suppressed by any government in the West. Soyinka penned both an epochal and very prophetic volume on Nigeria's military dictatorship under Abacha, in which he called the military government the "open sore of Africa." Also, he wrote a powerful piece for the April 18, 1999 issue of the *New York Times Magazine,* that was included in the magazine's cover story on "Best Ideas, Stories and Inventions of the Last Thousand Years." His specific three-page piece was subtitled, "Every Dictator's Nightmare."[54]

Seeing the actions of dictators in general as part of the obstacle to the attainment of human rights anywhere, Professor Soyinka characteristically made a potent opening observation in the magazine article: "The message, whether from Yoruba elders or the Founding Fathers, the Bible or the Koran, is the same: Humans have rights."[55] Seeing the blood-soaked banner of religious fanaticism billowing across the skies as a prominent legacy of the soon-to-end millennium, Dr. Soyinka considered Martin Luther's famous theses against religious absolutism as "a strong candidate for the best idea of the last thousand years."[56] The appearance of the article is not very surprising because Professor Soyinka has always been known—similar to Nigeria's late leading rebel and pamphleteer, the indomitable Dr. Tai Solarin—as a rebel with a cause. He risked his life as a youngster when he seized a western Nigerian radio station to espouse his cause against dictatorial and corrupt tendencies. Indeed, if his fellow Nigerians had listened to his messages, possibly the bloodbath that they witnessed in the January 15, 1966 coup and the subsequent civil war between the strong-willed Igbos and the rest of Nigeria would have either been avoided completely or minimized. Most certainly, Soyinka has continued on his warpath against authoritarian rule in Africa, as he has spoken out forcefully against all shades of abuses everywhere in Africa, including risking everything to travel to Rwanda so that he could write about it as an informed African. He wrote in anguish because of Rwanda's sad state of affairs: "The next morning, however, I learned that I had just enough time to see Rwanda before our next appointment in Tanzania. . . . Nostalgia lost out to nightmare, and I headed off to keep tryst with the dreaded moment, the proving ground of faith."[57]

Describing Rwanda as the "land of a thousand hills," Professor Soyinka wrote about the country, with poetic beauty, as being "still as breathtakingly beautiful as I remembered it, so pastoral and idyllic that it did not take long to recall that Rwanda was the land that gave birth to H. Rider Haggard's *King Solomon's Mines,* and the legend of Prester John."[58] Bemoaning the fact that the party of genocide in Rwanda had used its Radio des Milles Collines to incite Hutus to kill other ethnic groups, including the Tutsi, Professor Soyinka—who had been in the area in 1962 and returned there in the 1990s—wondered:

Could any one of us, in the sixties, have suspected the possibility of a massacre on this scale? Not even the rabid slaughter in Liberia, home of the poet Lenie Peters, or the random killing in Sierra Leone of that urbane critic, Eldred Jones, had prepared us for this; not the genocide in Nigeria that led to the secession of Biafra and the war in which Christopher Okigbo lost his life; not the agonies of Robert Serumaga's and Okot p'Bitek's Uganda. These writers were the representative voices that dominated the 1962 Kampala conference: their humanism defined for us the new Africa. Where was that Africa now? How does a nation like Rwanda overcome its history?"[59]

In fact, most of the African press is so badly censored that, but for *Transition Journal* of 1999 and a few overseas-based pan-African publications, the precious criticism by Professor Soyinka would hardly see the light of publishing day on the African continent. Soyinka suffered arrest and detention without trial for over a year in the prisons of the Gowon regime in Nigeria, all because he spoke out against what he still sees as the genocide in Nigeria perpetuated by the warring factions: a situation where young women had their breasts slashed off, and their wombs publicly cut open, and innocent children were either killed or maimed so that they would neither give birth to nor grow up to become "another Ojukwu, the secessionist leader."[60] That time, to Professors Soyinka, Chinua Achebe, and other leading African writers, was Africa's period of shame.

Achebe in a 1968 interview with the hard-working Rajat Neogy, founder of *Transition Journal* in Uganda—offered readers a clear-cut picture of life in the civil war–torn Nigerian Eastern Region, for which he reportedly served as the "unofficial ambassador for the breakaway Republic of Biafra."[61] Nigeria's censored "wartime" press—although still led bravely by men of journalistic integrity like Peter Enahoro (the popular local Peter Pan), Alhaji Babatunde Jose, Dapo Fatogun, Lateef Jakande, and a few other stalwarts—was unable to publish words by Achebe, Soyinka, and some of the voices of reason that needed to be heard, especially if that senseless genocide was to stop on both sides, on the part of Gowon's Nigeria and, of course, on the part of Ojukwu's Biafra.

Neogy, who died not long ago, asked Achebe to describe an average day in the last eight months for the average Biafran, or Igbo. His responses include the following account:

It depends [on] where you are. If you are very close to the war zone, you hear the sound of war. You get used to sleeping with the sound of shelling and all the other things. From about seven A.M. to about six P.M., there is the tenseness. At any moment, they might come. It does not take long—a few seconds—and 120 people are charred to ashes, charred black, and perhaps twenty buildings wrecked. I only realized how nervous I had become when I got to London about three weeks ago. My reaction to the sound of the first airplane I heard was to take cover. This has become a way of life for everyone, children too.[62]

Again, a military regime in Nigeria would not allow the local press, which has always had some of Africa's best writers as editorial leaders and reporters, to publish materials—indeed, interviews—from Nigerians who were considered saboteurs and nation-wreckers. Such intimidation, in the absence of a formal political opposition to the military dictatorship, often added to the instability that a typical military regime introduces to the continent's political arena, which creates the overall ingredients that invite coups d'etat.

Apart from its shabby treatment of the African press, another area that many military regimes—and, sometimes, even elected governments—in Africa have lacked wisdom in handling is "Big Power" politics, a situation of rich politicians that has helped in festering other forms of insatiability on a large scale. Indeed, Liberia's Rev. B. Carr, in his foreword to Ann Seidmann's *The Roots of Crisis in Southern Africa* (1985), eloquently showed that, in spite of South Africa's pernicious apartheid policies, which made it a pariah in African politics, Western capital and investments flowed freely into the country, helping its stability. He, *inter alia,* writes:

> South Africa is changing for the better, and the U.S. government and business influence are in the vanguard of the forces that are responsible for peaceful change. Moreover, the changes in South Africa are of benefit not only to Africans in that country but to the entire region, for South Africa is a source of modern technology and stability in [the entire] southern Africa. The evidence offered to support these claims points to the elimination of some aspects of "petty" apartheid. . . . Sometimes it is even claimed that Africans in South Africa have a standard of life and opportunity superior to Africans anywhere else on that continent.[63]

Although South African Blacks were—in the 1980s, when Rev. Carr wrote this piece—treated inhumanely in the nation of their birth, Rev. Carr was still of the opinion that South Africa's Blacks were better off than other Africans living outside the then apartheid enclave. After all, these Blacks lived in a very "stable" environment without threats of coups d'etat, although they were dominated by repressive and, sadly, racist Whites, whose national origins were traced to Holland. It is sad that South Africa's "stability" was being measured against the acts of hooliganism, torture, and undemocratic tidings that had become the lot of many Africans whose regimes fell prey to military take-overs and lawlessness. For example a female Ghanaian lawyer played an active role in the PNDC regime in Ghana until her own father became a victim of the same administration that she was extolling in public statements. However, she did not like the fact that the very press that she and her PNDC supporters had supported was being used to publicize her father's alleged crimes against the country. To her, the published picture of her humiliated father, standing among those styled as "economic saboteurs" should not have been published. That was a hypocritical and an unfortunate reaction on the lawyer's part; she was angry as her father could easily be identified, she was much more opposed to the caption under the published photo: "A parade of alleged economic saboteurs in Accra. Some were given long prison terms."[64]

It is true that President Rawlings of Ghana, as an elected leader, has followed democratic norms to a large extent, although what happened under his watch during the PNDC regime left a lot to be desired. With such sad incidents in mind, Liberia-born Rev. Carr was, in fact, correct in his assessment that Blacks in South Africa, in spite of their sufferings under the apartheid regime, did seem to be better off than those elsewhere in Africa. In Mike Adjei's 1994 book, he gives an account of events that took place immediately after the 1981 coup in Ghana:

> A few days after the coup, the [new military] government announced the freezing of all bank accounts with more than 50,000 Cedis deposited in them and the owners of such assets were called to appear before a Citizens Vetting Committee (CVC). Mr. Amissah, who had a couple of million [Cedis] in his account was one of the first people called to the CVC, which was then sitting in Parliament House. Kwamina Ahwoi, Ato's younger brother, [and] the co-ordinator of investigations, was on this committee. Mr. Amissah was ordered to pay 5,612,166 Cedis on his undeclared income from 1977 to 1979. His two cars, a Mercedes and a Scirocco, were confiscated to the state. When Justice Daniel Annan was appointed a member of the [ruling] PNDC in July 1984, he [allegedly] moved into Madam Fathia's house [she was Nkrumah's widow]. The Mercedes Benz saloon car given him for his official use was Mr. Amissah's confiscated car. Mr. Amissah was allowed two days to pay his fine but could not raise the rest of the money. When one day the security people arrived in his house to arrest him, he was tipped off and left the house by the back wall, and fled to Togo. The couple of millions in the bank and his house were confiscated to the state and some PDCs were sent there to take it over. The new tenants [allegedly] stole the louvre blades and other properties left in the house.[65]

The foregoing instance makes one wonder if Mr. Amissah was a known rogue or nationally-certified thief, since the new PNDC regime picked on him for punishment. That, of course, was not so, because, by Adjei's account, "Mr. Amissah, a very quiet man in his middle fifties, [who] enjoyed the company of friends."[66] Yet, a military government did not care if an individual was quiet or not: he could become a victim of the ongoing instability and "revolutionary experiment," which included instant "justice."

Apart from the deaths of very prominent Ghanaians, there were, reportedly, several deaths of less prominent citizens that went unreported by the local press for fear of intimidation, including that of Madam Larmiokor, a 63–year old Kaneshie New Market woman, who was allegedly killed by a stray bullet. Allegedly, the incident happened, as reported by Mr. Mike Adjei in his 1993 book, when a group of military men and price control officers allegedly accompanied by Mr. Amartey Quaye, PNDC member, challenged a boy who was selling *domedo* (roast pork). The boy was alleged to have confronted the soldiers for telling him how much he should sell his commodities, and the soldiers fired at the boy—2 gun shots—but missed him and shot Larmiokor. When she fell, the soldiers left without attending to her and she subsequently bled to death. The Kaneshie Police removed the dead body later.[67] She was one of many Ghanaians who died between January and June 1982, reportedly at the hands of agents of Ghana's then-ruling PNDC: Reportedly, there were 28 people killed from the greater-Accra region; 44 people killed in the Ashanti region; 22 people killed in the eastern region; 7 people killed in the Tema area; 28 people killed in the Volta region, from where coup leader Rawlings (like the late General Kotoka of the 1966 Ghana coup) hailed; 29 people killed in the western region; 16 people killed in the central region; 10 people killed in the northern region; and 12 people killed in the upper region.

Among arrested and detained persons under various military regimes—including the PNDC regime—were very prominent Ghanaians, including Mike Adjei. Others were Chris Asher, a well-known newspaper editor in Accra, and John Kugblenu, who allegedly died in prison. Interestingly, laws or decrees could be passed to subvert the existing legal court system, which created a lot of instability. As Adjei reported: "Our case was never tested in court. For, a few days later we were sent to the Army's Gondar Barracks. Then a new law was passed. From then on the courts will entertain *no writs of habeas corpus* in the country. Now the way was open to detain people indefinitely without recourse to a law court."[68]

Indeed, what seems to be contradictory is the fact that the successive military regimes in Ghana did not behave much differently from the mainly civilian regimes they had overthrown. For the notorious prisons and jail-cells that the politicians had used were the very same terrible places that the new military regimes utilized to detain and often torture their suspected opponents. Written about a so-called condemned block or cell, supposedly meant for convicted people awaiting execution or hanging for heinous crimes, including murder is the following:

> Perhaps it is not even correct to say that the Condemned Block is meant for only people going to the gallows. Kwame Nkrumah sent his worst opponents here. Obetsebi Lamptey, a prominent Accra lawyer, who was one of the leaders of the United Gold Coast Convention (UGCC), which started the fight for independence in Ghana, died in this block when he was detained on October 5, 1962, although he was a very sick man. . . . He died [in Nsawam Prison] on January 29, 1963. Dr. J. B. Danquah, the leader of the UGCC which invited Nkrumah to Ghana to join the struggle for independence, was later detained twice by Kwame Nkrumah and also died in the Condemned Block.[69]

From the available facts, one can conclude unequivocally that many of the actions of military regimes often created instability, similar to the way corrupt and tainted actions of politicians persistently to invited military interventions in numerous African situations. Sadly, however, when the behavior of a military leader is out of line in an African country, it is simply not possible for civilians to do anything about it. What is called for then is either a palace coup d'etat or a full-blown military intervention, as the citizens of Niger learned in April 1999: The ruling president, Ibrahim Bare Mainassara, was allegedly assassinated by his own body guards—a dangerous phenomenon, of course—and a new military regime appointed 49–year-old Major Daouda Malam Wanke, the head of the deceased president's body guard unit, as the new President of Niger.[70]

Knowing that military dictatorships foster instability, the former colonial master of Niger—France—reacted angrily to the assassination of President Mainassara. A spokesman in the French Foreign Ministry added, in an official statement: "The interests and development of Niger require the rapid return of democracy [to Niger]."[71] France became so enraged that it decided to suspend aid to Niger after the event. The French reaction is, indeed, in consonance with Ghanaian President Nkrumah's contention about the army's involvement in politics generally, which was contained in his February 1, 1966 sessional speech to Ghana's National Assembly in Accra. Many of Nkrumah's critics have seen this speech as prompted by self-interest. After all, barely three weeks after he made it, Nkrumah's own government was overthrown in a coup led by then Colonel Kotoka. Nkrumah's assertion that it is not "the duty of the army to rule or govern, because it is no political mandate" to do so became a moot point.[72]

Even if a former African military leader transforms himself into a civilian leader through democratic elections, it is still a possibility that many acts of instability will crop up, especially if such a leader's followers continue to believe in armed struggle and also behave in a paramilitary fashion. It has happened in several African nations, irrespective of the good intentions of the new leaders. Uganda is a typical example, as it was reported in April 1999 that President Yoweri Museveni had found it necessary to reshuffle his cabinet and make several changes in leadership commands, including the replacement of Prime Minister Kintu Musoke with Education Minister Appolo Nsibambi as well as "stripping the post of Minister of Agriculture from Vice-President Specioza Wandira Kazibwe, who has [allegedly] been implicated in a corruption scandal."[73]

To the applause of several Ugandans, President Museveni had led armed Ugandans to seize power and install a regime of national reconciliation. Therefore, it is hoped that it would not deteriorate into an anarchy. Already, the civil war and destruction of lives between Ethiopia and Eritrea has produced anarchical anecdotes. After the violent but much-needed overthrow of Mengistu Haile Mariam and his military cohorts, the new paramilitary regime agreed that the people of Eritea could have self-determination and, as a result, Eritrea is a sovereign nation today. As reported, one of the serious acts of recklessness on the part of the earlier Mengistu military regime was that, in the face of an imminent killer famine in 1984, "the Mengistu regime in Ethiopia strenuously denied reports of an impending famine."[74]

Among Africa's respected but autocratic leaders was Emperor Haile Selassie of Ethiopia. In a 1974 coup d'etat, the Emperor was removed from office and put under a virtual house arrest in his extravagant palace. Allegedly, circumstances of Emperor Selassie's death and the aftermath of the Ethiopian coup included the following details:

> The ailing emperor was [allegedly] suffocated with a wet pillow, and his body was buried in an unmarked grave. Scores of his relatives were murdered or chained to walls in the cellars of the imperial palace [of Ethiopia]. Thousands of suspected counter-revolutionaries were gunned down in the [Ethiopian] streets. More than 30,000 people were jailed. . . . Since 1977 the Soviet Union has [reportedly] poured over $11 billion worth of arms into Ethiopia, largely on credit. Much of the Soviet military hardware was used to carry out indiscriminate bombings, shellings, and slaughter of civilians. Even famine relief centers in the north [of Ethiopia] and along the Sudan border were bombed and burned.[75]

Although Ethiopia under Emperor Selassie, was not the best place for non-royal citizens, what followed the military takeover was more nightmarish for all citizens of the Horn of Africa nation; even the original coup leaders were replaced by younger officers, led by Mengistu. Then under a capricious and hastily-promulgated land reform act, the new Ethiopian military regime nationalized all land and, subsequently, instituted a so-called "villagization program in which Mengistu proposed moving 34 million people (roughly 75 percent of the total population of Ethiopia] into state-controlled communes, guarded by the army—300,000 strong and the largest in Africa."[76]

Sadly, Ethiopia and Eritrea have become enemies, if temporarily, instead of brothers. They are currently at each other's throats, locked in what the London-based *Africa Confidential* of February 19, 1999 described as "pride and prejudice," adding in its detailed report that "Both sides seem to be keen to fight to the death in one of the least explicable wars."[77] In May-June of 1998, Eritrean forces reportedly took over disputed areas between their nation and Ethiopia. It was on February 6, 1999 that "Ethiopia launched the first of several attacks to test how deeply Eritrean forces were dug in along the disputed border areas which they had taken over."[78]

As reported, Ethiopia's second attack of February 8, 1999 was on the Tserona front, which was intended to cut off the Eritrean troops that had seized Zalembessa. The war has been nasty, and, indeed, the Organization of African Unity (OAU)—which is headquartered in Ethiopia—and the United Nations—now headed for the first time by an African, Secretary-General Kofi Annan—have tried to settle the dispute. Yet, as reported, "both sides remain intransigent on mediation, refusing to give up an inch of land."[79] A ray of hope was that Ethiopia reportedly accepted the U.S.-Rwandan mediation initiative, which later came under the guidance of the OAU and the United Nations. However, Eritrean President Issayas Aferweki and Ethiopian President Meles Zenawi are so much opposed to each other that they tried to do more than the other in their respective support for Somali warlord Hussein Mohamed Farah Aydeed, who visited Ethiopia in October 1998 and Eritrea in January 1999.[80]

While the Ethiopia-Eritrea military fracas was in the news, the north African nation of Algeria, which has had paramilitary regimes since France was "driven" out of the country as a colonial power, was making efforts to use the ballot box to settle its seven-year civil war between the army and Islamic guerrillas "that has cost more than 80,000 lives."[81] In fact, subsequent to the electoral preparations, the Algerian army—like many military forces elsewhere in Africa—had, reportedly, "made clear its preference for Abdelaziz Bouteflika, a former Foreign Minister, making him a strong favorite."[82] Meanwhile, to show how religious groups can also meddle in African politics, the rebellious Islamic Salvation Front of Algeria "urged voters to support former Foreign Minister Ahmed Ibrahimi in the presidential election on April 15 [1999]."[83]

Similar to the spring 1999 Nigerian presidential elections, which ushered in a democratically elected leader on Saturday, May 29, 1999, former Foreign Minister Bouteflika, who was heavily favored by some powerful elements in Algeria's armed forces—just as retired General Obasanjo reportedly enjoyed both financial and political support from former leading Nigerian military brass—won the electoral mandate to rule Algeria as the next president. In both instances, since democratic elections were used to determine the new civilian leaders of both Algeria and Nigeria, one can underscore that whenever military authorities mean well, stability can have its place in national elections in Africa. The only difference is that, in the Nigerian case, President Obasanjo was a former military head of state.

Indeed, in his own words, the retired General, as the elected president of Nigeria, expected success to crown his efforts for the benefit of his fellow Nigerians and to serve as a shining example for other Africans, as he said enthusiastically: "Nigeria is wonderfully endowed by the Almighty with human and other resources. It does no credit to us or the entire black race if we fail in managing our resources for quick improvement in the quality of the lives of our people."[84]

To show overwhelming international support for the Nigerian military regime, led by General Abdulsalami Abubakar, the inauguration was, reportedly, attended by "more than a dozen African heads of state, including [retiring] President Nelson Mandela of South Africa. . . . Washington sent a delegation headed by the Rev. Jesse Jackson, President Clinton's special envoy for Africa, and Rodney E. Slater, the Secretary of Transportation. Prince Charles represented Britain."[85]

Most certainly, the presence of high-powered delegations from the United States of America and Great Britain was an indication that democratic nations and their leaders believed that the latest Nigerian experiment at democratic rule, indeed similar to that of Algeria, would succeed. Seeing the second coming of Mr. Obasanjo—this time as a civilian leader—as another chapter in his remarkable political journey, it was recalled, *inter alia:* "Exactly a year ago, he was in prison serving a 15–year sentence for having allegedly plotted a coup against General Abacha."[86]

Although President Obasanjo's appearance on Nigeria's political scene is seen in stable terms, since experts and political analysts feel that he will continue to bring about quality leadership, his critics still bemoan and even criticize the way he was supported by a powerful section of the current, as well as retired, military and Nigeria's business community. It was reported, "Backed by retired generals and the country's wealthiest businessmen, General Obasanjo easily won the elections in February despite suspicions surrounding his military past and a wide-spread anti-military mood in the nation."[87]

Before Obasanjo's election in February 1999, Nigeria's future was deemed bleak by experts and analysts. The reasons for that state of affairs was well captured in the following words:

Years of misrule, corruption and theft have shattered the country's economy, facing the new Government with a restive population lacking basic needs like reliable electricity and drinking water. In recent months, economic conditions have worsened as the Government engaged in an as yet unexplained spending spree that is estimated to have reduced foreign reserves of $4 billion by more than $2 billion.[88]

The outgoing military regime and Obasanjo encountered unrest from the Niger Delta of Nigeria, where, as reported, "almost all the country's oil" is produced. It had become "a focal point of unrest and violence in recent months," as a result of neglect by previous governments. Happily for all Nigerians, President Obasanjo, in his inaugural speech, "fully acknowledged these problems and the failures of government. . . . Pledging to tackle the problems, he pleaded for patience and sacrifice."[89]

Although Mr. Obasanjo's vice-president is from northern Nigeria, critics made sure to point out the fact that Obasanjo was from southern Nigeria, because: "In a country ruled by northern Muslims, Mr. Obasanjo is the first Yoruba—from southern Nigeria—to lead the country since he himself was a head of state."[90] Indeed, the fact that the new Nigerian leader is from the southern part of the country and that he is seen as acceptable to the military leaders— including those retired, retiring, and still in uniform—prompted many people to hope for stability in Nigeria for several years to come. Otherwise, it is a well-known fact that a military leader could easily refuse to hand over power if the incoming administration is to be headed by anyone from another ethnic group that he and his colleagues could not trust, as it happened in the case of Chief M.K.O. Abiola, a Yoruba from Southern Nigeria, who died in detention.

The Abiola episode, both sad and tragic, is recalled in the following words:

The hand over [of the government to Obasanjo] was the culmination of a tumultuous year in Nigeria that began with the unexpected death of General Abacha last June [1998]. A month later, the equally sudden death of Moshood K. O. Abiola, the presumed winner of the 1993 presidential elections annulled by the military and the country's most popular politician, plunged Nigeria into a crisis quelled only by the promise of elections.[91]

After the foregoing events, Nigeria—with its teeming and diverse population—most certainly needed a leader who could command overwhelming respect and, subsequently, bring about stability, two precious qualities that the electorate found in President Obasanjo, a Yoruba like Chief Abiola. In fact, his "second coming" is heralded by some of his antidictatorial words of the past, including his recollection that African nationalist leaders teamed up with the people to drive away colonial leaders. He is often being reminded of his famous quote: "Yet no sooner had colonial rule ended than our new rulers set about converting the revolution into one of fire and thunder against their own people."[92] What an indictment! However, it is hoped that new leaders of Africa, whether they emerge from partisan politics or military retirement, consider patriotism and the progress of the nation as their main priorities, especially as they place their hands on the Holy Bible or Holy Koran to take their oaths of office!

Also, since many Africans, in their patriotic zeal, often claim one should not blame political indigenous forces alone for Africa's massive problems, we have utilized the next chapter of our study to focus on the international dimensions, coupled with the various ideological forces, that either openly supported or were suspected of actively playing roles in African military interventions. This section, like the earlier chapters, is very important in view of the fact that in *Dark Days in Ghana,* Nkrumah claimed that his regime in Ghana was overthrown with the tacit support of the CIA. However, a former CIA officer, John Stockwell, later wrote in his own book, *In Search of Enemies,* that the Ghana-based CIA operatives (in the American Embassy in Accra) did not actively plan and executive the 1966 coup in Ghana (as they did the anti-Allende coup in Chile), but did encourage the anti-Nkrumah plotters.

CHAPTER SIX

African Coups Galore:
Foreign and Ideological Influences

As an avowed socialist-cum-Marxist, Ghana's President Kwame Nkrumah always suspected that his government was under the threat of capitalism from nations like the United States of America and Great Britain. In fact, Nkrumah was so suspicious of these countries that, when in Guinea in exile from 1966 until his death in 1972, he blamed the American Central Intelligence Agency (CIA) for the setbacks in his plans to regain political power in Ghana, when the military-police regime of the National Liberation Council (NLC) was in power. This was why, in *Panaf Great Lives: Kwame Nkrumah* (1974), his literary editor, Mrs. June Milne and other writers of the biographical study noted:

In 1967, Guinean naval forces intercepted a fishing trawler containing convicted criminals released from prison in Accra, who had been engaged by [Mr. J.W.K.] Harlley to capture Nkrumah dead or alive. The criminals, who were all Ewes, the same tribe as Harlley and Deku, were arrested and interrogated by the Guinean police. At about the same time, it was [allegedly] discovered that an Ewe security officer of Nkrumah's entourage, by the name of John Ketsowo Kosi, had been bribed through American connections in Conakry, to report regularly on Nkrumah's activities, his visitors, the security surrounding him, and any other information likely to be of interest to the NLC. For these services he was paid a salary of about 25,000 francs a month. According to the Guinean police report on Kosi's activities: "Kosi consciously worked for the American Intelligence Service and is the root cause of the non-realization of many of the plans relating to President Nkrumah's return to Ghana."[1]

Those who knew the inner workings of Nkrumah's affairs in Guinea, coupled with the intelligence operations for and against his plans to regain power from the NLC regime, knew that the CIA had nothing to do with the futility of Nkrumah's anti-NLC plots. Instead, they were aware that the ruling military junta in Ghana had its own elaborate plans conceived and carefully executed by well-trained security men like former Special Branch Director Charles Kwashie Mawuennyegah and other foreign service intelligence officers of Ghana's erstwhile Research Bureau. The CIA reportedly did not pay any sum of money to Kosi: if any payments were made, they came from a friendly African Embassy in Conakry, Guinea, with whose government the NLC mutually shared intelligence. However, Nkrumah and his supporters were, unfortunately, blinded by the thought that a socialist leader with Soviet connections during the Cold War era would be subverted and have his government unseated by the CIA and other capitalist intelligence forces.

Indeed, when military takeovers began to surface as a mushrooming cascade of regular events in the 1960s on the African continent, many Africans and scholars of the continent's affairs thought that it was a temporary matter that would abate over the years. Unfortunately, the coups became popular occurrences, and, peculiarly they also became part of the "legitimate" ways of changing democratically-elected regimes in several areas of Africa ("legitimate" in the eyes of coup makers because nobody dared to challenge them whenever they took over national radio and television stations.) Early on, these military events were never identified within the spectrum of either the ongoing Cold War between the Capitalist West and the Socialist East or an ideology in general, which, in Webster's interpretation, is the "integrated assertions, theories, and aims that constitute a socio-economic program."[2]

Historically and politically, it was not until the successful or attempted overthrow of regimes headed by radical African leaders who showed an ideological bent in their nationalist rhetoric and developmental programs that experts on African history and politics and enlightened citizens of many nations on the continent began to see coups d'etat in ideological terms. Citing examples from several countries on the continent, this chapter concerns itself with the international and ideological forces that shaped African military intervention; the Cold War era as a partially precipitating event has also been dissected.

To many researchers on Africa, the Cold War could be seen, in its heated waves, as a minor factor in the way Third World nations—including those in Africa—were "required" by the big powers to "behave" politically, economically, and even ideologically. Professor Edmund Keller, Director of the Coleman Center for African Studies at the University of California at Los Angeles (UCLA) and a serious scholar on African political history, offered an enlightened and very instructive overview of Africa and the demise of the Cold War. Also, his 1996 study—coupled with his thinking toward a new African political order—helps his readers to deduce that there was no excuse for seeing the Cold War as a major reason for the rampant overthrow of many regimes in Africa between 1960 and 1970. Also, Professor Keller, with true scholarly precision, has reiterated several of the momentous historical and political events that spelled doom for the Cold War beast: They included, from the mid-1980s to the 1990s, the collapse of the Berlin Wall; the use of organized labor in the ten-year struggle of the Polish Solidarity Movement to topple an entrenched Communist regime;

and how then Czechoslovakia fashioned, in characteristic Keller jargon, its "velvet revolution."[3]

For the future, as Professor Keller further stipulated, the world had come to assume unquestionably that the Cold War would always be with us. Hence, many of the historical and political "ills" of the Third World, particularly in Africa, were seen within the context of that icy and deadly war. Earlier in postcolonial African history, European incursions into Africa for political and economic gain were largely seen by critics of colonialism as the area's bane, in much the same way that many Blacks in and outside of Africa have often seen slavery as the dooming event that led to the abysmal plight of the ancestors of enslaved Africans.

After all, as Weber State University economics professor John Mukum Mbaku spelled it out, "Africans regarded colonialism as an alien, despotic, and non-democratic system designed by the Europeans to help the latter exploit African resources for the benefit of the metropolitan citizens."[4] Furthermore, Keller, as a specialist on the Horn Africa, also made the comparison that—in the same way that weak and corrupt regimes of Africa were swept aside by the avalanche of military coups d'etat, the Cold War became nonexistent. He writes, "almost overnight a unipolar world was created, as a result of the fact that the United States and what was left of the former Soviet bloc had decided to cooperate rather than compete on the world stage."[5]

Even as Keller postulated about the Cold War political stance, Africa was not immune to all of the dramatic shifts in the world where political, economic, and other factors were concerned. Also, just as the nations of the former Iron Curtain, or socialist Eastern Bloc, were struggling for their very survival, the nations of the African continent were, themselves, engulfed in their own political, economic, and social crises. These were eventful upheavals that would pave the way for the reasons and excuses that military officers—who have long been in search of power, prestige, and affluent lifestyles—would use to plot and topple several of the old regimes on the continent, including the West African nations of Benin (the former Dahomey), Nigeria, Ghana (Gold Coast), Mali, Ethiopia, and Liberia. Keller, *inter alia,* wondered: "If the Cold War has ceased, what does this mean for Africa? Will there be a peace dividend that will enable Africa to recover from its debilitating economic [and political] crisis? Or will Africa simply be relegated to the dustbin of history?"[6]

Apart from the Keller treatise, Nigerian President Obasanjo, a soldier-turned-intellectual-cum-politician, offered a very useful discussion in *Africa in the New International Order* (1996), which dovetailed with African problems to Cold War realities. In doing so, Obasanjo further supplied answers to some of the queries raised by Professor Keller, especially as he wrote eloquently:

> As the Cold War years advanced, growing inequalities between the industrialized nations of Europe and North America, on the one hand, and the underdeveloped countries of the Third World, on the other, introduced new tensions and new fears and added another dimension to the already

tense international atmosphere. . . . In a nutshell, the effects of Cold War politics on Africa were mixed. In a positive sense, Cold War politics encouraged and assisted the course of political emancipation from what was perceived as Western colonial domination. Cold War rivalry also impelled the superpowers and their allies to provide economic assistance for the newly independent African states in the 1960s and 1970s. In a negative sense, the involvement of the new states in superpower ideological politics aggravated their internal conflicts and encouraged stability. Furthermore, the readiness of the superpowers and their allies to supply arms to Africa encouraged an unnecessary arms buildup and diverted resources meant for development to unproductive and wasteful ends.[7]

Apart from the foregoing nuances, in which the Cold War played center stage, some experts, too, saw the "dirty hands" of the erstwhile Cold War in many problems that nations and institutions throughout the world suffered. The problems included some of the early shortcomings that plagued the United Nations and several of its integral outfits, especially in the business of the all-powerful Security Council, which has a chairmanship that is often rotated among member nations. For example, former Executive Chairman Richard Butler of the United Nations Special Commission in Iraq, who later resigned to become the Diplomat-in-residence at America's Council on Foreign Relations, wrote in *Foreign Affairs* about how the end of the Cold War had benefited the operations of the U.N. Security Council, from which he took his instructions for two years while serving in the commission's leadership in Iraq. From his thesis, the Security Council eventually became veto-less, as the permanent members rarely used their veto powers in post–Cold War U.N. business.[8]

In his own words, Butler had many confrontations with the Iraqi leadership, led by President Saddam Hussein, resulting in the unfortunate Iraqi accusation that his commission and its staff were made up of pro-American intelligence officials. Butler, *inter alia,* wrote:

> For the first half of the decade since the Cold War's end, the atmosphere in the U.N. Security Council was decidedly improved. With less East-West divisiveness, the council met more frequently and did more business. Only seven vetoes were cast in the post–Cold War period, versus 240 in the first 45 years of U.N. life. Twenty peacekeeping operations were mandated, more than the total for all the preceding years. But then the initial optimism about the Security Council's ability to get its job done in a veto-less world turned sour. Particularly dismaying were the last 12 months, during which the council was bypassed, defied, and abused.[9]

Indeed, the Cold War had a special place in almost all of the historical and political actions that played in the world's political theater until its demise. This came about thanks to powerful world leaders who wanted to see less ideological confrontations and more collaborative efforts where they could act without the hindrance created by ideological differences. However, earlier military takeovers in Africa were, at the time, merely seen as military-cum-police exercises to remove "bad" leaders whose styles of governance were often at variance with what either former colonial leaders or the electorate wished to see.

For example, when President Nyerere announced his socialist program and the January 1963 one-party rule in Tanganyika, several successful and attempted coups d'etat, some of which were suspected to be Western-influenced, were taking place in various African countries. The specific attempt to overthrow Nyerere's regime was certainly seen in ideological terms, mostly because of his socialist rhetoric. In the nearby island state of Zanzibar—which would later team up with Nyerere's Republic of Tanganyika to form the Tanzanian union—a military takeover on the island "ended the reign of the Sultanate of Zanzibar."[10]

Kenyan President Jomo Kenyatta—President Nyerere's good friend and political compatriot within East Africa—did not waste time in recognizing the new leaders of Zanzibar. However, Nyerere reportedly refused to endorse the new leaders of the island's coup d'etat. In fact, on January 20, 1964, President Nyerere nearly met his own military Waterloo: There was a serious mutiny in a section of Tanganyika's armed forces, which basically rose up against Nyerere's leadership. This serious threat to the stability of the government that Nyerere headed was "quelled by Brigadier Patrick Sholto Douglas, the British commander of the Tanganyika Rifles. Nyerere escaped harm."[11]

In some respects, Nyerere's refusal to endorse the new Zanzibari leadership, did not completely erase the suspicion that he possibly had a prior knowledge of the military event on the island, the leaders of which would pave the way for the subsequent union of the mainland and the island. The suspicion deepened when, on April 23 of that year, it was announced that Tanganyika's leaders, led Nyerere, had met with the new Zanzibari leaders to create the union of Tanzania, with Nyerere as its first president and Aboud Karume, from Zanzibar, as its first vice-president. After that, events unfolded very fast. For example, a revised constitution was put in place for Tanzania in the spring of 1965, and a government *White Paper* was passed simultaneously, which, by June 1965, made the new Tanzanian nation a one-party state like that of the erstwhile Tanganyika, with African Socialism as its main ideology. The new parliament of the unified nation approved all of the foregoing actions. In September 1965, the new regime of Tanzania held its first general elections, through which Dr. Nyerere was retained as president by receiving 99 percent of the vote cast, a familiar African political phenomenon, although Nyerere was not, necessarily, suspected of rigging the elections.[12]

Meanwhile, what prompted a suspicion about external interference, where military takeovers were concerned, in Africa, was that it was around the same time that Nyerere was creating a socialist form of governance and a one-party nation that his regime was almost overthrown. Also, to compound the area's ongoing political problems, shortly after all of the foregoing events, Prime Minister Ian Smith of Rhodesia made his 1965 Unilateral Declaration of Independence called UDI, a historic event in which Smith unilaterally declared Rhodesia (Zimbabwe) independent. Kenya's Kenyatta, Ghana' Nkrumah and Tanzania's Nyerere—among other African leaders—reacted angrily to the visible British tolerance of UDI. At the point of threatening to break up diplomatic relations with Great Britain, common sense prevailed, and the three radical nations and several others suspended their memberships in the British Commonwealth organization instead. Coincidentally, on February 24, 1966, the publicly-avowed socialist government of Nkrumah in Ghana was swiftly overthrown by the country's armed forces under very suspicious circumstances.[13] The anti-Nkrumah coup incident was seen by socialists as a typical example of a so-called socialist nation in the Third World that, arguably, suffered at the hands of pro-Western forces, which publicly condemned Nkrumah's socialist ideology and economic program. These have been varied theories and accusations about Nkrumah's overthrow in 1966.

In Nkrumah's own words, the downfall of his regime was engineered by anti-socialist Western nations, including the United States, Great Britain, and even Germany. Also, he implicated the American Ambassador to Tanzania Franklin H. Williams, who had attended the Pennsylvania-based Lincoln University, like Nkrumah. Nkrumah's allegation has never been proven, not even after the release of several doctored CIA documents on such events through the Freedom of Information Act. In *Dark Days In Ghana,* in which Nkrumah catalogued his impression of what happened in the Ghanaian military and police overthrow of his regime in 1966, he wrote pointedly:

> In Ghana the embassies of the United States, Britain, and West Germany were all implicated in the plot to overthrow my government. It is alleged that the U.S. Ambassador, Franklin Williams, offered the traitors 13 million dollars to carry out a coup d'etat, Africa, Harlley and Kotoka were to get a large share of this if they would assassinate me at Accra airport as I prepared to leave for Hanoi. I understand Africa said: "I think I will fail," and declined the offer. So, apparently, did the others. It is particularly disgraceful that it should have been an Afro-American ambassador who [allegedly] sold himself out to the imperialists and allowed himself to be used in this way.[14]

Nkrumah, angrily associating antisocialist ideological interpretations with his 1966 overthrow, had earlier written that "it has been one of the tasks of the CIA and other similar organizations to discover those potential quislings and traitors in our midst, and to encourage them, by bribery and the promise of political power, to destroy the constitutional government of their countries."[15] Nkrumah did not hide his ideological leanings, as he underscored in 1957, the year of Ghana's independence: "Today I am a non-denominational Christian and a Marxist socialist and I have not found any contradiction between the two."[16] Therefore, it was a lot easier than in many other cases to pinpoint the CIA and other Western intelligence organizations as having teamed up to effect Nkrumah's removal from power, with no confirmed evidence.

To Bob Fitch and Mary Oppenheimer, Nkrumah's socialist experiment was an illusion of sorts. Both authors discussed "the myth of Ghanaian socialism," of which the Nkrumah experiment was a version. Therefore, in the words of Finch and Oppenheimer, one of the most popular explanations, for failure was to "put all the blame on the CIA."[17] Afrifa, one of the 1966 Ghana coup d'etat leaders, spelled out the real reasons for Nkrumah's overthrow to coauthor Assensoh, who quoted him as saying that, as far back as in November 1964, he had conceived an idea for a military overthrow of Nkrumah. Afrifa added: "It was very unfortunate that Nkrumah could not realize that his armed forces were not happy with the way he was handling the affairs of state."[18] Misrule of Ghana was the general belief among Nkrumah's opponents in and outside of Ghana. Again, the story of the anti-Nkrumah coup was told in variation, depending on the teller.

About the Ghanaian military and police forces, *per se,* Afrifa wrote in his published memoirs, *Ghana Coup:* "Our [military] clothes were virtually in tatters. We had no ammunition. The burden of taxation was heavy. The cost of living for the ordinary soldier was high. The Army was virtually at the mercy of the politicians who treated it with arrogance and open contempt."[19] Apart from the suspicion cast by Nkrumah and other socialist forces that his overthrow was the work of Western intelligence agencies, former CIA operative John Stockwell confirmed in his book, *In Search of Enemies,* that, indeed, his employers, the CIA had something to do with Nkrumah's downfall: "For example, the CIA station in Ghana played a major role in the overthrow of Kwame Nkrumah in 1966, in violation of a 40 Committee decision not to, but CIA cables and dispatches infer that all contacts with the plotters were undertaken solely to obtain intelligence on what they were doing."[20] In fact, where ideological implications were concerned, Stockwell went on to add, "So close was the [CIA] station involvement that it was able to coordinate the recovery of some classified Soviet military equipment by the United States as the [Ghana] coup took place."[21]

Socialist embassies were so much suspected of involvement in Ghana's socialist policies, under Nkrumah's rule, that Stockwell claimed this was what the CIA agents wanted to do after Nkrumah's overthrow:

> The [CIA] station even proposed to headquarters through back channels that a squad be on hand at the moment of the coup to storm the Chinese embassy, kill everyone inside, steal their secret records, and blow up the building to cover the fact. this proposal was quashed, but inside CIA headquarters the Accra station was given full, if unofficial credit for the eventual coup, in which eight Soviet advisors were killed. None of this was adequately reflected in the agency's written records.[22]

Though Stockwell's version of events have been repeated by others, U.S. Ambassador Williams—up to the time of his death in New York of cancer—denied his personal involvement in the Nkrumah overthrow. Interestingly, however, Stockwell also confirmed that the CIA went after suspected radical or socialist leaders like Congolese first Prime Minister Patrice Lumumba and others. Although such plots to assassinate these leaders were often denied, Stockwell added: "In each case there are documents which place CIA officers in supportive contacts with the eventual assassins, but the link seems to break before the final deed."[23]

Certainly, the ideological interplay in Third World political events was very important during the hectic years of the erstwhile Cold War. In fact, in a recent recollection of some of the East-West accounts, some of Africa's budding political leaders who played active roles in the anticolonial nationalist struggles were tainted as being communist before they even became national leaders. An example is Zimbabwean President Mugabe, who in his early years was a freedom fighter. *African Business Journal* editor Anver Versi wrote about how Mugabe, as a freedom fighter in the 1970s "was the 'Communist scourge' that Britain and the US did their best to undermine and prevent from gaining the Presidency [of Zimbabwe]. They failed when Mugabe rolled over the 'President designate' Bishop Abel Muzorewa and took his seat on a thunderous wave of popular support."[24]

To a large extent, there were varied reasons for why Mugabe could be seen in either socialistic or communistic terms, although there has never been a bona fide, full-fledged communist leader; all the world has ever known are true socialists, since the October 1917 revolution that V. I. Lenin led. However, since then, many world leaders have aspired to become communist in outlook and leadership style. Precipitated by the March 7, 1917 strike of the workers of the Putilov factory and the March 15, 1917 abdication of Russian Czar Nicholas II as well as the right of his hemophilic son Alexeis to the throne, the Lenin-led revolution would become a world model for individuals interested in revolutions, including true and pseudorevolutionaries on the African continent. In fact, similarities exist between the Russian events and subsequent African revolutionary events.

For example, Nigeria had a situation comparable to the refusal of Czar Nicholas's brother, Grand Duke Michael Alexandrovich Romanoff, to occupy the throne that the Czar had abdicated.. In the midst of the 1966 counterrevolution, in which General Ironsi was killed, the most senior military leader to become the next Head of State was Brigadier Ogundipe, who saw that he would not last for 24 hours as leader of Nigeria if he agreed to lead the new post-Ironsi regime. Instead, he agreed to become Nigeria's new High Commissioner to Great Britain, and left the country quietly to assume that position so that General—now Dr.—Yakubu Gowon would become Nigeria's new military leader. Similarly, the Nigerian revolution had its bloody aspects like the one that toppled Czar Nicholas's Russia: General Ironsi, who was visiting the western region's Governor Fajui, was abducted with the governor, and both of them, reportedly, with several security personnel, were assassinated. In Russia, the Czar and his entire family were wiped out as part of the Lenin-led revolution.[25]

Then, there is the Zimbabwe scenario. In the case of Zimbabwe, Dr. Mugabe was neither being suspected nor accused of any bloody revolutionary ties. However, it was still a fact that he had lived and worked in Ghana, where he reportedly taught at St. Mary's Teacher Training College at Apowa, during the hectic socialist revolutionary years of Nkrumah's regime. Because of that, as well his own rhetorical statements, he was seen as coming from a socialist or Marxist mold. These were coincidents, too. In fact, as the existing records have confirmed, Dr. Mugabe was in Ghana—together with other liberation movement leaders—when Che Guevera paid a rousing official visit to the West African nation. It was indeed not surprising that—as already discussed elsewhere—Nkrumah's regime would be overthrown in February 1966 by pro-Western military and police officials of the Ghana armed forces, showing the extent to which antisocialist (and anti-Marxist) forces would go to do away with individuals with Marxist leanings.

It was, indeed, the era of politics by elimination, especially when ideological interests were concerned. Assuredly, both the socialist world and the capitalized one behaved similarly. That was why the Western press and other sources delighted in accusing socialist Ghana of involvement in the 1963 overthrow and assassination of Togolese President Olympio, a pro-France West African political leader. That happened three years before Nkrumah's own overthrow in a military takeover, in which some of his top military leaders, including the much revered and feared Brigadier Hassan, were murdered. Nkrumah lamented their deaths bitterly in *Dark Days in Ghana,* one of the books that he wrote while in political exile in Sekou Toure's Guinea (where he was also designated co-president of Guinea when he and his entourage arrived at Conakry airport on March 2, 1966[26]).

Where African monarchies and royalty were concerned, there was marked difference in the way and reasons for their overthrow. An example was the 1969 Libyan military overthrow of King Idris. The king who had been foisted on Libyans by a December 1951 United Nations resolution, making Libya the first country to be created by a resolution of the United Nations. Motivated by the earlier Nasserite revolution in Egypt, the Libyan revolution of 1969, led by Colonel Muammar Gaddafy, was seemingly led by anti-monarchy revolutionaries. Behind the scenes, however, there were ideological underpinnings as well. There was also the ethnic dimension as Idris was from the dominant Senussi ethnic or tribal group, and the bulk of the leaders of the 1969 coup were from the unsophisticated Bedouin ethnic group. Ideologically, King Idris was seen as a Western stooge when he agreed to retain the sprawling American air base in Libya. In reaction to this image, 29–year-old Gaddafy led the violent and very radical revolution that toppled Idris from power and proclaimed a socialist Arab republic modeled on Gamal Abdul [Abdel] Nasser's Egypt.[27]

Also, the new Gaddafy regime underscored its anticapitalist nature by taking several measures. These included the fact that Libya nationalized British and American oil companies that operated in its territory. Gaddafy played a major role in leading the Organization of Petroleum Countries (OPEC). The Western world saw that their economic and, to an extent, external political interests were at stake, and Libyan-American relations have not been good for many years since. Similarly, in Ethiopia, Emperor Haile Selassie had created a virtual fiefdom in his ancient empire, resulting in a coup by the country's military leaders. The ideological nature of the 1974 overthrow of Selassie was captured by Martin van Creveld, author of *The Encyclopedia of Revolutions and Revolutionaries: From Anarchism to Zhou Enlai.* Van Creveld made sure to point out that the regime was pro-Western and, as was openly known, several Western countries—including America—maintained very healthy relations with Ethiopia under Emperor Selassie's rule; there was even the rumored claim that some of these countries maintained foreign-operated military and satellite bases in Ethiopia. After the overthrow of Selassie's long-reigning monarchy was replaced by a Provisional Military Administrative Council (PMAC), known then simply as the Derg, or committee, which was made up of 120 soldiers, with the radical Major Mengistu Haile Mariam as its the most influential member.[28]

> The new regime's prosocialist (or pro-Russian) slant could be seen in these words: On December 20, 1974, Ethiopia was officially declared a socialist state. More than 100 companies were nationalized or partly taken over . . . all rural land was nationalized. . . . The 1974 revolution also led to a change in Ethiopian foreign policy. Ethiopia turned away from the West, expelled the US military advisory mission and signed a treaty of friendship and cooperation with the USSR. Close relations were also developed with Cuba, which provided substantial military assistance in the war with Somalia (1977–1978). There were also close contacts with the [former] German Democratic Republic (GDR) and other Eastern European states and with the Marxist-Leninist People's Democratic Republic of Yemen (PDRY).[29]

Ethiopia

The ethnic yardstick in Ethiopia's new leadership, however, emerged when General Teferi Banti, a leading figure of the Derg, was seen principally as a member of the Oromo ethnic group, the Kushitic people that invaded Ethiopia during the 17th century in search for new lands. Reportedly, Banti tried very had to conceal his Oromo background; he was recalled from his military attache position in Washington, D.C. to later become the commander of the second division of Ethiopian troops in Eritrea. When the Derg's first Chairman, General Aman Andom, was assassinated on November 22, 1974, Banti was appointed, by seniority, to become the new chairman. This was the height of the Ethiopian revolution's nationalist fervor, whereby the slogan, "Ethiopia *Tikidem*" or "Ethiopia First," was in vogue. Banti's had the good fortune of not been shunned from or deprived of Ethiopia's leadership for being an Oromo.

Reportedly, it was in a shoot out between Banti and Mengistu/Anafu loyalists at an August 1976 Derg meeting that Banti consolidated his position by replacing pro-Mengistu and pro-Anafu Abate members of the ruling Committee, hoping that his continuing leadership would, therefore, be assured or solidified. That was not so at all, as—on March 2, 1977—Mengistu, known to be a very ambitious young officer, angrily left in the middle of a Derg meeting and a group of his military supporters entered the room and killed all the people present, including Teferi Banti himself, the head of state of Ethiopia. Mengistu, as the emerging new leader, had Marxist-Leninist leanings. Since Ethiopia was officially declared a socialist nation on December 20, 1974, it was easier for Colonel Mengistu to institute Marxist-oriented measures in the country, actions which would later make him an enemy of the West. Subsequently, they would lead to his overthrow and exile in Zimbabwe, which is considered a socialist regime under Dr. Mugabe. There have been attempts by agents of the new

Ethiopian regime to capture and bring Mengistu to Ethiopia to face trial for several alleged crimes, but these attempts have been foiled.[30]

The Oromo dimension of Ethiopia's ethnic politics—coupled with Banti's background and eventual assassination by Mengistu's agents—does explain very well some of the reasons for today's Oromo opposition to the Mengistu regime and, unfortunately, even to the present regime. Certainly, the Oromo people have genuine national concerns, but it is historically and politically apt to place all events in their proper contexts. In his preface to Dr. Addisu Tolesa's *Geerarsa Folksong as the Oromo National Literature* (1999), Professor Asafa Jalata of University of Tennessee in Knoxville lamented that Ethiopia had played a colonialist role in stifling the development and growth of the Oromo linguistic expression, known as Geerarsa in Ethiopia. In addition to Dr. Tolesa's own authoritative study of the issue of Ethiopia's linguistic imperialism, as contained in Tolesa's 1999 book, Dr. Jalata, a sociologist by training and author of a book on Oromia and Ethiopia (1993), wrote:

> The Oromo [of Ethiopia] are an oral society; hence *geerarsa* played a key role in transmitting historical knowledge and cultural values from generation to generation. . . . For almost a century, recognizing that Oromo transmit their history mainly through oral discourse, such as *geerarsa,* the Ethiopian colonialists have discouraged the development of this oral literature, [and] Oromo scholars and others have been discouraged or prohibited by the Ethiopian colonial state from studying oral traditions.[31]

This, certainly, is a scenario of great historical and political import, although it would take an entire book-length study to debate both sides of the Ethiopia-Oromo issue to do justice to the squabble, which has been going on for many years. However, the Ethiopia-Oromo problem does offer a lesson in ideological implications in African politics to court socialist sympathies, as Mengistu came to power through these orchestrated events and announced that his country, Ethiopia, would follow a Marxist line of ideology in its rule and economic matters. Reportedly, a statue of Karl Marx was erected in the center of Addis Ababa, the capital, during Mengistu's rule in order to enlist socialist sympathies.

The foregoing are, indeed, only examples of several situations in which a new "coup" leader had cause to tilt the national policies toward a specific non-African ideology of either capitalism or socialism. At that point, Ethiopian nationalism—punctuated by "Ethiopia Tikidem"—went out the window. After Mengistu's overthrow in a counter-coup, which was more like an invasion led by leaders of the various Eritrea and Tigerenya liberation forces, the Marxist line of thought was replaced with a mixture of pro-western ideologies, including capitalism and social-democracy as practiced in Sweden and other places in Ethiopia. In the midst of these polarized ideological situations, one wonders: Whither Africa?

Several socialism-inclined leaders began to carve out ideological fiefdoms, becoming what was known as Afro-Marxist, which Professor Mbaku saw as nations in which "the state combined regulation with the control of many market functions and became all-encompassing. In fact, in many of these countries, the state took control of most market functions and gradually became the primary employer of national labor resources."[32] Many military officers, often Western-trained, became intolerant of these pseudo-socialist and Afro-Marxist nations. For, as well illustrated by Dr. Mbaku, "by the mid-1980s [or even much earlier, in the mid-1960s] most industrial activities in the Afro-Marxist countries were controlled by the state as the private sector had almost been regulated to extinction."[33] The intolerance of the military hierarchy in many of the newly-created socialist nations of Africa—including Nkrumah's Ghana and limitedly, Nyerere's Tanzania—was for good reasons, especially as citizens of these countries began to suffer untold economic and political hardships as a result of half-baked policies and empty socialist political slogans that could not feed them. Soldiers of both nations wanted to end the socialist experiments at the expense of human suffering.

In Ghana, a discussion reportedly took place between President Nkrumah and President Bronz Tito of Yugoslavia, during the latter's official visit to Ghana. As claimed by antisocialist elements at the time, Nkrumah took Tito on a ride in an official car, so the Yugoslav leader could see the capital of Ghana, Accra, in the afternoon. There, Tito saw a throng of long lines of Ghanaians, and he instantly thought that they were at voting booths. "I didn't know that your people were voting today," Tito reportedly told Nkrumah. "No, not quite so. They have queued up to buy what we call essential commodities: soap, sugar and other imported canned goods," Nkrumah explained. Nkrumah reportedly further told Tito that he wanted to find out if Yugoslavia could help Ghana establish more factories to produce more essential commodities so that, as was shown, his fellow countrymen would not have to line up just to buy the few items they needed. Allegedly, Tito responded that it was a good socialist practice to have the people in serious economic want, reportedly adding: "After all, the more impoverished the people are, the more subservient and obedient they become, as they look up to you as the ultimate leader from whom they can have relief."

Indeed, with such a foregoing political mentality all over the place in many countries, military officers of postcolonial Africa felt the need to help the impoverished citizenry of many nations and, in the end, to use their guns to effect changes in leadership and ruling styles. Hence coups d'etat mushroomed in many places in Africa. Indeed, in times of need and economic misery, the military officials, too, suffered, sometimes compelled to wear tattered clothes and shoes, as Ghana's military strongman, General Afrifa, documented in his published memoirs, *The Ghana Coup*. According to Afrifa, it became an embarrassment to belong to the Ghana armed forces, as both soldiers and civilians in Nkrumah's Ghana were in similar impoverished economic misery. In fact, the officer, who later became one of Ghana's military leaders, used familiar personal experiences to explain some of the reasons behind the 1966 coup in which he teamed up with his boss, General Kotoka, to overthrow the Nkrumah regime.

For example, he recalled the time that a female shopper at a Ghanaian store saw him dressed in his military uniform, and said within earshot: "If you want to see a soldier, go to Nigeria; there, they have real and bold soldiers."[34] This was after the first Nigerian military coup d'etat of early 1966, which had claimed the lives of several top civilian leaders of the country. Not very long after that incident, Afrifa and Kotoka came together to effect the February 24, 1966 overthrow of the CPP regime of Nkrumah, after which the regime's socialist ideology was maligned and discarded instantly.

In a nutshell, therefore, economic realities and ideological experimentation played major roles in most of the coups d'etat that took place—and continue to take place—in Africa. However, where ideology is concerned, Professor Robin Cohen, a sociology professor at University of Warwick, was correct in asserting in *Democracy and Socialism in Africa* (1991) that the "debates about the relationship between socialism and democracy are as old as the social movements for these practices and the ideas themselves."[35] In this context, one sees how advocates of democracy and socialism can tear each other apart to make sure that the other's preferred mode of governance prevails. Therefore, when military coups were effected, the successful leaders would announce, as part of their program, their willingness to hand over power to democratically elected leaders. So, lack of democracy and, sometimes, too much ideology were a big part of the grievances of coup makers, as some Africans would say cynically, "Is it ideology we can eat and survive?" Above all, corruption in all forms, including what Dr. Mbaku has tantalizingly labeled as "bureaucratic corruption," was a major obstacle in efforts to minimize coups d'etat. In many places in Africa, corruption is a profession in itself, and even men and women convicted of corrupt practices find their way into governance. As Mbaku reported in *Corruption and the Crisis of Institutional Reforms in Africa,* Nigerian tribunals, for corrupt practices, sentenced former Anambra State Governor Jim Nwobodo to over 900 years in jail, and Bendel State Governor Samuel Ogbemudia was also convicted of corruption. Yet, in 1993, Nwobodo was appointed a cabinet minister, and, similarly, Ogbemudia "was subsequently appointed a minister under the general Ibrahim Babangida regime."[36]

Sadly, this same regime deemed it necessary to repeal the tough, anticorruption Decree No. 54, passed in 1976 in Nigeria, which authorized the ruling government to seize all assets that had been acquired through proven corrupt practices. The examples cited by Dr. Mbaku are a mere tip of the iceberg of corrupt practices throughout Africa, although the cited circumstances of the publicly-proclaimed corrupt people being able to find their way back into cabinet positions are unique. Under such situations, the governed look up to coups and counter-coups to remove such corrupt leaders from political power. For, no matter how much noise the ruling elite makes against corruption, as Mbaku stipulated, "a weak, corrupt, fragile, repressive and insensitive state cannot wage an effective campaign against corrupt practices, so long as the state itself does not command any respect or loyalty from the majority of the people, its attempt to create a new basis for public behavior through corruption cleanup programs is doomed to fail."[37] And where failure crowns all efforts to erase corruption, a coup d'etat, sadly, becomes the main yardstick by which to measure and remove the entrenched leaders in many places in Africa, especially as the governed masses of Africa loudly pray and yearn for change—in Malcolm X's parlance—by any means possible.

Although Oxford-based Anthony A. Akinola has offered a useful study of the history of corruption, published in *West Africa Magazine,* it is still unfortunate that there are many reasons why corruption cannot easily be either defeated or removed from African governance. Professor Mbaku puts it well, in writing:

> Another conclusion that we can draw from both disclosures on corrupt practices and the discourse on corruption in Africa is that there is a well-established international connection to fraudulent and corrupt behavior in Africa. In many cases, multinational corporations, foreign governments and expatriates are the main conduits for corruption in Africa.[38] There-fore, it should take international leaders, working with patriotic Africans, to help minimize—not necessarily to end, as it is hard to do so com-pletely—institutionalized corruption, which would continue to invite the Armed Forces in many African countries to dabble in politics via coups d'etat. Otherwise, the loud hew and cry by many patriotic voices of Africans, would go unheeded: that "today, the continent remains the poor-est region of the world—Africa's development potential appears to have been squandered through perverse economic policies, corruption, and other forms of opportunism."[39]

Above all, if economic and political matters continue to deteriorate in Africa, indeed to a point of no return, then again the hard-to-answer query would be: Wither Africa, one of the mothers of civilization? As Anthony Akinola also put it, African nations should take on seriously the pervading incidents of poverty, "the very root cause of corruption in [African] society."[40] In the next chapter, we have offered a political and theoretical context for the unending spate of coups d'etat in Africa including what seems to be the impatience of many African political interests, which results in quick and ad hoc solutions to many of the continent's multifarious problems. Indeed, when compared to situations in developed societies like the United States, Great Britain, and other places, many African nations fall short in arriving at political decisions.

An example of Western political patience is seen in the Florida electoral seg-ment of the November 2000 American presidential election. There were chal-lenges upon challenges as well as court suits and countersuits, all in efforts to arrive at the "truth" of what the press has referred to as an electoral maelstrom. Indeed, when a deadline of Tuesday, November 14, 2000, exactly a week after the presidential election was set for the verification of votes in Florida by Secre-tary of State Katherine Harris, basically to stop the tallying of large volumes of votes, it was reported that a "U.S. Judge [refused] to block hand tallying of votes."[41] As many Africans and experts on African issues have noted, if the electoral stalemate had taken place in an African country, or in many places in the Third World, military adventurers would have announced a coup to stop what they would describe as a messy situation. The next chapter is, therefore, crucial as we place most of the coups d'etat, the reasons for them, and their instigators in varied contexts.

CHAPTER SEVEN

African Coups in the Political and Theoretical Contexts

Several writers have said beneath all the norms of legal and institutional behavior in society lies the great beast—the people's capacity for outraged, uncontrolled, bitter, and destructive violence. This is very often utilized either for self-defense or to make a political statement of sorts.[1] Most certainly, the prevailing circumstances have shown that all of the foregoing factors can often converge, historically and politically, to prompt many African military officers—including those in the air force, naval, and police—to decide when the time is ripe for an armed rebellion, rather than an election, to overthrow a particular unwanted regime.

Many of such overthrown regimes might have been either established through the electoral process or instituted by an earlier military upheaval. Armed rebellion in an African nation could come in the guise of either a palace coup or a full-fledged coup d'etat, which might bring about the swift elimination of an entrenched leadership. However, African countries may be different from other nations, as we found out when completing research for this study, in the fact that it does not necessarily have to be a very serious political event for a violent conflagration to be used to bring about change. In this guise, what comes to mind is a leader's violation of various taboos, traditions or customs, and outright dictatorial regimes, as pretences to effect coups. In doing so, several leaders who were known to have been obsessed with power have declared themselves "Presidents-for-Life," "His Excellency Dr. President-for-Life," and "Our Supreme Ruler," among other outrageous titles.

Our research has shown what today are called coups d'etat, employed to effect change were seen as terrorist acts in the early 1900s. In a study of early nineteenth-century Elmina in the Gold Coast, for example, Professor Larry W. Yarak, a Texas A & M University historian, has categorized the actions of the citizens of the city, who endeavored to undermine Dutch efforts at instituting a form of internal slavery as nonrational and terrorist. In Yarak's 1990 study for Oxford University Press, the Dutch officers in the area quoted prosecutor J. Cremer as reporting that he recognized the normative basis of Elmina's social and political order. However, the rebellious actions of a section of the citizenry prompted the officials to conclude that the indigenous Elmina citizens could not be said to be rational creatures or humans.[2]

Also, it is a historical fact that the rancorous and protesting actions of eighteenth-century *Tabwa* tin miners in northern Nigeria, along with other nationalist acts, were seen in banditry terms by competing European merchants and colony seekers. Therefore, evaluations of such actions basically depended on who was writing about these events. Hence, insulting terminologies were utilized by colonialists and their scholars at the time. An example to the contrary is that of Guyana's great historian, the late Professor Walter Rodney, who has been well-known for his Howard University Press-published book, *How Europe Underdeveloped Africa* (1967). He had done the bulk of his major research about Africa while in Africa, and he did not see the eighteenth-century revolutionary actions of the indigenous populace of the Futa Djallon mountainous area of Nigeria in terrorist terms when he wrote about Jihad and social revolution in the area.

Dr. Rodney, a revolutionary intellectual himself, invariably suffered at the hands of the regime of Prime Minister Forbes Burnham in Guyana. His tribulations were very much akin to what scholars and other writers go through in Africa, mainly because of his partisan political activism. In the end, he was like the sacrificial lamb; he paid the supreme price of his life when, allegedly, a planted bomb exploded in his face, killing him instantly and seriously maiming one of his siblings. It was a dastardly act that was similar to what some of the very dictatorial and desperate regimes in Africa would do to an opponent or a mere public critic in order to get him off their backs. Indeed, it was similar to what happened to Dele Giwa in Nigeria during the military rule of General Ibrahim Babangida; Giwa's murder has never been successfully investigated nor the perpetrators punished.[3]

When Dr. Rodney was reportedly killed in the timed bomb that was reportedly hidden in a "walkie-talkie" device, pro-Burnham supporters, in trying to justify his murder, described the celebrated historian's political opposition and some of his tactics as being "terrorist" in nature. That, of course, is not surprising, because, whenever a coup d'etat was unsuccessful in Africa, its planners and would-be leadership were seen in banditry, terrorist, saboteur, treasonable or "nation-wrecking" terms. Some of these accusatory terminologies are often brandished about or listed at the trials of abortive coup planners in several African countries.

Coauthor Assensoh and Giwa shared an interest in ensuring that journalistic standards in all of Africa would be raised to the highest professional levels so that, in the end, the profession and its practitioners would become as celebrated and fearless as they were in democratic societies. As examples, both journalists often remembered the cherished writings of some of Africa's leading journalistic icons, including Alhaji Odenewu of Nigeria's defunct *Morning Post;* the indomitable Tai Solarin, whose "Thinking With You" column appeared regularly in the mass-circulating *Daily Times* newspaper of Nigeria, Peter Enahoro, who wrote under the admirable pen name of Peter Pan and, of course, Alhaji Lateef Jakande of Nigerian *Tribune* newspaper. Assensoh's particular respect for

Enahoro was enhanced when both of them served in different journalistic capacities for *Africa Magazine* at the Africa Center on King Street, London. At the time, Enahoro was based in Germany, working for a German radio station, but he paid frequent editorial visits to London.[4]

Also, Giwa's editorial representative in London, Wole Soyinka, reportedly suffered a partial hearing loss due to the letter-bomb blast that ended the youthful and bubbling life of Giwa, whose widow and small children had to soldier on in life without a loving husband and father. But, as expected, the Babaginda regime handled the incident like an ordinary murder case and, in over a decade, the perpetrators of such a criminal act have never been found. However, caring professional colleagues and extended family members rallied to ensure that the Giwa family was never left in material or spiritual want, and that they were well cared for. This incident and others are being narrated to illustrate the extent to which some Third World institutions, even governments and their leaders—whether elected or imposed by a coup d'etat—would go to perpetuate their rule. These acts are very much part of some of the shocking and corrupt activities of several regimes in Africa and elsewhere, which could invite soldiers to plan and stage coups d'etat to topple leaders that they considered to have fallen short of the standards of societal decency and general governance.[5]

The spate of political killings in many military—and sometimes civilian or elected—regimes in Africa often drove away not only journalists, but also some of Africa's very celebrated authors and future leaders into either voluntary or forced exiles outside the continent. For example, it was not an exaggeration when the *New York Times,* in its issue of December 7, 1994, reported the unorthodox escape of Professor Wole Soyinka, the distinguished writer and Nobel literature laureate, from his native Nigeria. Wole, as he is affably called by admirers and friends alike, had to sneak out of Nigeria abruptly. Irrespective of the fact that he was the author of some of Africa's excellent publications, including *Death and the King's Horseman* (1975); and *Art, Dialogue and Outrage* (1990); *The Man Died (1972),* which detailed his political prison experiences under the Gowon regime, he did not receive red carpet treatment, but reportedly made his exit through the bush.[6]

Kenya's Ngugi wa Thiong'o, now occupying an endowed professorial chair at New York University; Malawi's Jack Mapanje, who went to Britain to teach immediately after his release from a Malawian prison; and several other African writers now living in voluntary exile have documented their prison experiences. Ngugi shared his Kenyan political prison experiences in *Detained: A Writer's Prison Diary,* while Mapanje, a former professor of Malawi's premier university before his detention under the regime of President-for-Life Kamuzu Banda, detailed his own Malawian prison experiences in his 1993 book, *The Chattering Wagtails of Mikuyu Prison* (1991). At an International P.E.N. writers' association annual meeting in Vienna, Austria, coauthor Assensoh met Dr. Mapanje for the first time and, while they were traveling together on an Air Austria flight from Vienna to New York, they had a very delightful discussion about the plight of African writers, especially about how many African leaders were intolerant of the open criticisms by these writers or journalists.[7]

Very interestingly, Dr. Banda's political friend in Ghana, Nkrumah, also did not spare his political critics, as Ghana's *Pioneer* newspaper's city editor Kwame Kesse-Adu captured his own political prison odyssey in his 225–page book, *The Politics of Political Detention,* published in 1971 by the Ghana Publishing Corporation. Mr. Kesse-Adu was well-known nationally and internationally because of his column, "The Accra Diary," which appeared during the week and on Saturdays in the *Pioneer* newspaper (for which Assensoh served as the subeditor). Yet, the Nkrumah regime did not care about Kesse-Adu's stature, and detained him without trial for several years. As he explained it himself, Kesse-Adu had used the column to castigate "the [Nkrumah] Government time and again, pointing out its faults and defects."[8]

However, those who knew Kesse-Adu very well did not believe that he was among active saboteurs or nation-wreckers, then described by the leaders of Nkrumah's Convention People's Party (CPP) as subversionists who needed to be uprooted for the famous official description of "the public good," to protect the very public that was being trampled upon by many of the postcolonial nationalist regimes.[9] It is useful that many of these writers lived to share their experiences in their published "prison" notes, as several imprisoned authors, unable to withstand the hardships of political prisons or detentions, perished during their years of detention without trial, while many others were simply eliminated by killer squads on behalf of the regimes that they critiqued in their writings.

Yet, the sad political fortunes of the time—reported vigorously in the political memoirs—made both necessary and germane the plans of military officers to plan and execute coups d'etat. Such military officers wanted to remove from power corrupt and dictatorial regimes, whether elected through the ballot box or not, which had lost the confidence of the electorate or a majority of a particular African nation's voting constituency. Sadly, such coups happened to be one of the few avenues through which unwanted regimes and their leaders, who had often ruled for decades, could be removed from office. Again, it had become impossible to use the ballot box to change unwanted political leaders, as such leaders had the resources and the sheer ability to rig national elections.

In comparison, the colonial era in Africa did not witness the same amount of human destruction that was witnessed in postcolonial Africa, where a critic or a political opponent could either be arrested and imprisoned without trial or blown to bits and pieces by a letter-bombing device. Africans were poised for all forms of revolution in the 1900s: anticolonialist revolution and, of course, anti-indigenous imperialism, colonialism, and neocolonialism in the mid-1960s. That is why Nigerian president Obasanjo's words about postcolonial tyranny have become memorable, where indigenous colonialism, neocolonialism and outright oppression in several areas of Africa are concerned.

When General Obasanjo was seeking the Nigerian leadership for the second time, this time through the ballot box, many researchers or scholars of African politics and history agreed that the general would be a model leader. The reason for such a reassurance is that, apart from having earlier served as Nigeria's leader and been "baptized" by fire he had also often, in the past, spoken out loudly against all forms of indigenous thievery and oppression on the continent. However, some of his critics did not think that Obasanjo's earlier leadership of Nigeria, upon the assassination of General Muhammed and as a fighting army battalion commander during the unfortunate Nigeria-Biafra civil war, was totally free of high-handed military and political tactics. Yet, it is a fact that it sometimes takes very drastic measures to be able to govern countries of the Third World, including those in Africa.

It is on record that, apart from voluntarily handing power back to an elected civilian leadership in Nigeria, Obasanjo also simply retired to his Ota Farm, from where he played an active role in world politics through the "barrel" of a pen, but not a gun, and also through dynamic speeches. After all, observers of his actions are familiar with the proverb that the pen is always mightier than the sword! Admirably, Obasanjo furthermore did not, in his retirement pronouncements, see indigenous colonization to be anything better than European colonialism. Hence, he lamented postcolonial dictatorships![10]

To subjugate their citizens to the point of driving them into docility and complacency—sometimes through a culture of silence or fear to express themselves—many of the nationalist leaders, as elected prime ministers and presidents, comfortably occupied the colonial offices and mansions that the departing European officials had "abandoned" in haste. To safeguard their newly-acquired status, most of these indigenous leaders both retained and re-invented repressive colonial laws or totally introduced their own, just to make sure that nobody undermined their authority. Writers, including journalists, seemed to have suffered the most because they wielded the "power" of communication through which the masses, the postcolonial electorate, could know what was actually going on in these newly independent nations. As the late President William V. S. Tubman of Liberia used to say at his famous Friday press conferences, he was never prepared to allow journalists to undermine his authority and, subsequently, plan to overthrow his regime by what he called "the stroke of the pen."[11] That was why Liberian writers and journalists like Albert Porte, Rufus M. Darpoh, Tuan Wreh, Stanton Peabody, and many others did not operate their professional or journalistic outfits in unfettered peace.

In some nations of Africa and, in fact, in several other Third World areas of Asia or elsewhere, a new leader would utilize repressive laws from the colonial era and, when there was a hue and cry over the indiscriminate use or excesses of these laws, such a leader would point to the fact that he (or she) met the laws on the books. Often these repressive postcolonial and indigenous leaders forgot that utilizing the inimical laws against their own people was much different than when strangers from Europe did so.[12] An interesting but sad scenario outside Africa happened in Malaysia in 1986 during coauthor Assensoh's Fulbright-Hays faculty research visit to several Asian nations. Upon the arrival of Assensoh's group at the Kuala Lumpur airport, two Australian nationals were hung for allegedly importing illegal drugs (called *dada* in Malaysia). When the Australian and other European governments, supported by protests from institutions like Amnesty International and human rights organizations, described the hangings in inhuman terms, the Malaysians said loudly that they learned how to hang people from British colonial rule. They added that, as a Muslim nation, Malaysia was familiar with act of beheading offenders or criminals to provide quicker deaths. It was hoped that after colonial rule, hangings would cease, even if they had been bequeathed by colonial authorities as punishment for capital crimes.

However, the colonial administrators of Africa neither eliminated their critics through killer squads nor saw the need to arrest and clamp them into jail for long periods of time without trial, as postcolonial African leaders have been doing, although this does not necessarily mean that the colonial rulers allowed their known political or editorial critics to act with impunity. What was admirable, however, was that the British colonial authorities would use existing laws of sedition, for example, to deal with a journalist who dared to undermine their authority. Nigeria's first indigenous President, Dr. Nnamdi Azikiwe, and Nkrumah, Kenyatta, and Nyerere, among several imprisoned or convicted nationalists, were typical examples. In Dr. Azikiwe's 1970 instructive memoirs, *My Odyssey,* he has devoted an entire chapter—titled "My Trial for Sedition"— to his own trial as the editor-in-chief of the *African Morning Post,* which was based in Accra, Ghana. He was charged with seditious libel for an anticolonial rule article titled "Has the African a God?" When it appeared in the May 15, 1936 issue of the newspaper, the colonial administration of the then Gold Coast did not merely arrest and detain Dr. Azikiwe in a colonial prison without trial. Instead, he was brought before an Accra court, tried, and he was found guilty. There were three assessors sitting as jury (including one White), and though the two Blacks did not find Dr. Azikiwe guilty of the seditious libel charge, the White assessor as well as the presiding judge, Mr. Justice St. John Yates, found Azikiwe guilty according to Section 330 of the existing criminal code (retitled Section 326 of the Criminal Code 1936 Revision, Subsection 2). Indeed, very swiftly, the presiding judge, *inter alia,* pronounced: "The sentence of the court is that you shall serve six months in prison and, in addition, you shall pay a fine of fifty pounds, and, in default of payment within 14 days, be imprisoned for three months."[13] As expected, Dr. Azikiwe was marched to jail to mix with the other imprisoned persons there.

A unique aspect of all of these matters in the colonial administration in Ghana was that Dr. Azikiwe, after his conviction, was granted bail, and later the West African Court of Appeal, which was presided over by Sir Donald Kingdom as president, "allowed the appeal, quashed the conviction, remitted the fine, and acquitted and discharged the accused [Dr. Azikiwe]."[14] Interestingly, one wonders, in retrospect, if such a trial would even take place, leave alone the acquittal on appeal, in most of the postcolonial regimes of Africa. In fact, in some countries in postcolonial Africa, judges and chief justices or defense lawyers could be either dismissed outright or arrested and jailed for merely daring to acquit, defend, or release persons that a regime wanted to see in prison, and that is if their political charges ever saw the light of day. Sir Arku Korsah, a chief justice of Ghana under Nkrumah's regime, suffered summary dismissal for freeing politically-charged persons that the regime was anxious to have in jail; the regime arrested the freed men and detained them under later the notorious Preventive Detention Act (PDA).[15]

In retrospect, it is very interesting that, with all the many civilian leaders that post-independence Africa has seen, it took a former military leader—who was recently transformed electorally into a civilian President of Nigeria—to speak out clearly and loudly about tyrannical rule in Africa. Obasanjo's statement, made in semipolitical retirement, was a truthful but painful admission that only a few honest and truly patriotic leaders of Africa could either make or even accept. To put it mildly, accepting and sometimes uttering similar truthful comments, laced with condemnation of repression, could cost many elected or militarily imposed leaders of Africa their leadership roles and, where care is not taken, even their lives. Of course, there are a few ultraconservative African scholars who would now become perpetual hecklers and anti-Africa authors simply because of the good lives they live abroad through the monetary handouts from their richly endowed paymasters, which include affluent foundations and educational institutions.

Meanwhile, in the midst of man's inhumanity to man, where Africa is concerned, several researchers and ordinary citizens of some of the nations on the continent have often tried to seek paradigms and, indeed, external examples to see if Africa is not really "unique" in events that call for coups d'etat and the multiplicity of such military upheavals. Sometimes, comparisons can give solace. For example, the plight of several South American or Latin American nations within the contexts of Third World politics, including that which has prevailed in the past in Argentina, comes to mind. Therefore, a brief discussion of the Argentine political-cum-military history has been offered here to help readers who may have been wondering if Africa is being singled out, among Third World areas, for a rough deal where coups are concerned.

It is, in fact, very fascinating to learn from our research that Argentina saw its first full-fledged coup d'etat in the 1930s, long before any African nation or military officer thought of staging one. Yet, Argentine military leaders, who have seen the repercussions of such coups, would still not hesitate to seize power in the 1990s if they deemed it to be in the national interest, just as several African coupists would claim that they took up arms against constitutionally-elected regimes to protect national interests. These new regimes often had the word "liberation" or "redemption" firmly entrenched in their names: National Liberation Council, National Redemption Council, Council for the Liberation of . . . , for example.

A Brief Argentine Comparison

Sometimes, in comparative terms, African scholars look at a place like Argentina, with its numerous military takeovers and conclude that Africa can afford more of such revolutions, even if they are bloody and costly. It is true that the Argentine military takeovers date back to September 4, 1930, when General Jose Urburu led the country's first military overthrow of the regime of Hipolito Irigoyen, which was under the Radical party's banner. Apart from that, there were these minor revolts and coups: a 1943 revolt during Ramon Castillo's leadership; the 1955 revolution, in which Juan Peron's regime was overthrown by General

Lonardi, forcing Peron to seek exile; the 1962 coup, which overthrew Arturo Frondizi and brought General Raul Poggi to power; and the 1966 revolution, led by General Juan Carlos Ongania, which banned all political parties, allowing the military officer to become the new leader. Ongania was considered dictatorial and, as a result, a 1970 coup replaced him with General Roberto Levingston; a 1976 coup toppled Peron's three-year-old rule, which had been completed by his second wife, Eva Peron, since his death in 1974, and general Jorge Rafael Videla became the new leader of Argentina. There was also the 1987 rebellion against Raul Alfonsin's presidency, although he had transformed Argentina by arresting and subsequently prosecuting former Argentine military leaders who had led coups d'etat.[16]

This sampling of military takeovers in Argentina does not, necessarily, mean that respective African nations have not had enough or their share of military coups, as it would be catastrophic for African military officers to sit back and say that, comparatively, they have not had enough of coups as a continent. Using the Argentina situation as an example is neither an exaggeration nor out of place. For, comparatively, Professor Baffour Agyeman-Duah, in a short study of West African coups d'etat concluded that very "blatant forms of foreign intervention occurred in Latin American and East European countries in the cold war era."[17]

Africa's share of active military dictatorships has been a long standing problem, ever since old kingdoms and empires were invaded by armies of other ambitious leaders. However, coups d'etat began to be a constant, bothersome feature of African politics in the 1950s. Apart from pockets of military revolts in precolonial times, whereby civil wars and internal conflicts were concerned, among the early mainstream coups d'etat in African affairs was the July 22, 1952 overthrow of King Farouk of Egypt. The coup paved the way for an Egyptian republic to be declared in June 1953, with Gamal Abdul Nasser as its effective leader. Sadly, outright coups d'etat have always been planned and executed with brutality.[18]

In some instances, military and civilian opponents had to be eliminated if the event was to succeed, just as Nigerians saw in the first full-scale coup led by Major Nzeogwu and other radical military leaders. In Nasser's Egyptian revolution, he had to be swift in performing some of these tough acts. For example, for him to succeed as the coup leader, he had to place the army chief, General Muhammad Nagib, under house arrest and to repress the Muslim Brotherhood, a Muslim organization that an Islamic nationalist leader would not have ordinarily repressed. Like latter-day coup makers, Nasser stayed in power until his death in 1970, having ruled for a total of almost two decades in military-cum-civilian style leadership. Unlike the modern-day coup leader in Africa, Nasser did not seem to lose his aura of invincibility and dynamism for the many years that he ruled his beloved Egypt. He was so popular that his handpicked heir-apparent, Anwar Sadat, easily ascended to Egypt's political "hot" seat after his death. However, unlike Nasser before him, Sadat's leadership was abruptly ended by a 1981 assassination, which was supposedly sponsored by an ultraconservative Islamic leadership of Egypt, often referred to as being religiously fundamentalist.[19]

Nasser's radical coup seemed to have paved the way for revolutions in northern

Africa. For example, the Algerian revolution of the Front de Liberation Nationale (FLN) was launched as a very "bloody" guerrilla warfare on November 1, 1954. Although not as successful as planned, it would have been a follow-up to Nasser's revolution in Egypt if it had succeeded. Instead Algeria's neighbors—Tunisia and Morocco—succeeded in attaining independence by bloodless revolutions in 1956, and some of Algeria's FLN leaders—including World War II–decorated officer Ahmad Ben-Bella—went underground as part of the anti-French rebellious tactics but from 1963 to 1965, Ben-Bella ruled Algeria.[20]

North Africa's revolutions continued unabated, as Libya's revolution in 1969 had a history of its own. Originally under Italian rule, from 1911, the British conquered Libya in World War II. But, in December 1951, the UN played a role in making Libya a kingdom under King Idris, until Colonel M. Gaddafy toppled his regime in September 1969. Meanwhile, West African regimes were also having their field days with coups. Apart from several military takeovers in former Dahomey (now called Benin), the most serious and full-fledged coup d'etat in the area was that of 1963, in which President Olympio lost his life. Nigeria, seen at the time as very stable under Sir Alhaji Tafawa Balewa, subsequently experienced its own first successful coup in 1966, costing the lives of Prime Minister Balewa and several of his officials, including regional governors.

The aftermath of the 1966 coup in Nigeria proved radical African leaders correct in their assessment that Nigeria, although free from colonial rule, still clung to the neo-colonialist apron strings of Great Britain. Reportedly, Queen Elizabeth II of Great Britain was so distraught over the death of Sir Tafawa that she, as later claimed by several sources, lamented his assassination and described him as having a golden voice that she reportedly liked to hear at British Commonwealth conferences.[21] Then, a mid-1966 counter coup, led by Lt.-Colonel (later General) Yakubu Gowon brought the young officer to power. As recounted elsewhere in this study, there was a secessionist rebellion led by Colonel Chukwuemeka Odumegwu Ojukwu, an Oxford-educated military officer, whose Igbo people unsuccessfully attempted to secede from the Nigerian Federation and form a Republic of Biafra. Invariably, the February 24, 1966 overthrow of the Nkrumah regime was a big deal, followed by the unsuccessful counter-coup led by Lieutenants Arthur and Yeboah, both of whom were executed later. However, the 1966 coup leader Kotoka was also murdered, together with some army officers, in the unsuccessful military uprising; Nkrumah treated Arthur and Yeboah as heroes in his book *Dark Days In Ghana,* in which he catalogued the events of the coup and castigated the military-cum-police leaders who overthrew his regime. He could not regain power and died in exile in 1972.

Ethnicity, Royalty, and Coups

The September 12, 1974 overthrow of the Ethiopian Emperor Selassie shook the foundations of African politics because Selassie was considered so powerful, the proverbial "Lion of Judah," that few people ever envisioned his overthrow and subsequent, replacement by the Derg of radical and conservative army officers. These events would also precipitate Selassie's untimely death. American-educated

General M. Ja'far Numeiri led the May 1969 coup in Sudan and, between 1969 and 1985, ruled the country with an iron hand, as usual, until his removal from power in a counter-coup of April 1985, led by General Bashir. Unlike other overthrown leaders on the African continent, who often lost their lives, Numeiri was fortunate enough to have been able to leave the country to live in exile in Egypt until recently in mid-1999, when he was welcomed back to Sudan by former supporters as a hero of sorts. For his own safety, however, Numeiri made it abundantly clear that he was no longer interested in Sudanese politics.

There have also been coups and counter-coups in Uganda, the first one led by Idi Amin Dada. Then came the revolutionary movement, led by Ugandan President Musoveni, that drove Amin out of power and into exile in Saudi Arabia, which was a logical place for a Muslim like Amin. In fact Professor Anthony H. M. Kirk-Greene (affably called Tony) of St. Antony's College, Oxford, put it best in his extraordinarily useful discussion of ethnic factors in various military set-ups around Africa in his publication on ethnic ranking and the martial races' imperative in Africa . For example, he saw both colonial and ethnic hands in the early upheavals that would lead to Uganda's first successful coup d'etat. Just like what prevailed in other African countries, certain ethnic groups rejected being enlisted in the army as a result of thinking that being enlisted in the army was beneath them. In Uganda, Kirk-Greene reported how, in the colonial and post-colonial periods, the Baganda people "either rejected the army as a career or had been rejected by it as a non-martial people."[22]

As the first elected indigenous head of state of Uganda, President Milton A. Obote saw the ethnic imbalance in the Ugandan army, with the Acholi people outnumbering every other ethnic group. The Acholis were deemed the military aristocracy of Uganda by colonial officials, mostly to create and perpetuate a divide-and-conquer mentality. Obote attempted, fruitlessly, to change things around by trying to ensure a recruitment of more of his own Lango people. That failure would cost Obote very dearly, as it would mean that he did not have enough men and women from his ethnic group to defend him in case of trouble arising from military indiscipline. Surely enough, as Professor Mazrui has aptly described in a 1975 study, Amin cashed in on the situation and seized power from Obote in a coup, driving the deposed leader into exile in President Nyerere's Tanzania. As one of his prompt actions as the new leader of Uganda, Amin decided to purge both the Acholi and Lango elements in the Ugandan Army in order to create a predominantly Kakwa-controlled army, as that was his own ethnic group, through which he thought that he could create a military ethnocracy.[23] In the end, all of these ethnic contradictions created the convoluted ethnic-cum-military chaos that sank Uganda into its political and economic abyss until Musoveni, using invasion and guerrilla tactics, took power from Amin, drove him into exile in Saudi Arabia, and tried very hard to correct problems of Uganda. He needed to reintroduce multiparty rule and reinvigorate moribund economy, which was that way partly due to the crude manner in which Amin had driven Asian businessmen and women out of Uganda.

In fact, while in the tight-grip of the Americo-Liberians since 1847, there had been unsuccessful coup plots and political murders of several Liberian political leaders. However, the West African country saw its first successful, full-fledged coup in April 1980, with the overthrow of the True Whig Party regime and the assassination of Tolbert by Doe, the master-sergeant. Accompanied by the summary execution of several of Tolbert's cabinet members, the coup marked one of the most bloody military exercises to remove an unpopular leader from power. Not long after these events, Kenyan president Daniel arap Moi was snared in an unsuccessful coup attempt led by one officer, Oyoga; also, Cameroon suffered an unsuccessful military coup that prompted President Biya and his top officials to go into hiding for several hours. In the same West Africa subregion, the former Upper Volta, now called Burkina Faso, was under Thomas Sankara's military regime until his deputy, Blaise Campore, overthrew his regime in a sort of a palace coup in which Sankara, a close friend of Ghana's Rawlings in his revolutionary days, lost his youthful life. Still, as some experts have concluded, Campore has, for a long time, been among the African leaders who base "their right to rule on revolutionary purity or paternalism."[24]

The ECOWAS/ECOMOG Factor

A new way of discouraging coups d'etat in Africa took place in Sierra Leone, where there have been successive military regimes since independence. The most recent coup, led by Major Paul Koroma, became a pariah regime, as it was later confronted by troops from Economic Community of West African States (ECOWAS) countries in a military alliance (called ECOMOG), led by Nigeria. Having toppled the elected Sierra Leonean regime of President Tejan Kabbah, the ECOMOG forces succeeded, at an expensive price in human lives and material destruction, in dislodging Koroma's forces. ECOMOG drove them out of the country to join the guerrilla-like liberation army called the Revolutionary United Front (RUF), four of whose leaders later accepted the July 7, 1999 peace agreement because, as President Kabbah modestly said, "there are people in the international community who are ready and willing to help us rebuild our country [Sierra Leone]."[25] These developments in Sierra Leone are exemplary because, for peace to return to the country, it took the detained leader of the RUF, Foday Sankoh, to cooperate with ECOWAS and Kabbah's officials to complete negotiations between the RUF and the Kabbah regime. Very reassuredly, Baffour Ankomah, editor of the much-respected London-based journal, the *New African,* reported that, despite calls by war-mongers or hawks, including some Western journalists and mercenary groups, for an all-out war to wipe out the RUF rebels in Sierra Leone, officials of the United Nations and ECOWAS were insisting, appropriately, on a negotiated settlement if genuine peace was to return to the mutilated country, adding that there was hope for Sierra Leone.[26]

Apart from ECOWAS and the United Nations, which is sending a large contingent of soldiers to Sierra Leone to safeguard the peace accord, the United States tried, on its own to help Somalia and other places to settle ethnic differences that had cost countless human lives. The response was, indeed, an escalation of the strife by the tribal warlords, which cost the lives of many American soldiers who were there to help maintain peace and order. The entire conflagration flared up when President Siad Barre, who ruled Somalia as a military dictatorship for over a decade, dragged his feet about multiparty politics. However, when he agreed to such politics, as Professors Michael Bratton and Nicolas van de Walle contend, his "declaration of multiparty reforms appeared to be a particularly cynical attempt to convince the United States to restore cuts in foreign aid."[27] Fortunately for Barre, he was able to flee from Somalia to settle in exile, although in poor health; Somali warlords then took over the country in civil wars.

Indeed, military takeovers in Africa have been so numerous that our efforts to discuss most of them here, coupled with our research interests to offer the reasons for many of them, cannot be seen in exhaustive terms. There are, certainly, many reasons for these coups, but, interestingly, many experts contend that the main cause is relative deprivation, as it encourages discontent and, sometimes, anger, which can bring about all types of violence. How true, indeed, because whenever a military takeover is announced, citizens of the country affected look forward to the fact that the new leaders will right wrongs and satisfy the people's needs, though sometimes these aspirations have been repeatedly dashed. It is like the case of a drowning person in a big river: He or she holds on to whatever has the semblance of a life-saving device but, in the end, the person drowns anyway. In Africa, the hopes of many people have been dashed by false alarms of new dawns when military takeovers were announced.[28]

Again, Professor Agyeman-Duah's study for the *Armed Forces and Society* journal offers a very systematic investigation of the obvious linkage that has existed among West Africa's coups d'etat: regime change and Africa's interstate conflicts. His study stemmed from the fact that 55 percent of all substantive or successful coups d'etat and, indeed, an entire third of all abortive or unsuccessful coups, coupled with one-half of all reported coup plots on the continent took place in the West Africa subregion.[29] One can see that he does not exaggerate if one looks at the rapid succession of coups in the area, especially since some countries have had several of such coups. As of 1985, the number of recorded coups included the following: the Republic of Benin (former Dahomey), had seen six successful coups by 1985; Mauritania had had three; Sierra Leone then had had two, but now up to four; Ghana had had four; Liberia had had one; Guinea had had one; Guinea Bissau had had one; and the giant of the region, Nigeria, had had about four.[30] These, again, are only the military takeovers that were successful, leaving out those which failed, but were nonetheless destructive.[31]

Interestingly, it is also a fact that the occurrences of these coups were so many in West Africa that, as reported by *The Europa Yearbook,* the area also leads all of Africa's subregions in what has now come to be known as "civilianized" military regimes. They include such countries as Togo in 1967, Mali in 1968, Benin in 1972, Niger in 1974, and Liberia in 1980. There have also been military-cum-civilian coalitions in the following countries: Nigeria in 1985, Ghana in 1981, Burkina Faso in 1987, Guinea in 1984, and Mauritania in 1984.[32] Apart from the reported tragedy of electoral corruption or election rigging on the part of some of Africa's military rulers who were bent on turning their regimes into "civilianized-military" rule, it has been very instructive for some countries in Africa to have a foretaste of what is in store for them when such military strongmen succeed in shedding their military khaki for civilian suits, *agbada, batakari,* and other clothing. In Ghana, General I. K. Acheampong tried hard to retain political power through the rigged "Union Government" or so-called "Unigov" elections, which would have made him a civilian and elected president. That made Acheampong so unpopular that his second-in-command, General Fred Akuffo, unseated him in a palace coup, ruled briefly, and was toppled in the June 4, 1979 very radical coup d'etat that heralded Flt.-Lieutenant Jerry Rawlings's rule in Ghana. In Paul Nugent's *Big Men, Small Boys and politics in Ghana: Power, Ideology and the Burden of History, 1982–1994,* he narrated how the early hours of the December 31, 1981 People's National Defence Council (PNDC) coup by Rawlings, his second coup which toppled the regime of the late Dr. Hilla Limann, saw muted reactions until "after some days during which Rawlings elaborated on the motives of the takeover, [then] Ghanaians rallied to the side of the regime."[33]

Although President Rawlings, as a civilian leader, has done many good things for Ghana, to the point that the international community has, fondly, embraced his leadership, the elections that brought him into Ghanaian politics as a "civilianized-military" ruler were questioned by some of his opponents. Professor Adu Boahen, one of his main political opponents in the first post-PNDC elections, wrote a treatise on what he termed "The Stolen Ballot" in the London-based *African Affairs* journal of the Royal African Society. The fact that President Rawlings was overwhelmingly reelected to a second four-year term by the Ghanaian electorate possibly erased the taint of the Ghanaian opposition's claims. Though resting on some tantalizing facts, the claims of the opposition, led by Boahen, were not supported by the international observer teams that went to Ghana to monitor the elections. The election results, although part of a democratic exercise, suffered similar suspicions as the December 1981 PNDC coup, which Nugent indicated was colored from inception: "The fact that the PNDC came to power through a military coup rather than by virtue of a popular uprising was to color the revolution from the moment of its inception."[34]

Yet, one may state that many military takeovers in Africa are initially treated coolly or even with scorn by a section of the citizenry until the people get to know some of the sordid details of the unusual acts of corruption, nepotism, and, sometimes, murderous acts of the deposed regime. In some cases, however, like that of the anti-Nkrumah coup of 1966, the people are afraid that, possibly, the coup was a ploy to find out who is for and against the regime that had been in power for so long. In that case, there is be no jubilation at the overthrow of the old regime until the entire country is sure that, indeed, the coup has succeeded. When success is ascertained, there is a rapturous joy for the new leadership, and subsequent calls for a counter-coup by the dethroned leaders are often ignored.

Taking Stock: Why Coups Galore in Postcolonial Africa?

Though southern and eastern Africa have not had much of a share in the prevalent coups d'etat that West, Central, and North Africa have experienced in postcolonial Africa, Professor Richard Hull of New York University was correct with the title of his book *Southern Africa: Civilizations in Turmoil*. His study pointed to the turbulent nature of the historical and political processes of the southern belt of Africa, including its neighboring southeastern portion. Though they haven't experienced many military takeovers, they have still undergone stresses and impacts from revolutions, which include the various violent liberation and anti-apartheid struggles.[35] As a result, a lot of lives and valuable properties, both private and public, have been lost.

Remarkably, postcolonial southern and eastern Africa have ceased to take the abuses that some of the liberation struggles unleashed: one need only look at the fierce Mau Mau struggle in Kenya, the FREMILO's anti-Portuguese war, or the combined forces of the African National Congress (ANC) and the Pan-African Congress (PAC) against the entrenched apartheid system of South Africa. Yet, these areas of Africa have not escaped from French agronomist-turned-political commentator Rene Dumont's "fatalistic" depiction of Africa after decolonization as a continent of doom in his prophetic book *False Start in Africa* (1966).[36]

Professor T. Balogh describes in the introduction to Dumont's book, former British prime minister Harold Macmillan's description of the wave of protests for political change in Africa and the momentous "wind of change blowing in Africa" prediction. To Balogh, Africa's "wind of change" had been characterized by a "bewildering violence," although he agreed (as President Obasanjo did in his often quoted "thunder and fire" statement) that the violent "wind of change" helped in converting "the most universally colonial continent into the greatest jumble of independent states."[37]

Leaving the academic field for a civil service job, Balogh became an official of the newly-created Ministry of Overseas Development in 1965. In his analysis, he used an economic developmental perspective in arriving at some of the conclusions that his introduction evoked in Dumont's book. For example, he agrees with several of Dumont's stringent conclusions about the behavior of postcolonial African leaders, especially about how many of these new African rulers inherited colonial institutions but never modified them, resulting in some leaders ruling like colonial officers. The Oxford don saw these leaders as "inheritors of the imperial institutions, especially in administrative structure and education, which suddenly lost such socio-economic relevance as they had ever possessed."[38]

Professor Dumont's *False Start in Africa* (1966) is seen by some nationalist leaders as being either too critical of postcolonial Africa or simply anti-Africa in the postcolonial period. There is even the silent claim that he became a persona non grata in several postcolonial African countries, basically because of the stringent manner in which he took new leaders of the continent to task. His criticisms are similar to several of the already-discussed faults pointed out by indigenous African writers, particularly when they wielded their pens freely and dared to take many of their postcolonial leaders to task.

For Dumont, there should have been a change in attitudes, style, and developmental strategies on the part of the new rulers, especially those articulated very early by opposition leaders, clarion calls that were ignored to the peril of many of these leaders, whose regimes fell prey to the wave of coups. Essentially, the second wave of Africa's axiomatic "wind of change" engulfed several areas of the continent when the citizenry could no longer accept the dictatorial and corrupt leadership that had been foisted on them by their own kith and kin. Balogh, therefore, did not see Dumont as a mere colonial agent out to undermine the indigenous leaders of Africa, who had fought relentless anticolonial battles to "free" the continent from what many of the nationalist leaders and others saw as the balkanizing and neocolonizing attitudes of former colonial powers and their agents. Indeed, it was not strange, then, that Nkrumah, who was being accused of dictatorship and economic mismanagement by his opponents, would write his stringent attack on colonialism and neocolonialism in his book, *Neo-Colonialism: The Last Stage of Imperialism.* It was a publication that reportedly enraged Western leaders, especially President Lyndon B. Johnson of the United States. Published in 1965, it was followed by Nkrumah's overthrow in the February 24, 1966 coup d'etat, barely a year later, which made observers speculate Western conspiracy was the cause.[39]

To Balogh, therefore, Dumont's work on Africa, no matter how critical it was of several post-independence African regimes and their leaders, made him "a shining example of how constructive thought can be fused with a fearless political attitude."[40] Looking at deteriorating African politics, Balogh went further in claiming boldly that, to an extent, Dumont really stood on the side of the exploited masses of the Third World and even of some "First World" nations as, *inter alia,* he wrote:

> [Dumont] has been a matchless champion of the most disinherited, oppressed, exploited, wretched and physically most ailing class in the world, the primitive peasant who is living in primeval misery at a time when the privileged population are able to flourish while wasting an untold mass of resources on national rivalry in the arms and space-race; resources amply sufficient, if well applied, to lift Adam's curse and to eradicate poverty from the face of the earth. . . . His [Dumont's] merciless investigation of the feudal battening of a tiny minority on the toil of the multitudes in the Mediterranean, in Latin America and in Asia, has earned him the detestation of the callous profiteers who benefit from the maldistribution of private property. His equally famous analysis of the defects of Soviet, Cuban and Algerian collectivism were no less disliked by the respective rulers of those countries.[41]

Dumont was a friend to the downtrodden of Africa and, therefore, the summation by Balogh above is admired by many. After all, Dumont did not mince words where poverty and suffering of the common people were concerned. For example, the Ivory Coast, under the late President Houphouet-Boigny, was often compared to several of its English-speaking neighboring countries like Nkrumah's Ghana, as the former was a success story within the realm of French collaborative efforts in Africa. In a critique, Dumont wrote that Houphouet-Boigny dressed his air-conditioned palace's ushers in French style while "turning his back resolutely on African civilization."[42]

To Dumont, most of the countries of Africa with elected leaders at the time exhibited only caricatures of democracy, but not true democracy as it existed in America and other Western nations. In this connection, the undemocratic ways of the postcolonial leadership made it possible for many of the new leaders on the continent to behave in ways that hampered progress or happiness for their people. Again, in the Ivory Coast, Dumont lamented the fact that, apart from Mr. Houphouet-Boigny emulating Europe in climate and dress, he also made sure that "breweries and Coca-Cola or private car factories are springing up in Abidjan, while the Senoufa people around Korhogo cannot get enough to eat from the exhausted land, despite a great deal of hard work."[43]

Certainly, Dumont did not shy away from the fact that, among the farming community, there were well-to-do planters. However, they would often work their indigenous farm laborers very hard. Also, rich planters from the prosperous south of the Ivory Coast would often be well endowed enough financially to "drive up to have a spree in the capital."[44]

In several African nations the inhabitants of poor neighborhoods, which date from colonial times to the post-independence period remained poor, seeing none of the affluent lifestyles of the rich. Instead, Dumont, in an example, looked at the very poor circumstances of Ivory Coast's Treichville and the Plateau areas and, in a melancholic way, wrote that they were "already similar to the Rio slums [in Brazil]."[45]

There are inconsistencies and outright disparity between the socioeconomic and political fortunes of the poor and the nouveau riche of postcolonial Africa. Hence, one wonders why the majority of the citizenry, in its economic misery, would not celebrate and support a military upheaval that would remove from political or economic power leaders that they simply saw as their tormentors or as part of the root cause of their sufferings. To Dumont, therefore, African independence was like owning a taxi, operated by another driver. Later, the taxicab owner feels a measure of being cheated by the employed driver, resulting in his taking his cab away from the cheating driver so that another driver could try his luck in operating it: axiomatically, it is that the vehicle is the same taxicab but with a different driver! However, as John Hatch also wrote, if a national government in Africa wants to be national, then it "ought to govern by the people and for the people, for the outcasts and by the outcasts."[46]

Africa's problems were complicated in places where the post-independence leaders began to harp on foreign ideologies as they searched for economic and political survival. Hatch has an interesting interpretation of the socialistic approaches of these leaders, as he expatiated on the notion of some African leaders basing their policies on so-called African socialism. Hatch writes:

> Whatever adjective is used to qualify the term [African socialism], the concept "Socialism" must always be directly related to the welfare of the mass of the people and to social equality. Yet it seems obvious from the present trends that many African countries are running the risk of becoming Latin American racketeering oligarchies—or Arabian oil plutocracies. The masses—who are still the peasants—are being not merely neglected but

exploited by the new politico-commercial regimes. This is inevitable; it is the product of man's policies.[47]

Maybe, in some instances, several of the new leaders and their political associates did not understand what "socialism" and other ideologies that they were harping on really meant. Here, we may cite an example from Nkrumah's Ghana. Hatch underscored that it was in Ghana that the dichotomy between progressive economic development and destructive misuse of resources could be seen most vividly.[48] Along with Tanzania, Nkrumah and his political colleagues experimented with an African socialism approach. Yet, after the 1966 overthrow of their CPP regime, one of Nkrumah's cabinet members was, reportedly, brought before a commission of enquiry that was probing graft and corruption allegations and asked to give his own interpretation of socialism. Jokingly, he said that, to his understanding, socialism meant "Eat and let me [or your friend] also eat"; the idiom in the Ghanaian Akan or Twi language is simply "Dibi mma menso m'endi bi."[49] In the name of socialism, many Africans suffered tyranny and outright dictatorship, hence one of Nkrumah's staunch opponents, Baffour Osei Akoto, the chief linguist of the King of the Ashanti people (or the Asantehene, as explained elsewhere) plainly stated in his published memoirs, *Struggle against Dictatorship* (1992), that he had a "deep-rooted conviction that dictatorship must be resisted at any price."[50] It was, therefore, not surprising that Akoto—although a respectable royal person—was among the many opponents of Nkrumah's regime arrested and detained in the colonial forts or castles where slaves were stored before being exported to the so-called New World or the Americas. Indeed, about his arrest and subsequent detention at James Fort Prison, he wrote: "At exactly 1:00 A.M. on Wednesday, 11th November 1959, my house was surrounded by a team of armed police personnel, who had come to cause my arrest."[51]

In other African countries, such political detentions were rampant, thus fulfilling the claim by Dumont, Hatch, and others that, in postcolonial Africa, dictatorship and repression became the order of the day. Although the days of active slavery were gone, these detention orders were effected to perpetuate political dominance, as Kenya-born Ngugi wrote, in detail, about his own December 31, 1977 arrest and detention under the Kenyatta regime, until his release on December 12, 1978. To him such official actions in his native Kenya, as also happened in other parts of Africa, were usually meant to "turn Kenyans into slaves.[52]

While efforts are being made by many thoughtful and worried Africans to either stem or halt some of these dictatorial and repressive measures, another subject of great concern for enlightened Africans is corruption. As we were completing this study, *African Voices,* a newsletter on democracy and governance in Africa issued by the Office of Sustainable Development of the United States Agency for International Development (USAID) had a fall 1998 front page story titled, "USAID Supports Anti-Corruption Efforts in Africa: Africans at the Forefront of Anti-Corruption Activities." It reported that anticorruption efforts in Africa were the topic of a recent hearing before the Subcommittee on Africa of the U.S. House of Representatives' International Relations Committee, and that the "United States and others in the donor community are concerned about governance and the fight against corruption."[53]

Ms. Carol Peasley, the acting assistant administrator of USAID's Bureau for Africa, among·other details, further testified:

> But even more important, Africans themselves are in the forefront of the effort to improve governance, increase transparency and accountability, and fight corruption. USAID strongly supports these African-led efforts both through our overseas programs and our coordination with the donor community.[54]

USAID, an American agency, is so serious about the anticorruption fight that, reportedly, it is providing $35 million, over the next two years, for activities aimed at improving governance as well as the fight against corruption in Africa.[55] It is very interesting that during these noble efforts on the part of USAID and other external, non-African agencies, Russia was engulfed in massive corruption and money-laundering problems. Since some of these African nations were once client nations of the "old" Russia's socialist and Marxist ideology fervor, many scholars concluded the scenario to be instructive. The Russian situation has been viewed so seriously by American officials that Treasury Secretary Lawrence H. Summers had to mount a vigorous defense of the Clinton administration's policy of supporting aid for Russia, although he "warned that the Russian central bank had to comply with safeguards to maintain American backing for assistance."[56]

The U.S. Congress, in its relentless fight against corruption in any place where American tax dollars are utilized, deemed it necessary to open congressional inquiries into alleged corruption and money laundering that have reportedly included at least $4.2 billion diverted through the Bank of New York in the last 18 months.[57] Indeed, the Russian monetary fiasco, especially concerning the reported money laundering, cannot be seen in isolation from African situations, as capital flight also exists in Africa, whereby billions of dollars have reportedly been stolen by some of the unscrupulous leaders of the continent and stashed in foreign banks.

Meanwhile, though many experts on African problems often felt that highly-educated Africans living overseas should return to their respective countries to help improve things for their societies, evidence has shown signs of deteriorating conditions on several fronts, including economic and political stances. It was very sad to note that, at the time USAID was in the forefront of the anticorruption (and antifraud) struggle in Africa, a Washington, D.C.-based African foundation, run by some Black African scholars, reportedly received a jolt in the area of fraud. Although its leaders claimed to be struggling for true democracy, freedom, and progress and were openly vocal against corruption in Africa, the leadership was embroiled in a fraudulent incident, in which one of its top administrators was accused of having lied about a graduate degree that he, reportedly, never earned. As the Internet (and email) reports were having a field day with this sordid incident, many African scholars and foreign experts on

Africa wondered if the said pro-African center in Washington really meant what it were preaching, or if its activities were a mere smokescreen to amass wealth! Although the other leaders of the said foundation, reportedly accepted the resignation of their fraud-tainted colleague, there was no public evidence that they had helped to either expose or punish the "black sheep" colleague. The situation is similar to instances where corrupt postcolonial African leaders very easily "let off" known corrupt colleagues, often because they did not want to be exposed in corruption themselves. The Washington episode, to a large extent, showed that the highly-educated Africans outside the continent may be as dangerously corrupt as those still inside Africa reportedly responsible for the corrupt practices that have undermined every facet of life, economically, politically, socially and otherwise, on their continent.[58]

Apart from the corruption discussed above, including that of corruption, many other African situations call for serious redress in order to prevent military officers from cashing in on them. These include the existing deliberate power vacuums: Many of postcolonial Africa's ruling elite shied away from designating a successor in case of an incapacitation. As could be seen in the circumstances of post–Sekou Toure Guinea, the acuteness of the succession problem prompted the military leaders to take power after Toure's death, something that they could not do when the anti-France nationalist leader, who ruled with an iron hand, was alive.[59]

This is why Kenyans breathed a sigh of relief when Professor George Saitoti was appointed the substantive vice-president of the East African nation. The mass-circulating Nairobi-based publication the *Weekly Review* published a cover story titled, "Heir Apparent?" The opening paragraph of the story confirmed the state of confusion of many African nations, lacking clear-cut successors to their existing dictatorial rulers. The Kenyan situation was still deemed so confusing by the editors of the publication, as they felt that the situation:

> looks as confused and unpredictable as ever, and the political future of the country [Kenya] remains uncertain. Indeed, even with last week's appointment of Prof. George Saitoti as vice-president, the big question that remains is whether the appointment has indeed closed a power vacuum, and whether it shows that the president [Mr. Moi] has at last started grooming a successor."[60]

The Kenyan publication raised several other fundamental issues that can very easily apply to many other African nations, where the successors to the ruling elite have not been clearly designated. The *Weekly Review* cover story went on to point out that their query was:

> a pertinent question indeed because the recent clamor for the appointment of a vice-president was predicated on the presumption that the country faced the risk of having a power vacuum in the event that something happened to the president. Clearly, even with the appointment of Saitoti, the shape of the new order that is likely to succeed President Moi

when he leaves the scene in the year 2002 is far from clear. Technically, the country now has a successor who can assume power in the event of the president's incapacitation. But in reality, President Moi is still reluctant to reveal his hand on the matter of his successor.[61]

Indeed, Kenyans were better off than other Africans whose rulers never made an appointment of a heir-apparent. Sadly, the Kenyan issue of a successor was muddied further when President Moi, upon his return to Kenya from fraternal visits to Malawi and Namibia, reportedly spoke at the Kenyatta International Airport as if he were "forewarning the [Kenyan] public not to give too much political significance to his naming of a vice-president. He fell short of categorically asserting that the vice-president he was about to name was not necessarily going to be his heir apparent."[62] This is a departure from other instances in Kenya, when possible successors to the political rulers died under clouded circumstances. One of the most recent of such deaths was the assassination in February 1990 of Dr. Robert John Ouko, Kenya's Minister for Foreign Affairs and International Co-operation. Reportedly, Dr. Ouko had been seen as a possible credible replacement for Mr. Moi, who had been tainted politically by his association with former regimes in Kenya and who critics wished to replace. A few days after Ouko's return to Kenya, after an official trip to Washington, D.C., official trip, he was killed. The Scotland Yard detective appointed to investigate the death, Superintendent John Troon was reported to have thought that "Ouko's death had something to do with that trip. Troon implicated the [Kenyan] government in the death and the subsequent cover-up. He suggested further interrogation of some government officers and politicians. His advice was ignored."[63] Kenya's retiring President Moi was quoted as saying that, allegedly, "Ouko's killers had also tried to kill his then vice-president, George Saitoti, implying that he knew who the killers were."[64]

In comparison, Ghana's President Rawlings, whose two elected terms of office ended in the year 2000, is to be commended for coming out boldly to endorse Vice-President Atta Mills as his apparent successor. The ruling NDC political party had Mills as its standard bearer and presidential candidate in the 2000 general elections in Ghana. In several instances, African nations have seen the heir-apparent eliminated, sometimes as a result of rumors or false speculation, a palace coup, or an arrest, as happened to Nigeria's deputy leader and army chief under Abacha's regime, General L. Diya. He was accused of a coup plot, arrested, tried, and sentenced to death by a pro-Abacha military court until he was pardoned and released by General Abdulsalam Abubakar. Abubakar came to power after Abacha died of the usual "heart attack" that afflicts many African political leaders.

Therefore, whenever coup-happy soldiers look at the disgraceful manner in which a country's politicians are treating one another, they use the incidents to plot "acceptable" grounds to wrestle power from them causing the numerous military takeovers that African countries continue to witness. To stem the tide of these adventurous coups, it is hoped that African politicians will become more tolerant of political opposition and meaningful criticisms. Otherwise, since elections are often rigged to help these rulers perpetually stay in power, the only way open for political leadership change, is through the barrel of the military gun.

A reputable organization like Amnesty International, headed now by an African, thinks it its duty to critique all nations' human rights abuses. However, instead of the guilty nations taking steps to amend their corrupt and undemocratic ways, their leaders turn around to accuse Amnesty International and other well-meaning non-governmental organizations (NGOs) of trying to foment troubles in their countries. These accusations reached absurdity in Togo when visiting French president Jacques Chirac, received by General Eyadema in an elaborate ceremony in Lome, openly "accused Amnesty international of engaging in 'manipulation' in its report on Togo released in May [1999]. Amnesty accused Eyadema's government of widespread killing of opponents prior to the presidential elections held earlier this year."[65] Just like the U.N., the London-based Amnesty International is headed by a West African diplomat, Secretary-General Pierre Sane, who would not frivolously support any empty critical annual reports against African nations, including Togo, unless it had substance, as he found the report have.

Sadly, if international human rights organizations are to be intimidated in refraining from issuing impartial reports that may help correct some of the abuses in several African and, indeed, other Third World nations, one wonders where anti-coup elements want change to come from. For example, a large segment of the African press has been "tamed" by many of the dictatorial regimes and their leaders to a point of reportorial impotence. In fact, as we were completing this publication, it was reported that Kenneth Best from Liberia, one of Africa's best journalists and owner of the Gambia-based newspaper, the *Daily Observer,* had "suddenly sold the paper recently to a businessman with close ties to the government [of Gambia]."[66]

As also reported earlier, the newspaper had been founded in 1992 by Mr. Best, a well-meaning journalist who simply wanted to see decent publications in African countries, including his native Liberia, where he once held high-level subcabinet ministerial positions, and Gambia, but as expected, the 1994 coup leaders saw it as an opposition publication. Subsequently, "Kenneth Best himself and five other foreign reporters were deported in 1994."[67] Indeed, the problems of the fine newspaper, which served as a watchdog of national affairs, did not end with the deportation of the six journalists. In January of 1999, "a government circular banned government departments from subscribing to the paper."[68] This, of course, is the extent to which some African nations will go in trying to silence a newspaper that could help in correcting the abuses that several military leaders feed on to plot and effect coups d'etat.

Apart from the intimidation of publications and political opponents alike in several African nations, even the voices of students have often been silenced with brutal force. That is why Indonesian protesting students were hailed for forcing out of political power the three-decade old "civilianized' military rule of President Suharto, who had come to power through a palace coup against President Sukarno. Sukarno's daughter, Megawati Sukarnoputri, is now president of Indonesia. As in some African nations, the protests against the Indonesian government did not make matters better, as several antigovernment citizens suffered dearly. Indeed, when Dili, the capital of East Timor voted to end its ties to Indonesia, it saw a violent and destructive program reportedly implemented by the Indonesian armed forces. For example, when Marcos N. Soares returned to his compound in Dili, he met only the burned-out shell of his home, although what mattered most to the 27–year-old Timorese man was the sad fact that "right now," as he said, "the most valuable thing we have lost is my mother, my sisters, and my two small brothers."[69] Because of this situation, the antimilitary protest in Indonesia shifted from Jakarta and Dili—after the deaths of six protesters in Jakarta—to Medan, a city of 1.2 million people on the island of Sumatra, and "smaller anti-military protests were also reported Friday in Surabaya and Bandung, the nation's second- and third-largest cities, and on the island of Bali."[70] Many Africans have been wondering why the Indonesian armed forces, as has happened in African nations, did not step in to seize power in the name of trying to end anarchy in their country. Instead, in contrast to many of Africa's politically active military officers, when the head of the Indonesian armed forces was proposed for the position of vice-president, he declined and, as expected, Sukarno's daughter, although in opposition, was elected overwhelmingly to occupy that position, the first time since her father achieved independence in the 1940s for Indonesia that a woman has come that close to the presidency.

Maybe the voice of the United Nations, now headed by Secretary-General Kofi Annan of Ghana, would be able to help stem the tide in many of these civil wars and internal conflicts, not necessarily dictatorships, that contribute to some of the ingredients that lead to coups d'etat in many Third World areas. Sometimes, there is need for a force or a voice of reason if the world is to end much of the brutal strife in the Third World. As recently reported at the U.N., when the twentieth century emerged, the world's civilian populace accounted for only fifteen percent of such war or crisis casualties, compared to the current ninety per cent. According to the *New York Times,* the reason is that "most wars today are not international conflicts waged by armies on a battlefield, but internal conflicts fought in streets and villages."[71] The newspaper added that the fact made intervention more difficult, because national sovereignties were at issue. It is only gratifying that "at last the world's conscience is catching up with the changing nature of war," and that "the challenge for the U.N., as Mr. Annan points out, is to find ways to honor what that conscience urges [the world]."[72]

It is hoped that the rejuvenated Organization of African Unity (OAU), with several newly-elected purposeful and serious African leaders, including Nigerian President Obasanjo, will redefine the meaning and tenets of national sovereignty, under the cloak of which the organization has become impotent, almost like the proverbial toothless bulldog, even though it happens to have some of Africa's top civil servants, including Tanzania's Dr. Salim Ahmed Salim, at the helm of its affairs.

In looking at issues of national sovereignty, the continental organization may also take a close look at and recommend appropriate succession idioms for some nations, providing alternatives to what Professor Ali A. Mazrui calls the "monarchical tendency in African political culture."[73] For example, when Moroccan

King Hassan died in July of this year, his 35–year-old son, now King Sidi Mohamed VI, inherited the throne, similar to Jordan, whose late King Hussein was succeeded by his 37–year-old son, King Abdullah II. Following traditions and customs, these sons, succeeding their deceased fathers, should not be blamed. However, if succession is by a democratic fiat, done in America and other advanced democratic nations through the electoral process, soldiers would think twice before they decide abruptly to overturn the popular will of the elec- torate anywhere in Africa or in other Third World countries, including Morocco and Jordan. This is especially important as some leaders of Africa, at the 1999 annual summit of the OAU, led by Egypt's Hosni Mubarak, Uganda's Yoweri Museveni, Nigeria's Olusegun Obasanjo, Zambia's Frederick Chiluba and South Africa's Thambo Mbeki pushed a concerted idea that makers of coups d'etat would no longer be tolerated as OAU members. This grand idea could mean either the end of the multitude of coups d'etat in African nations or an effort to reduce their occurrences to the barest minimum.

Otherwise, Africa could remain the laughingstock of the non–coup infested nations of the world, thus confirming the details in Elenore Smith Bowen's 297–page anthropological treatise *Return To Laughter,* which detailed part of her years of research in the Tiv areas of the former northern Nigeria between 1949 and 1953. To go back to the African continent—as expatriate scholars often do—is deemed by cynics and critics as a "return to laughter," as heralded in Bowen study, which is dubbed a novel with cynicism. Indeed, that was how Bowen, the nom de plume for Laura Bohannan, saw matters in northern Nige- ria in terms of laughter. Oxford-educated, Bohannan was a serious researcher.[74] Above all, when African leaders and their military learn to tolerate each other and govern in collaborative terms, then Rene Dumont's depiction of African independence as being false may, alas, prove no longer to be true!

To succeed in implementing some of the suggestions made in this publication to help redeem Africa's past glory—what Camara Laye once called "radiant Africa"—a major area that needs immediate corrective measure is that of national leadership and succession. Nigeria's celebrated author Professor Chinua Achebe once opined in a very curious book, *What Is Wrong with Nigeria,* that his country's main problem rested on unpatriotic and bad leadership. Such also seems to be the multifarious problems facing many countries in postcolonial Africa, which have often prompted their armed forces to poke their military noses into national politics. Therefore, the OAU may take it upon itself to ensure that leadership succession matters, irrespective of national sovereignty seem to be more important and—as enshrined in the OAU's 1963 charter—are firmly embedded in the constitutions of all postcolonial countries of Africa. Apart from making succession procedures clear-cut, the OAU should also stress that ruling a nation for life, or even for decades on end, is an anathema to democracy and good governance. OAU should additionally inscribe regulations ensuring that departing national leaders receive retirement benefits, similar to what is done in the major democracies, including America and Britain.

Otherwise, many leaders in Africa would be afraid to step down from public or elective office, no matter how old or sickly they turn out to be. Staying in power perpetually would, in turn, multiply the mistakes of these old and feeble politicians, giving their ever-ready soldiers the excuse to taste power by plotting and executing coups d'etat. Indeed, there should be a way out, if Africa is to be saved from political and military autocracy and, sadly, rampant corruption as well as self-serving governance.

Above all, apart from the OAU, an important institution like the Ethiopia-based Economic Commission for Africa (ECA), a body of the United Nations that is usually also headed by an African civil servant and technocrat, should continue to assist in finding economic avenues for the progress of postcolonial Africa. The first African Development Forum (ADF) of the ECA, held in Addis Abba, emphasized Africa's need for a new paradigm for development in the twenty-first century, in addition to "highlighting domestic private sector, science and technology, good governance and key requirements for a progressing Africa."[75] The ECA wants to see progress for Africa on many fronts, including in the private sector, the sciences and in governance.

In an opening speech loaded with foresight, Ethiopian Prime Minister Meles Zenawi pointed out forcefully that the ongoing process of globalization would be a major determining factor of the destinies of the countries on the continent. He added: "If present conditions remain unaltered and the trend we see were to continue, then being more enmeshed within the globalized economy would only mean that by force of circumstances, Africa would be made to stay on the margins of the global economy."[76]

About 600 experts met to discuss some of Africa's economic problems and offer solutions at the ADF from October 24 to 28, 1999, mainly from governmental sources, the private sector, civil society, and bilateral and multilateral organizations from inside and outside of Africa. With the theme, "The Challenge to Africa of Globalization and the Information Age," the forum was also addressed by U.N. Under-Secretary-General and ECA Executive Director K. Y. Amoako. Amoako emphasized that some of the most important issues facing Africa today, required networking and alliances, which meant that no nation in postcolonial Africa could afford to behave in a way that would force its citizens into voluntary, economic, or forced exile in Europe, Asia, the Middle East, or the Americas. Other well-meaning speakers included Dr. Salim Ahmed Salim, the OAU Secretary-General and, on behalf of the African Development Bank (ADB), President Omar Kabbaj. ADB's Finance and Planning Vice-President Ahmed Baghgat gave a speech that addressed the prospects that information technology afforded African development as well as the role of the continental bank in promoting Africa's entry into the global information society.[77]

A crucial situation that is still confronting African nations is population explosion in midst of abject poverty and scarce resources. Therefore, it was very reassuring that, at the ADF, U.N. Deputy Secretary-General Louise Frechette based her own speech on the world's population problems, noting that the total population of the world was about to reach six billion but, sadly, nearly half of that number would enter the new millennium in abject poverty, adding that "violence, brutality and discrimination as well as negative climatic change were also threats to survival."[78] The deputy U.N. boss appealed to humanity and, of course, to Africa, stating that the challenge facing all nations is to make the twenty-first century "more secure, more equitable and more human."[79] It is, indeed, hoped that many of postcolonial African rulers as well as other Third World leaders were listening to these speakers, especially the searing and profound words of Ms. Frechette. For the points they have made, if adhered to, would reduce tensions as well as such debasing and undemocratic measures as outright corruption, discrimination based on ethnic differences, and human rights violations within the context of "man's brutality against man," all of which—coupled with lack of equity in sharing the accrued national resources— prompt African soldiers to abandon their barracks for the state houses. In the opinion of Africans and experts on African political history, with respect to economic development and political growth—coupled with respect for the human condition—the time has come for the military authorities to end the coups- galore in order to build durable democratic and very humane institutions for Africa's meaningful progress.

CHAPTER EIGHT

Conclusion

Nobody expected that Cote d'Ivoire [the Ivory Coast], too, would experience a *coup d'etat*. . . . But after all, is this *coup* not a bad thing for the entrenchment of democracy in Cote d'Ivoire?[1]

—General Robert Guei

On January 10, 2000, former London-based *West Africa Magazine* editor Adama Gaye held an interview with retired Ivory Coast General Robert Guei. The retired army general had, as Gaye wrote, "seized power on December 24, 1999 after unrest among soldiers protesting against their living conditions."[2] In his response to several queries, retired General Guei behaved like many of Africa-based coup leaders. He was in self-denial that his act was a military putsch: "Let me say bluntly that the term coup d'etat does not apply here. It is not in line with the situation we went through on December 24 and 25, which resulted in a change at the helm of affairs of our country."[3]

Given the long-existing air of stability that has characterized the politics and economy of the Ivory Coast, it was a shock to many observers that the first coup, in December 1999, took place to unseat the seemingly well-entrenched government of President Henri Konan Bedie. It simply meant that no African nation would be spared coup-mania if even the Ivory Coast, which its founding president, Felix Houphouet-Boigny, described during his long reign as "an African miracle in terms of stability and development,"[4] could not avoid military intervention.

Retired General Guei held power until October 2000, when he tried to rig national elections that observers felt that his only civilian opponent, Laurent Gbagbo, had won. As editor Gaye promptly pointed out, "General Robert Guei, the man who has just lost power, came in and thought that he could outsmart everybody to cling to power. Like many dictators, he refused to listen to the many voices of reason, warning him of the dangers ahead of him. He refused to listen."[5]

The Ivory Coast coup events recalled above are very similar to past military takeovers. It is auspicious to recount them here because, as the latest military seizure of power in an African country, the coup confirms our assertions throughout this study that the armed forces of African nations would continue to use their guns to seize power from corrupt and sometimes arrogant politicians. In the Ivorian situation, however, Guee, who led the coup d'etat, was himself thrown out of office through popular demonstrations backed by the very soldiers who once supported him.

Although the Ivory Coast was part of the French colonial entity, the December 1999 coup in the West African nation showed no visible ideological persuasion. However, in the midst of the hectic Cold War political atmosphere, several of the past military takeovers in various African countries and their subsequent military leadership that emerged in the aftermath, often demonstrated amply that, in the midst of the ever—increasing military incursion into African politics, indigenous and foreign ideologies of different types have contributed their own share in these events. This is especially so as one used to see both old and new military regimes in Africa as being either procapitalist or prosocialist.

The funny side of Africa's ideological politics is that ideologies seemed to play vital roles in a variety of ways on the continent even though most of the independent nations claimed to be members of the defunct or currently inactive nonaligned movement, which meant neither subscribed to socialism nor capitalism, and were basically ideologically uncommitted. In fact, several leaders from Africa seriously attended nonaligned movement conferences, at which heavy denunciations were made of capitalist economies. In the end, as Kofi Batsa of Ghana has confirmed in a book, *The Spark* (1985), the nonaligned activities, which had a powerful lobby of radical and conservative African diplomats, prompted African countries to be divided into two camps:

> The newly independent countries of Africa gradually sorted themselves out into two groups, the progressive and the conservative—called the *Casablanca Group* and the *Monrovia Group,* after the names of the locations of where the two conferences were held in 1961. The need to bring these two groups together was paramount, and fitted in with Kwame Nkrumah's vision of united Africa.[6]

However, now that the East-West divide seems to have been dissolved with the downfall of the erstwhile Soviet Union, the ideological warfare of the capitalist West and the former socialist East has ceased. The cessation of hostilities has been particularly marked since the demise of communism in the Warsaw Pact countries, led by the Soviet Union, which former President Ronald Reagan often described as the "Evil Empire." To many, there is need to help complete the anticommunist propaganda and events, which were begun by Western capitalist leaders, and coupled with the institution of pro-Western leaders like former Russian President Boris Yelstin and the Czech Republic's Vaclav Havel. In completing these events, the tangled results and spin-offs helped in minimizing the ideological dimension of African revolutions that are sparked by military takeovers. One may look at the Cuban presence in such matters, but, with Cuba's ever-increasing economic and political problems, it is not easy for its leaders—led by President Fidel Castro—to play active or very pragmatic political or military roles in ongoing armed revolutions in various areas of Africa. It is a fact, however, that old Cuban friends on the continent still gratefully maintain cordial contacts with their "big brother" in the Western Hemisphere, sometimes to the point of trying to do so to irritate the United States of America, Great Britain, and other capitalist nations.

Sometimes, as a way of courting socialist countries as well as warding off perceived attacks by capitalist forces, some of Africa's military leaders pretended to espouse socialist slogans when they initially emerged on the political scene through the barrel of the military gun. Yet, they would turn out to be merely radical, not truly committed socialists or communists, especially once pragmatic needs set in. A typical example is the circumstances of Ghana's outgoing President Rawlings, who initially seized power in June 1974, reportedly with a lot of help from Libya. In fact, it was widely speculated that President Rawlings, whose two terms of four years each came to an end in the year 2000, was an ardent believer in Gaddafy's ideological document the *Green Book,* which was published in 1975 and 1979 to propagate the goals of the Libyan revolution. Today Ghana, is one of America's good friends on the African continent.

However, just like other military regimes on the continent of Africa, Rawlings with his young and radical military colleagues overthrew a democratically-elected regime in 1981, which was led by the Western-educated President Hilla Limann, now deceased. Rawlings was fearful for various reasons, including the worry that Dr. Limann's friend's in Western capitals might intervene to restore him to power. After enjoying popular support and the sweetness of leadership, Rawlings later retired as a military ruler and, subsequently, ran for democratic elections to become a two-term elected Ghanaian president; before that, he felt the need for a stronger military and an ideological arm to lean on in order to ensure that Western nations, with political and economic interests in Ghana, would not help in fomenting problems in the country that might lead to a counter-coup. After all, Western investments were often considered much safer in a civilian administration like that of the moderate Limann. In the end, Rawlings, as an elected civilian president, approached national politics with such pragmatism and democratic zeal that he became a very good friend to many Western leaders, including America's President Bill Clinton. That was ironic, since the earlier military regime of Rawlings had a serious clash with the American Central Intelligence Agency (CIA), which Ghanaian intelligence saw as having plotted to have Rawlings, as a military leader, either killed or overthrown.[7]

While ideology may be seen as part of the motivations for military takeovers in Africa, it can additionally be underscored that economic starvation has, very often, prompted military leaders to intervene in political processes on the continent. It is also true that some military officers were anxious to line their own pockets and cushion up their existing or new foreign bank accounts, as our research showed in several instances. These selfish ends could be the sole motivating yardstick by which to measure the need for some of the military takeovers that several African countries are saddled with for many decades, including counter-coups d'etat. Thus when coups take place, many of the new military leaders begin to think about their families and personal interests, indeed how to enrich themselves. Sometimes, they might have had good intentions, as coup leaders, but such intentions do change.

There are various examples of how military officers "kick" elected civilian politicians out of power, but, sadly, many of the new military leaders, instead of being the new broom or anti-corruption crusaders—like retired General Obasanjo becoming a decent elected civilian president of Nigeria—have become corrupt liabilities. In fact, in *Corruption and the Crisis of Institutional Reforms in Africa* (1998), Professor Mbaku and several of the contributors to the 325–page edited volume have very well discussed in detail the examples of Nigeria, Sierra Leone, and Zaire, among several other examples of "bureaucratic corruption" in general.[8]

In the end, our overall painful conclusion is that while some coups d'etat in post-independence Africa were inevitable and possibly necessary evils, most of them have become unnecessary intrusions into the political domain, which, as Nkrumah and other post-independence African leaders spelled out in their writings or speeches, should belong exclusively to the elected officials of the various nations that have suffered these takeovers. After the first successful Nigerian coup, Nkrumah seemed to have panicked so badly that he made his initial call on the Ghana armed forces to remain loyal and confined to their barracks. His British-born chief of staff, retired General Alexander, explained several scenarios, similar to those that happened in the armed forces of other independent African countries that could result in a military overthrow of Nkrumah's post-1965 oppressive regime.[9] To thwart the continuing occurrences of military coups, there is need for reexamination of the performances of rulers by independent and unbiased agencies, if possible as an elected term of office is coming to an end.

Although some of Africa's military coups were planned and executed to correct some of the transparently prevailing shortcomings of the elected officials, including pervasive corruption, human rights abuses, and economic mismanagement, it has also been borne out that in the outcomes of military rule in several nations that some of the new military leaders have performed either just as badly or even worse than the very elected officials that they removed from office. At least the elected officials in an African country owed allegiance of sorts—no matter how limited—to the electorate, especially if they still needed their mandate in subsequent parliamentary (or congressional) and presidential elections to rule. Though in a democratic process, the people, as electors, should always count, the truth remains, as coauthor Alex-Assensoh illustrated with the following 1952 Ralph Ellison quote in *Neighborhoods, Family, and Political Behavior in Urban America* (1998), the African electorate diminished in such importance that, in the end, it became utterly invisible and, indeed, irrelevant:

I am an invisible man . . . I am invisible, understand, simply because people refuse to see me. . . . When they approach me they see only my surroundings, themselves or figments of their imagination—indeed, everything and anything except me.[10]

Sadly, the conditions of most of the military-ruled countries on the continent have often become similar to those in the years that civilian leaders were in place, as one sees unlimited unemployment, abject poverty, and, indeed, heinous human rights violations. These pervade mostly because the new military rulers make it abundantly clear that since they came to power through the barrels of the gun, they owed nobody any allegiance. The common man or woman in the street, therefore, becomes invisible as according to Ellison.

In fact, the common person in the street of some of these countries become so dispensable that he or she becomes an invisible individual. Therefore, anything could happen to this individual at any time. For example, as we were completing this publication, the London-based Amnesty International was being sued by the Republic of Togo because of its May 5, 1999 report titled, "Togo: Rule of Terror." Reportedly, the Amnesty International document detailed "how hundreds of bodies, many of them handcuffed, had been found on the beaches of Togo and neighboring Benin around the time of [President] Eyadema's election fiasco in 1998."[11]

French President Jacques Chirac, a staunch supporter of Mr. Eyadema, who has ruled Togo since his 1967 coup d'etat, reportedly condemned the Amnesty International report on Togo, and he even described it as a manipulation. What is reassuring, however, is that since that report, it is known that Mr. Eyadema, who sincerely feels that Togo still needs him as its leader for stability to rule supreme, is supposedly brushing up his public relations. Among his immediate measures were the firing of "his Parisian lobbyists, *Image et Strategie,* under Thierry Saussez, deemed to have failed to make adequate excuses for the rigging of the 1998 presidential poll. We hear that his new United States public relations consultants, Judith Vincent & Associates, have advised him to appear conciliatory in the talks with the [Togolese] opposition."[12]

Certainly, many of Africa's fine newspapers and magazines have been driven out of business through several anti–freedom of speech and outright repressive tactics by some of the continent's dictators. For example, several countries require registrations for such publications. Also, to import newsprint to complete publication, a publisher needs the approval of those in power. Therefore, it is very easy for a vocally opposing publication to have its application for license renewal pending ad infinitum, while applications for permission to import newsprint can easily be denied for lack of "almighty" foreign exchange or simply delayed in order to starve the publication of its much-needed lifeblood, newsprint.

For coups d'etat and, of course, counter-coups d'etat to be either minimized or completely removed from the idiom of African politics, many of the foregoing sad abuses and incidents must be corrected. For example, it is a fact that Amnesty International—which was for several years headed by French-speaking

African Dr. Pierre Sane—would not deliberately falsify facts or undermine the credibility of an African nation with false accusations. Consequently, it was sad that Togo would resort to a court action to intimidate or even, in the words of experts, to threaten Amnesty International and its leadership.

At best, one simply wanted Togo to take steps to correct some of the human rights abuses reported. After all, President Eyadema might *not* personally be involved in the extrajudicial killings contained in Amnesty's May 1999 report, although he can be held accountable as Togo's leader. This is especially so if accountability is necessary in one's kingdom or home. In Togo's neighboring Ghana, there was the international and local hue and cry over the manner in which some Ghanaian high court judges and a retired army officer were abducted, killed, and even mutilated. When Amnesty and other well-meaning international organizations reported and subsequently condemned such heinous crimes, Rawlings's Ghana did not go to court to get the issue driven under the rug. Instead, nothing like that sad and sickening event ever happened again, and President Rawlings has ruled Ghana, since then, for two consecutive elected terms of eight total years.

Since Mr. Eyadema came to power through his 1967 coup, one wonders what his reaction would be if another Togolese soldier would, today, seize power from him on the basis of the Amnesty report that he is spiritedly contesting. With this scenario in mind, many patriotic Africans are correct in their assessment that, very often, some of the reasons adduced by coup makers for their actions are both flimsy and petty. In Ghana, for example, some of the military officers, in executing their February 1966 coup d'etat, later faulted Nkrumah for going to Egypt to marry Madame Fathia Nkrumah. Although Ghanaian women were disappointed in their president's choosing a foreign woman for a wife, the late Ghanaian president reportedly indicated to friends that he was doing so in the interest of continental unity, as he and Egyptian President Nasser were among the leading supporters of the Organization of African Unity (OAU), the medium through which Africa was to be united continentally. To reduce the occurrences of the continent's military takeovers, such petty ways of thinking, no matter how popular the issue at hand may seem—like Nkrumah marrying an Egyptian instead of a Ghanaian woman—should cease in the 21st century.

In fact, there is an interesting but undocumented anecdote as a result of the anti-Nkrumah coup story in Ghana. Reportedly, one of the military presidents of the various coup-infected West African countries visited Ghana shortly after the February 1966 coup d'etat that unseated Nkrumah. The new Ghanaian leaders of the NLC military-police junta reportedly tried to show off some of Ghana's economic developmental prowess by, reportedly, taking the visiting military leader to see several accomplishments of the deposed CPP government headed by Nkrumah, including the hydro-electric project at Akosombo and its man-made lake, the well-laid out Tema motorway that linked that metropolis with Accra, the capital, and the Kwame Nkrumah conference center that hosted one of OAU annual meetings. The visiting military leader paused to ask: "So, Nkrumah did all these marvelous things?" "Yes," his host answered. "If so, why overthrow him? We wished that the leader we overthrew did even one or two of these things. He just squandered our money on himself and his family, hence the coup that I led against him," the visiting military head of state, reportedly, said. This shows how others view the reasons another group gives for effecting a coup d'etat.

It is, therefore, hoped that—like some of the reported political and economic abuses of the Nkrumah regime, coupled with several of the obviously undemocratic measures to which some countries in Africa resort—internal political problems would be corrected in the interests of the citizenry in order to ward off military interventions, indeed not necessarily to attract investors and tourists. After all, the people of the nations, with corrupt leaders, deserve better. To begin with, all such corrective measure must be enshrined in new and existing constitutions and, in the case of military regimes, in decrees, which are used to govern most of these countries.

Also, such African constitutions should set term limits for current as well future leaders and, in the end, retired presidents or prime ministers should be entitled to retirement benefits as in Western nations. If well planned for African political leaders, retirement from active politics at a mature age, say at 65 years old, would become a sheer joy that all and sundry would look forward to. If not, many political leaders cling on to politics at all costs and die in office for the big national or state funerals![13]

Above all, measures should be taken to ensure that if the need arises for a military dictator to emerge on the political scene of an African country, he would be curbed by good laws to refrain from being attempted to steal funds from the national coffers. A typical example is what happened in Nigeria during the rule of the former military strongman, General Sani Abacha. In "Corruption Monster Out of Control in Nigeria," *West Africa Magazine* reported that the new Nigerian government of President Olusegun Obasanjo was on a crusade, which included visiting the world's major banking centers to recover money supposedly stolen by the military regime of General Sani Abacha."[14] Seeing the alleged thievery that went on during the Abacha military rule as stealing from the poor and making them poorer, President Obasanjo patriotically said: "We are leaving no stone unturned because, as you know, corruption impoverished Nigerians."[15]

It, therefore, seems as if military rule is no cure for the elimination of corruption. In "A Harvest of Double Standards," Uche Ezechukwu of *West Africa Magazine* further made it plain that "hardly any [Nigerian] government in the past, except that of President Ibrahim Babangida, failed to pledge to eliminate the scourge of corruption from the national body politic. And each government succumbed under the sheer weight of the evil."[16]

Tracing the history of corruption in "A History of Corruption," Anthony A. Akinola, compared several of the erstwhile military leaders, who claimed publicly that they overthrew their predecessor regimes for many reasons, including corruption. Akinola, Howard University and Oxford-educated, wrote that Babangida was a decent operator compared with General Sani Abacha, who ruled Nigeria from 1993 to 1998, adding allegedly that Abacha

"transformed Nigeria into a family company in which every member of his family was a shareholder: The Governor of the Central Bank of Nigeria was accountable to the family and had to make available whatever sum of money was demanded by any of its members. Revelations have continued to be made of Abacha's billions in foreign bank accounts, and the wealth of his collaborators is known to many Nigerians.[17]

Instructively, it is reported that the Obasanjo regime has succeeded in retrieving some of the stolen funds but, as also alleged Nigerian Senate Committee on Appropriations Chairman Idris Abubakar "claimed that the President [Obasanjo] had illegally spent the recovered monies according to his personal whims and caprices, without consulting the National Assembly, whose constitutional duty it is to appropriate funds."[18] What is important about these discussions is that, first and foremost, many Nigerians believe so much in President Obasanjo that they feel strongly that he would not misuse national funds; secondly, at least a discussion exists at all to find out what happened to the funds, instead of a handful of adventurous military-cum-police officers seizing upon the allegations and overthrowing a properly-elected government, as has happened in the past in Nigeria and other African nations.

Human rights abuses also invites coups and it is important that two African experts on human rights issues, J. Oloka-Onynago and Deepika Udagama, have authored a report on human rights issues that establishes guidelines for nations and institutions. Their report, which has a major focus on globalization and its impact on human rights, was supposed to have been requested by the special rapporteurs for the U.N. Sub-Commission on the Promotion and Protection of Human Rights, which is a panel of independent experts. For the first time in many years, the two authors are placing some of the blame of human rights abuses on several international organizations, including the World Trade Organization (WTO), the World Bank, and the International Monetary Fund (IMF.)[19]

Apart from describing policies as "a veritable nightmare for certain sectors of humanity, particularly in developing countries," the coauthors urged these international organizations to apply basic human rights principles.[20] They also complained about the lack of transparency and accountability of these organizations, adding that even the United Nations leaves much to be desired in its relationship with these organizations: The manner in which the United Nations Secretariat and the U.N. Development Program (UNDP) have sought to establish links with major corporations and multilateral institutions raises numerous concerns.[21]

With such reports, African and other developing nations may be able to deal with some of these powerful international financial groups and organizations on equal footing. In doing so, their resources will not be crippled by suicidal structural adjustment programs that prompt these countries to be so desperate that their leaders become overly intolerant. Happily, the coauthors confirmed that the World Bank, at least, made a greater attempt to address the criticisms against it, "especially those targeting its addiction to grandiose projects, its insensitivity to environmental, indigenous and minority concerns, and to the issue of gender."[22] As Amnesty International and other human rights organizations have always done, pressure will be put on respective African countries—especially those that are known to violate basic human rights—to ensure that human rights records are raised to such acceptable levels that no military or police officers would have the excuse, on that score, to overthrow a properly installed regime in Africa and, indeed, in other Third World nations.

A November 2000 incident in the Ivory Coast shows that, if they are willing, African leaders can safely entertain the presence of their political opponents without fear that such opponents may overthrow their regimes, especially if they allow reasonable unanimity to prevail. When the manuscript for this book was being revised, the military regime of retired General Robert Guei was "toppled in a popular revolt."[23] Reportedly, General Guei, who went into a temporary exile in a neighboring West African country, returned home and, "emerged in the capital, Yamoussoukro, and met with President Laurent Gbagbo."[24]

As a result of the meeting between retired General Guei and his successor, President Gbagbo, the new leader of the Ivory Coast promised that he would not pursue his predecessor, as many African leaders would have done. Toward that end, Guei has taken steps to urge his military supporters to turn their support to the Gbagbo government, indeed calling "on soldiers to return to their barracks and support Mr. Gbagbo. . . . General Guei plans to live in his home village, Kabacouma, in the southwest [of the Ivory Coast]."[25]

African political pundits and human rights organizations have hailed the reconciliation and magnanimity showed by President Gbagbo, whose electoral victory in the October presidential elections of the Ivory Coast was temporarily derailed by the retired General, who had planned to impose himself on the country as an elected "civilian" leader. It was, again, through the popular revolt of the people of the Ivory Coast that Guei was driven out of power into a temporary exile and, indeed, that Mr. Gbagbo was sworn in as the victorious candidate in the elections. For him to allow retired General Guei to return to the Ivory Coast and settle peacefully in Kabacouma is deemed remarkable and a bit unreal in Africa, where many of the vanquished in the political game are often not allowed to stay either free or alive unless they leave to stay in exile.

This, also, was why many Africans and experts on the continent's political history lauded the Sierra Leonean government of President Kabbah for agreeing with regional and international leaders to reach out to Foday Sankoh of the RUF in a variety of ways. For peace and tranquility, Alhaji Kabbah also agreed for Sankoh and his allies to have cabinet positions, at least, until the resurgence in rebel activities destabilized the government. Former British Broadcasting Corporation (BBC) correspondent Hilton Fyle wrote *The Fighter from Death Row: Testimony of Survival* (2000) while on death row in Sierra Leone.

Working for the BBC program *Network Africa,* Mr. Fyle, as he told a *West Africa Magazine* interviewer, was allegedly accused by the network editor of a conflict of interest for appearing "to be criticizing the BBC for allowing their facilities to be used by the RUF leader, Foday Sankoh, for propaganda purposes."[26] Fyle appeared before a panel of senior staff of the BBC African Service after which he left the service:

> In the end, the consensus among them was that rules were rules, and the fact that I was ignorant of the rule regarding conflict of interest was no

excuse. I was asked to leave. But it was an amicable parting. I stayed for two months and left with rosy memories and a handsome parting gift.[27]

Mr. Fyle returned to Sierra Leone after his BBC tenure, as he reported, to run a charitable organization to help the society. For example, in December 1993, he held a fundraiser and received support from the ruling NPRC, to which he also gave advice "whenever they asked for it. That was what every patriotic Sierra Leonean did for the NPRC. That was why James Jonah [formerly of the U.N.] agreed to conduct the elections."[28] After the removal of the military regime by the combined forces of ECOWAS countries, Mr. Fyle was arrested and, with other accused supporters of the military, charged with treason.

To give readers of his interview with *West Africa Magazine* fuller details of his circumstances beyond his BBC employment, his return to Sierra Leone, and the treason charges, Fyle disclosed the following:

At my treason trial, the Attorney General Solomon Berewa claimed that I allowed soldiers to broadcast on my FM radio station, WBIG. So, in a democratic environment it was all right for supporters of Kabbah's government-in-exile to criticize the AFRC on my station, but it was wrong to allow AFRC supporters to express their opinions. And his government calls itself democratic. . . . I opposed Kabbah during the term of the AFRC because, in trying to return to power, he was acting irresponsibly and endangering the lives of the citizens in Freetown and elsewhere. With the support of the Nigerian dictator, Sani Abacha, he seemed to see violence as the only way to return. I was against the AFRC coup, but I contended that a violent comeback was the wrong approach, and I campaigned against it."[29]

Imprisoned at Pademba Road Prison, Fyle, who was on death row, was freed on January 6, 1999, as a young soldier told him: "The boys [Sierra Leone's rebels] have arrived to free all of you. They sent me to come and warn you. So please get ready. You are going to be freed."[30]

Mr. Fyle now lives in Columbus, Ohio, where his older brother (Professor Cecil M. Fyle, a noted historian) serves as a full professor of history at Ohio State University. The Fyle scenario and circumstances are similar to those of many African journalists—including those executed in the aftermath of the abortive Dimka coup in Nigeria, in which then head of state Muhammed was assassinated—who were forced by circumstances beyond their control to "lend" often lukewarm support to coup makers and, in the end, got accused with high treason and other capital offenses. Since the press plays a useful role in the absence of viable opposition political parties, it is part of our concluding recommendation that when journalists are accused, they should always be given a fair trial. Also, like the example of the current regime in the Ivory Coast, African leaders should tamper kangaroo court trials and vengeful methods with mercy and understanding in their dealing with journalists. If that is done, Mr. Fyle, Mr. Kenneth Best of Liberia, and several very competent journalists in self-imposed or forced exiles may return home to help with the rebuilding of several nations on the continent.

It should not have taken the so-called rebel (RUF) soldiers to visit the Pademba Road Prison to free Fyle. A truly democratic elected government should realize that journalists everywhere perform their duties impartially, and that a particular journalist's association with people in political power often has a professional touch, especially when that person does accept any official or cabinet position from the regime.

One sometimes wonders: What can an unarmed journalist do if, as a news editor or an announcer-on-duty at a radio or television station, heavily armed soldiers arrive in an armored carrier to announce that a coup d'etat is taking place that moment? The only alternative to being brutally killed in resistance is, if time and logistics permit, for such a person to escape from the radio or television station into "freedom." Then what does the editor do if the coup in which he (or she) did not collaborate succeeds? Probably, he or she has to leave the country and live abroad in a form of exile until a counter-coup takes place. Conversely, if the coup failed, the immediate query from a military tribunal would be: Why did you allow the soldiers to use your radio or television station to announce their insurrection? An innocent journalist is, therefore, caught between a rock and a hard place. However, some of these deplorable and dictatorial circumstances have often accounted for the multifarious coups d'etat, instead of those in political power welcoming their opponents with open and unfettered arms, as has amply and patriotically been done by Ivory Coast's Laurent Gbagbo, who has "allowed" retired General Guei to return home from his temporary exile in Benin. With Guei back home, the chances of him or his supporters planning an armed insurrection to regain power are very limited. Consequently, the Gbagbo regime has the peace to govern, while already scanty national resources are not needed to counteract the inherent subversion that many exiles carry out against the home-based regime. Also, such a cooperative attitude on the part of the governing authorities toward their opponents ensures that the ballot box becomes the future avenue for changing regimes.

Most certainly, there are several cogent reasons—including the need for development and growth—why African governments should work in cooperation with their political opponents, especially if Africans want to succeed in undermining the mushrooming secret plans of various armed forces to intervene in national politics. Indeed, *West Africa Magazine* Deputy Editor Desmond Davies made an apt comment, when writing about retired Colonel Frank G. Bernasko's book, *Nigeria: The Rise and Fall of the Second Republic, 1979–1983* (2000). Davies, *inter alia*, wrote:

> It stands to reason that the army should take most of the blame for Nigeria's ills. But the soldiers have contrived to massage their image to the extent that they have been able to convince some sections of Nigerian society—and indeed the international community—that civilian rule is not suitable for Nigeria.[31]

Many politicians in Africa do not seem to learn that their mistakes often invite soldiers to return to the political arena. Where corruption, graft, nepotism, ethnic strife, and conspicuous mismanagement are concerned, the politicians should blame themselves. Hence Davies is on target in stating categorically: "Nigerian politicians did not learn any lessons from the collapse of the First Republic. Politicians in the First Republic (1960–1966) featured prominently in the Second Republic and they immediately continued where they left off."[32]

It does not happen only in Nigeria, although as Africa's most populous nation, its leaders can teach other Africans lessons. Nigeria's unfortunate era of "operation wetty," during which many political thugs and hirelings were paid to douse opponents of their masters with gasoline or kerosene and set them ablaze, has returned to the politics of many other countries. In some countries in Africa today, there is what is called "necklacing," whereby rubber rings or round rubber tubes are forced on the neck of a handcuffed political opponent and set ablaze.

Instead of many of these post-independence African countries and their leaders following through with promises and dynamic plans announced by their nationalist leaders in their struggles for decolonization, these sad and unpatriotic events are perpetrated on fellow Africans by agents of many rich politicians. For example, a lot of useful suggestions were made in June 1951 by Ghana's Nkrumah when he addressed the graduating class of his alma mater, Lincoln University of Pennsylvania. Nkrumah's developmental blueprint, enshrined in his public speeches, could have helped Ghana and, indeed, other African countries that followed its 1957 independence if the newly-freed nations and their political leaders had kept their hands on the plough of development, instead of performing rampant acts of political mischief, political detentions, and naked acts of corruption and outright greed. Among various details, Nkrumah said:

> I then spoke about my hopes for the future. We are aiming to work under democratic principles such as exist in Britain and in the United States. What we want is the right to govern ourselves or even to misgovern ourselves. I again spoke of the needs of the Gold Coast for technicians, machinery and capital to develop its great natural resources. . . . I said that there was much for the *Negro* people of America to do to help their ancestral country both then and in the future and that, upon the attainment of independence, it was the intention of my Party to re-name the country Ghana.[33]

Nkrumah's clarion call to Black Americans for help in his country was pursued diligently. Hence, the Ghanaian leader made sure that many prominent Black leaders were invited to Ghana's March 1957 independence celebrations: Rev. Dr. Martin Luther King, Jr. and his spouse, Mrs. Coretta Scott King; Dr. W. E. B. DuBois and Paul Robeson, who were denied passports to travel; A. Philip Randolph; Dr. Lawrence Dunbar Reddick; Lincoln University President Horace Mann Bond, and others. Dr. King, for the first time, came face-to-face at the Ghana celebrations with Mr. Richard Nixon, who was representing President Eisenhower's Government. As reported, Mr. Nixon, who initially did not know who Dr. King was, asked whether the young Black man was happy to be free in Ghana. "No, I am not free yet," Dr. King reportedly axiomatically answered. "Come on, didn't you like the independence gained by your country last night?" Mr. Nixon reportedly asked again. "Well, I am from Alabama. My name is Martin Luther King, Jr.," Dr. King replied.[34]

Anyway, the strong ties that bound Africans and their diaspora kith and kin helped build bridges for a relationship that should have been durable. For example, Black scholars from America, including Dr. DuBois moved to places in Africa to work or simply to live. Dr. DuBois became the founding editor of the *Encyclopedia Africana* in Accra, Ghana, took Ghanaian citizenship to protest the Vietnam War, and died and was buried in Ghana. The DuBois project did not succeed as Dr. DuBois and Dr. Nkrumah had wished, although a serious version of it has been produced in the *Encarta* series by two of Harvard's astute scholars, Professors Henry Louis "Skip" Gates, Jr., and Anthony Kwame Appiah. Also, Malcolm X included a trip to Africa during his Mecca pilgrimage.

Today, instead of post-independence African political leaders building on the quests of Nkrumah and other Pan-African leaders from Africa so that the continent would benefit from African-American technological know-how and capital, there is too much ongoing political bickering, ethnic strife, corruption, and "man-eats-man" political syndrome in many places in Africa. They have undermined what is left of the cordial relationship that Nigeria's first President Nnamdi Azikiwe (a Lincoln University graduate), Sierra Leone's Dr. Karefa Smart, Dr. Nkrumah, and other well-meaning African leaders endeavored to forge with Dr. W. E. B. DuBois, Rev. Dr. Martin Luther King, Jr., and others, for mutual benefit has been allowed to sink into a transparent abyss. In coauthor Assensoh's "Conflict or Cooperation? Africans and African Americans in Multiracial America" (2000), some of the reasons behind the bitter-sweet relationship have been pointed out.[35]

Any African who relies on such forthright Black publications and news outlets as *Ebony Magazine, Black Enterprise, Amsterdam News, Atlanta Daily World, New Orleans Tribune,* and *Black Entertainment Television (BET),* among several others, agrees that there is a lot of Black talent and capital that African nations can tap, if their leaders would straighten up and unquestionably end the corrupt pervading practices, civil and ethnic wars, and multifarious coups and countercoups, that have not done so much to aggravate and deepen the continent's ills.

It is true that, as pointed out in coauthor Alex-Assensoh's *Blacks and Multiracial Politics in America* (2000), many African-Americans genuinely have a sense of belonging to what Nkrumah once called their ancestral home. Yet, Africans and African-Americans have done things that undermine their relationship, although many African-Americans still say that the first and foremost quest is for Africans on the continent to address problems like the following appropriately:

Some Africans on the continent have met African Americans with either a sense of superiority or outright contempt. In fact, some U.S.-born Africans of African parentage have begun to call themselves American-

Africans, as opposed to being labeled African Americans. When it comes to criticisms of Africa and Africans by African Americans, many black scholars agree that, while the substance may be true, in the words of the Loyola University [now University of Montana] Professor Tunde Adeleke, "the color line mandates racial solidarity under all circumstances."[36]

It is, therefore, time for Africans and their leaders to "clean up" their political and economic acts. To do so, the spate of coups and counter-coups should be addressed. The politicians, too, have an obligation to operate within democratic norms as well as obvious honesty or transparency, and every African should have an equal shake at national leadership, instead of being faced with national laws contrived to disenfranchise certain citizens. When such circumstances happen, such persons often see themselves as desperate and, in the end, either opt for foreign citizenship through naturalization or support acts of sabotage or outright subversion to bring about political change through the barrel of the gun.

NOTES

Preface

1. Alexandria Zavis, "General leads a revolt in Ivory Coast coup," *Chicago Tribune*, 25 December 1999, sec. 1, p.3.
2. Ibid.
3. For a fuller account of the Liberian coup d'etat of April 1980, led by Master-Sergeant Samuel K. Doe, one may take a look at Edward L. Wonkeryor's *Liberia Military Dictatorship: A Fiasco Revolution* (Chicago, IL: Community Press, 1985). Also, Professor George Kieh, an erudite Liberian scholar formerly at Morehouse College, Atlanta, has done a lot of excellent scholarship on Liberia and the West Africa sub-region; Professors T. Tipoteh, a Nebraska-educated economist, and Dr. Amos Sawyer, a reputable political scientist, both from Liberia, have also done credible work on their country.
4. Michael Colin Vazquez, "An African Dilemma," *Transition* 75/76, anniversary issue (1999): 6.
5. N. Onishi, "Popular Uprising Ends Junta's Rule Over Ivory Coast," *The New York Times*, 26 October 2000, p. A1.

Acknowledgements

1. Sometimes, when a person offers help, he or she does not know the extent to which it aids the work or professional interests of the one being helped, and this was what happened with Dean Hanson. Therefore, the acknowledgment here is very genuine, as A. B. very much appreciated—and still appreciates—what Hanson did for him to speed his work, which had hitherto been "retarded" by lack of research funds. His help enabled us to move this manuscript ahead of schedule!
2. The named colleagues or professional friends were very helpful in varied ways, including offering excellent scholarly papers that provided some of the pieces of information that we needed, as coauthors, to compare notes. Several of them, too, have had books published on Africa that helped us in our research. They are, therefore, listed here for good reasons!

Introduction

1. In discussing corruption, as a topical issue in Third World politics in general but African political history in particular, with Professors Assensoh and Alex-Assensoh, they impressed me in having done their homework very well, as both of them referred me to some of the most recent publications on the subject, including the excellent 325–page book edited by Professor John Mukum

Mbaku of Weber State University, Utah, which is titled *Corruption and the Crisis of Institutional Reforms in Africa,* published in 1998 by the Edwin Mellen Press. Having been born in Cameroon, which is not far from my own Nigeria, Dr. Mbaku and the contributors to his edited volume do not mince words when it comes to the socioeconomic cankerworm called corruption, which has "eaten" away large chunks of African nations and their resources. I am particularly gratified that Drs. Assensoh and Alex-Assensoh have treated the issue of corruption extensively as a main reason that the military and police officers of Africa, some of whom tend to become corrupt later when dabbling in partisan politics seize power in coups d'etat from politicians.

2. I quickly want to raise a caution here, as the comparison between the performances of Nigeria's 1960–1966 civilian regime and the military regimes that followed is always subjective. Impartial economists and other analysts agree with the conclusion that the military did better than the politicians, but supporters of both eras might argue differently.

3. This quotation was part of the 1982 presidential address of African Studies Association (ASA) President Richard Sklar, in Larry Diamond's *Class, Ethnicity and Democracy in Nigeria: The Failure of the First Republic* (London: Macmillan, 1988), p. 1.

4. Ali A. Mazrui, *Cultural Forces in World Politics,* (London: Curry, 1990). While Professor Mazrui, our mentor and Spiritual Father, delves into Big Power rivalry in the context of African politics, he is also very much aware of the ethnic factors, which have played equally destructive roles in African affairs; one of his numerous studies that would be of help on the subject of ethnicity in Africa is "Francophone Nations and English-Speaking States: Imperial Ethnicity and African Political Formations," in Donald Rothchild and Victor Olorunsola, editors, *State vs. Ethnic Claims: African Policy Dilemmas* (Boulder, CO: Westview Press, 1983), pp. 25–43.

5. Okey Onyejekwe, *The Role of the Military in Economic and Social Development: A Comparative Regime Performance in Nigeria, 1960–1979,* (1981). Also, since several arguments have been developed from my own book, I took the liberty not to document them in this short introduction, although I urge readers interested in the fuller discussions, to consult it.

Chapter 1

1. Kwame Nkrumah, *Autobiography of Kwame Nkrumah* (London: Thomas Nelson and Sons Ltd., 1957), p.187.

2. Ibid., p.199.

3. Ibid.

4. Ibid., p.259.

5. Ibid.

6. Ibid., p.261.

7. Ibid., pp.261–262.

8. A. B. Assensoh, *African Political Leadership: Jomo Kenyatta, Kwame Nkrumah, Julius K. Nyerere* (Malabar, FL: Krieger Publishing Company, 1998), pp.131–133.

9. Ibid., p.133.

10. J. Isawa Elaigwu, *Gowon: The Biography of a Soldier-Statesman* (Ibadan, Nigeria: West Books Publisher Limited, 1985), p.1.

11. Very interestingly, the slogan became the clarion call for Nigeria to keep on fighting in the Nigeria-Biafra civil war so that national borders and unity would be preserved. The slogan always began and ended radio and other news bulletins.

12. Elaigwu, *Gowon,* pp.95–96.

13. Ibid., p.115.

14. Ibid., p.1.

15. S. C. Saxena, *Politics in Africa* (New Delhi, India: Kalinga Publications, 1993), p.315.

16. Ibid., p.41.

17. Ibid., p.42.

18. Boniface I. Obichere, *West African States and European Expansion* (New Haven: Yale University Press, 1971), p.2.

19. Saxena, *Politics,* p.42. Also, a full discussion can be found in Lord Lugard, *The Dual Mandate in British Tropical Africa* (London: Frank Cass, 1965), p.36.

20. Saxena, *Politics.*, p.75.

21. Ibid., p.76.

22. Ibid., p.91.

23. Obichere, *West African States.*, p.2.

24. Ibid., p.2.

25. In terms of Ghana's late President Kwame Nkrumah's opinions on colonialism and neocolonialism, one may take a look at his book, *Neo-Colonialism: The Last Stage of Imperialism.* (New York: International Publishers Co. Inc., 1984).

26. Saxena, *Politics*, p.109.

27. Nkrumah, *Axioms of Kwame Nkrumah.* (London: Panaf Books, 1980), p.22.

28. Ibid.

29. Ibid., p.59.

30. Samir Amin, *Neo-Colonialism in West Africa* (Middlesex, Eng.: Penguins Books Ltd., 1973), p.viii.

31. Ibid., pp.viii-ix.

32. The full title of Professor Kenneth O. Dike's book is *Trade and Politics in the Niger Delta, 1830–1885* (London: Oxford University Press, 1956).

33. Amin, *Neo-Colonialims*, p.xii.

34. Nkrumah, *Axioms*, p.49. Also, Nkrumah discusses these points in *Neo-Colonialism: The Last Stage of Imperialism* (1984).

35. Kwame Nkrumah, *Dark Days in Ghana* (New York: International Publishers, 1968), p.52.

36. Ibid., pp.45–46. Chapter 7 of this book, titled "African Coups in Political and Theoretical Contexts," will document the 18 coups listed in Nkrumah's book, along with other, earlier ones.

37. K. A. Busia, *The Challenge of Africa* (New York: Praeger, 1962), p.65.

38. To read more on this issue, see Kwame Nkrumah's *Revolutionary Path* (London: Panaf Books, 1974).

39. For a detailed discussion of Julius Nyerere's socialist path, readers and researchers should see his book, *Freedom and Socialism: Uhuru na Ujamaa* (Oxford: Oxford University Press, 1968).

40. Busia, *Challenge*, p.65.

41. When Dr. Busia returned to Ghana shortly after the military overthrow of Nkrumah's regime on February 24, 1966, he became an unofficial adviser to the new regime. Later, he served as the head of the Center for Civic Education, to reorient Ghanaians to partisan politics and in 1969 he was voted into power as post-coup *Ghana's* first Prime Minister.

42. Busia, *Challenge*, pp.65–66.

43. Nkrumah, *Axioms*, p.23.

44. Paul Robeson, *Here I Stand* (Boston: Beacon Press, 1988), p.119.

45. Ibid., p.39.

46. Ibid., p.63.

47. Ibid., pp.72–73.

48. Ibid., p.73.

49. Ibid., p.63.

50. Assensoh, *African Political Leadership*, pp.11–12.

51. This quote, originally from the *New York Times*, has also been enshrined on the front cover of the Beacon Press edition of Robeson's *Here I Stand*.

52. Martin Duberman, "A Giant Denied His Rightful Stature in Film," the *New York Times*, 29 March 1998, sec. 2, pp.1 and 38.

53. A. Adu Boahen, *Africa Under Colonial Domination,* (Berkeley: University of California Press, 1985), preface, p.vi. Professor Adu Boahen, in intellectual honesty, does not make claim to the assertion but, instead, attributes it to several of its original sources, including the following: L.H. Gann and P. Duignan, *Burden of Empire* (London: Pall Mall, 1967); L. H. Gann and P. Duignan, eds., *Colonialism in Africa*, 5 vols. (Cambridge: Cambridge University Press, 1969); and P. Gifford and R. W. Louis, eds., *Britain and France in Africa* (New Haven: Yale University Press, 1971), and, by the same editors, *Britain and Germany in Africa* (New Haven: Yale University Press, 1967).

54. Boahen, *Africa Under*, p.vii.

55. Ibid., p.29; also, the formal reasons for colonialism are well discussed in a paper presented by Lagos University's History Professor I. A. Asiwaju at the Nigerian National Open University Conference, Lager, Nigeria, 1984.

56. Boahen, *Africa Under*, p.28; also, in Asiwaju.

57. Boahen, *Africa Under*, p.58.

58. Ibid., p.59. For specific examples and other details of what is discussed on this page, readers and researchers can visit Britain's Public Records Office at Kew Gardens, where all colonial records have been stored; in the instance of the French, the National Archives in Paris is the logical place, as pointed out in several places, of Samir Amin's *Neo-Colonialism*. Reports by district and regional colonial officers will be helpful.
59. Samir Amin, *Neo-Colonialism*, p.viii.
60. Boahen, *Africa Under*, p.94.
61. Ibid., pp.94–95.
62. Ibid., p.95.
63. A fuller discussion of Dr. Kwame Nkrumah's notion of neocolonialism and imperialism can be gauged his the book *Neo-Colonialism*. The publication of the anti-imperialist and anticapitalist book in 1965 angered the administration of American President Lyndon B. Johnson, and the earmarked economic assistance to Ghana, reportedly pegged at $35 million at the time, was instantly cancelled. Also, it has been claimed in several quarters that the book's publication spelled doom for Nkrumah and his Convention People's Party administration in Ghana, as that year reportedly marked the beginning of America's active support of anti-Nkrumah political-cum-military forces that would, on February 24, 1966, overthrow his government in a combined military and police operation while Nkrumah was on his way to Hanoi, in what has been described by his critics as a self-appointed mission—although he was traveling in the capacity of a British Commonwealth leader—to mediate in the America-Vietnam war.
64. Nkrumah, *Axioms*, p.17. Also, Nkrumah has discussed the issue of the balkanization of Africa on p.25 of his book *Neo-Colonialism*.
65. Nkrumah, *Neo-Colonialism,* pp.15–16.
66. Boahen, *Africa Under*, p.95.
67. Nkrumah, *Axioms*, p.17.
68. Copies of the entire speech of April 15, 1958 are available at the Ghana National Archives, Accra, Ghana and the British Colonial Records Office at Kew Gardens; also, it is quoted in Nkrumah, *Axioms*, p.23.
69. Nkrumah, *Autobiography,* p.12.
70. Ibid., p.11.
71. Ibid., p.21.
72. Ibid., p.32.
73. Ibid., p.11.
74. Ibid., pp.12–13.
75. Kofi Buenor Hadjor, *On Transforming Africa: Discourse With Africa's Leaders* (Trenton, NJ: Africa World Press, Inc., 1987), p.3.
76. Pat Williams and Toyin Falola, *Religious Impact on the Nation State: The Nigerian Predicament* (Aldershot, Eng.: Avebury Ashgate Publishing Company, 1995), p.17.
77. Ibid.
78. Ibid., pp.16–17.
79. Ibid., p.17.
80. Michael Amoah, "Religion: Christianity, Libation and Utility (1)," *West Africa Magazine* (9–15 February, 1998), p.197.
81. Ibid., p.197.
82. Femi Vaughan, *Nigerian Chief* (Rochester: University of Rochester Press, 2000), p. 119.
83. Williams and Falola, *Religious Impact*, pp.216–217.
84. Okion Ojigbo, *Nigeria Returns To Civilian Rule* [Lagos, Nigeria: Tokion (Nigeria) Company, 1980], p.16.
85. Ibid.
86. Rupert Emerson, "Nation-Building in Africa," in *Nation-Building,* ed. Karl W. Deutsch and William J. Foltz, (New York: Atherton Press, 1963), p.85; this is also succinctly quoted in Okion Ojigbo's *Nigeria Returns to Civilian Rule*, p.16.
87. Ojigbo, *Nigeria*, p.16.
88. J. F. Ade Ajayi, *Christian Missions in Nigeria 1841–1891: The Making of a New Elite* (London: Longman, Green and Co. Ltd., 1965), p.xiii.
89. Ibid.
90. Amos J. Beyan, *The American Colonization Society and the Creation of the Liberian State: A Historical Perspective, 1822–1900* (Lanham, MD: University Press of America, Inc., 1991), p.xi.

91. Beyan, *American,* p.51. This information can also be located in the November 5, 1817 correspondence between Bushrod Washington and the two ACS emissaries, Samuel J. Mills and Ebenezer Burgess as noted in *First Annual Report of the ACS* (1818), London, England, pp.11–12.

92. Beyan, *American,* p.52.

93. America-born Alex Haley's book, *Roots,* has made Gambia a very well-known country, as he wrote in it that his Black ancestry, led by Kunta Kinte, came from there. The book, which won numerous spectacular literary awards, was made into a popular motion picture movie. Haley, who resided in Tennessee, died on February 10, 1992.

94. *Second Annual Report Of The ACS* (1819), pp.5–7. The report is based on an abstract of a journal written by the late Reverend Samuel J. Mills.

95. Ibid., p.5–7.

96. John Hope Franklin and Alfred A. Moss, Jr., *From Slavery to Freedom,* 7th Ed. (New York: McGraw Hill, Inc., 1998), p.167.

97. Ibid., pp.167–168.

98. A. B. Assensoh, *Rev. Dr. Martin Luther King Jr. and America's Quest For Racial Integration* (Devon, Eng.: Arthur H. Stockwell Ltd., Publishers, 1987), p.47; also in Franklin and Moss, *From Slavery,* p.168.

99. Assensoh, *Rev. Dr. Martin Luther King, Jr.,* p.47. Also, this historical fact has been elaborated in August Meir, "The Emergence of Negro Nationalism: A Study in Ideologies" in *Along The Color Line: Expectations in the Black Experience,* ed. August Meir and Elliot Rudwick (Urbana, IL: University of Illinois Press, 1967), pp.191–192.

100. Assensoh, *Rev. Dr. Martin Luther King Jr.,* p.47.

101. Assensoh, *Rev. Dr. Martin Luther King Jr.,* p.48; also, Franklin and Moss, *From Slavery,* p.168.

102. Beyan, *American,* p.149.

103. Harry Johnston, *Liberia,* vol. 2 (New York: Dodd and Company, Publishers, 1906), pp. 353–354; also, see Beyan, *American,* pp.148–149.

104. Nnamdi Azikiwe, *Liberia in World Politics* (West Port, CT: Negro University Press, 1970), p.49.

105. Azikiwe, *Liberia,* p.49.

106. Editor, "People, projects and pointers," *Africa Confidential* 15, no. 19 (20 September 1974): 8.

107. Ibid., p.8.

108. Dr. Justin Molokai Obi, an ethnic Igbo from Nigeria, was captured after he allegedly shot and killed an Episcopal Bishop, and was charged, tried, and convicted of the murder. His death sentence, passed when Dr. William V. S. Tubman was in power but carried out by his successor, President Tolbert, had nothing to do with ritual murders. Coauthor Assensoh, as a newspaper editor in Liberia, attended the trial of Dr. Obi and reported on it for the newspapers for which he worked, including the *Daily Listener,* the *Saturday Chronicle,* and the *Sunday Digest,* all owned by the Dennis family of Monrovia, Liberia.

109. At the time that Nigerian chemistry Professor Justin Molokai Obi was arrested, tried, convicted, and subsequently hanged publicly on orders of President William R. Tolbert, Jr., coauthor A. B. Assensoh was the editor of three Liberian newspapers, the Daily Listener, Saturday Chronicle, and Sunday Digest, all owned by the family of the Honorable Charles C. Dennis, Sr., a member of the defunct Liberian House of Representatives from Bomi Hills Territory of Liberia. Mr. Dennis—whose son, Cecil was Liberian Minister of Foreign Affairs, was among the cabinet ministers publicly executed in the aftermath of the April 1980 military coup in Liberia—was also a leading Americo-Liberian.

110. Tuan Wreh, *Love of Liberty,* (London: C. Hurst and Co., 1976), p.129.

111. Ibid., p.129.

112. Ibid., pp.129–130.

113. Ibid., pp.130–131.

114. Obichere, *West African States, p. 203.*

115. Ibid., pp.4–5; 203.

116. Obichere, *West African States,* p. 88. Also, there are well-preserved documents on this issue at Archives Nationale (in France), Papiers Ballot (MI 185/4), Cuverville to Ballot, dated December 11, 1890.

117. For a detailed study of African religions and philosophy, readers can consult John S. Mbiti's *African Religion and Philosophy* (Garden City, NJ.: Anchor Books, 1970).

118. Jahn, *Muntu,* pp.51–52.

119. Ibid., p.51.

120. Ibid., pp.52–53.

121. Ibid., p.52.

122. "People, Projects, and Pointers," p.8.

123. Jomo Kenyatta, *Facing Mt. Kenya: The Tribal Life of the Gikuyu* (New York: Vintage Books, 1965), pp. 270–296.

124. Jahn, *Muntu*, p.xxvii.

125. Boahen, *Africa Under*, p.16.

126. Ibid.

127. Ibid.

128. To make sure that we have access to up-to-date information on several aspects of our coauthored publications dealing with Africa politics, culture and history, we paid research visits to some areas in West Africa, including Ghana in 1994, and also to the British Colonial Records Office at Kew Gardens, near London, in 1997. In both travels, we benefitted from funds made available through our Dean's Summer Faculty Fellowships at Indiana University and, to an extent, private funds, for which we were grateful. Also, see the acknowledgements.

129. Several aspects of such marriages, as well as crosscultural marriages in particular, are discussed by the authors in Yvette Alex-Assensoh and A. B. Assensoh, "The Politics of Cross-Cultural Marriage: An Examination of a Ghanaian/African-American Case," in *Cross-Cultural Marriage: Identity and Choice,* ed. Rosemary Breger and Rosanna Hill, (Oxford, Eng.: Berg, 1998).

130. Micael Amoah, "Christianity, Libation and Utility," *West Africa Magazine* (9–15 February 1998), p.196.

131. Ibid.

132. Edwin W. Smith, *Aggrey of Africa: A Study in Black and White* (London: Student Christian Movement Press, 1929), pp.278–279.

133. Nkrumah, *Autobiography*, p.15.

134. A. B. Assensoh, *Kwame Nkrumah: Six Years In Exile, 1966–1972* (Devon, Eng.: Arthur H. Stockwell Ltd., Publishers, 1978), pp.20–21. In fact, in our research, as coauthors we visited Dr. Aggrey's grave site not far from Livingstone College in Salisbury in the summer of 1996, collected research materials, took pictures, and, later, wrote two published essays about Dr. Aggyrey in the fall of 1996 for London-based *West Africa Magazine.*

135. Assensoh, *Kwame Nkrumah,* pp.21. Also, Lincoln University, Pennsylvania, alumni records have carefully preserved the correspondence between Seminary Dean George Johnson and Kwame Nkrumah.

136. Assensoh, *Kwame Nkrumah.*, p.21.

137. Ibid., pp.21–22. Also, the letters exchanged by both men are lodged in the Alumni Files of Lincoln University, Pennsylvania.

138. Adu Boahen, *Africa Under*, p.88.

139. Adu Boahen, *Africa Under*, pp.46–47; 88–89.

140. Readers may want to consult Kwame Kesse-Adu's 225–page book: *The Politics of Political Detention* (Accra-Tema, Ghana: Ghana Publishing Corporation, 1971).

141. Assensoh, *African Political Leadership,* pp. 21–22. For a detailed discussion of arrests and detentions without trial in Ghana, readers may take a look at Bankole Timothy, *Kwame Nkrumah: From Cradle to Grave* (Dorchester, Eng.: Gavin Press, 1981).

142. Assensoh, *African Political Leadership,* p.21.

143. Ibid., p.21.

144. Andrew E. Barnes, "'Some Fire behind the Smoke': The Fraser Report and Its Aftermath in Colonial Northern Nigeria," *Canadian Journal of African Studies* 31, no. 2 (1997): p.197.

145. Ibid., pp.197–198.

146. Ibid., p.198.

147. Ibid., p.199.

148. Ibid., pp.198–199.

149. Ibid., p.204.

150. Baffour Ankomah, "Time for Some Home Truths," in *New African Magazine,* no. 363 (May 1998): p.27.

151. Ibid.

152. Boahen, *Africa Under*, p.1.

153. Orlando Patterson, *Slavery and Social Death: A Comparative Study* (Cambridge: Harvard University Press, 1982), p.13.

154. From Report of the League of Nations Advisory Committee of Experts on Slavery (Geneva, April 5, 1938, vol. 6, p.16). Several aspects of the report are quoted by Professor Orlando Patterson in his book, *Slavery and Social Death*, p.21.

155. Crawford Young, *The African Colonial State In Comparative Perspective* (New Haven: Yale University Press, 1994), p.89.

156. Ibid.

157. Nkrumah, *Autobiography*, pp.180–182.

158. Ibid., pp.182–183.

159. For a detailed discussion of tyranny and corruption in post-independence Africa, readers may peruse Rene Dumont, *False Start in Africa* (London: Andre Deutsch, 1966); the 1988 edition, translated from the French by Phyllis Nauts Ott, with a foreword by Lloyd Timberlake, was published by Earthscan Publishers of London.

160. Tuan Wreh, *Love of Liberty* (London: C. Hurst & Company in association with Wreh News Agency of Monrovia, Liberia, 1976). Also, Rene Dumont's *False Start in Africa* (1964) can share light on the assertion.

161. Wreh, *Love of Liberty*, p.xi.

162. Ibid., pp.xi-xii; and the book's back cover inscription.

163. Ibid., p.xii, and the book's back cover inscription.

164. Ibid., p.xii, 129.

165. Zaya Yeebo, *State of Fear in Paradise: The Military Coup in the Gambia and its Implications for Democracy* (London: Africa Research & Information Bureau (ARIB), 1995), p.1.

166. Ibid.

167. Ibid.

168. Ibid., pp.1–2. Also, Nkrumah's Independence Day speech, on March 6, 1957, is available at the Ghana National Archives in Accra, Ghana.

169. Yeebo, *State of Fear.*, p.2.

170. Ibid.

171. Ibid.

172. Ibid., p.4.

173. "People, Projects and Pointers," p.8.

174. Ibid.

175. Ibid.

176. Ibid.

177. Ibid.

178. Ibid.

179. Per Wastberg, ed., *The Writer in Modern Africa* (Uppsala, Sweden: Scandinavia Institute of African Studies, 1968), p.3. This same quote is also in Dennis Austin, *Politics in Africa,* p.155.

180. Dennis Austin, *Politics in Africa*, p.154.

181. Ellis Cose, "We are So Terribly Sorry," *Newsweek Magazine* (6 April 1998), p.31.

182. F. Abiola Irele, "In Praise of Alienation: An Inaugural Lecture," University of Ibadan, November 22, 1982, p.16.

183. Ibid.

184. Nnamdi Azikiwe, *My Odyssey*, (London: C. Hurst and Co., 1970), p.130. Dr. Azikiwe's categorization applied to Dr. Danquah being the first West African to earn the doctoral degree in philosophy from the University of London.

185. Part of the story of Dr. Joseph Boakye Danquah and the late President Kwame Nkrumah can be found in Nkrumah's *Autobiography*. Also, Kesse-Adu has discussed the Danquah-Nkrumah problem in his *Political Detention*.

186. Ngugi wa Thiong'o, *Detained: A Writer's Prison Diary* (London: Heinemann, 1981), p.xi. Also, these issues are thoroughly discussed in A. B. Assensoh, *African Political Leadership*.

187. Dennis Austin, *Politics in Africa*, pp.17–18.

188. Ibid., p.18.

189. E. Abotare Nani-Kofi, "The Crumbling of Nkrumaism," *West Africa Magazine* (7–13 July 1997), p.1099. Also, a series on Nkrumah's exile years, published by this London-based publication in the summer of 1997, discussed several aspects of the Limann connection.

190. In addition to Nani-Kofi's "The Crumbling of Nkrumaism," coauthor Assensoh pointed these facts out in his summer 1997 series in the same weekly publication, titled "Facts about Nkrumah in exile," *West Africa Magazine*, Summer 1997.

191. Dennis Austin, *Politics in Africa*, p.17.
192. James C. McKinley, Jr., "As Crowds Vent Rage, Rwanda Executes 22 for '94 Massacres," the *New York Times*, 25 April 1998, pp. A1, A5.
193. McKinley, "As Clouds Vent Rage," p.A5.
194. Joe Igbokwe, *Igbos: Twenty-Five Years After Biafra* (Lagos: Advent Communications Ltd., 1995), preface, p.x.
195. Ibid., pp. x–xi.
196. Busia, *Challenge*, p.3.
197. Ibid., p.139.
198. A. B. Assensoh, *African Political Leadership*, pp. xvii–xviii.
199. Busia, *Challenge*, pp.139–140.
200. Peter Woodward, *Nasser* (New York: Longman, 1992), p.8.
201. Ibid., p.15.
202. Alaba Ogunsanwo, *The Nigerian Military and Foreign Policy, 1975–1979: Processes, Principles, Performances and Contradictions* (Princeton, NJ: Center of International Studies, 1980).
203. Dennis Austin and Robin Luckham, *Politics and Soldiers in Ghana, 1966–1972* (London: Frank Cass, 1975), pp.4–5.
204. Terrence Neilon, "Egypt: Mubarak Sworn In," *New York Times* 6 October 1999, p.A10.
205. O. Onishi, "Popular Uprising Ends Junta's Rule over Ivory Coast," *New York Times*, 26 October 2000, p.A1.

Chapter 2

1. Major-General H. T. Alexander, *African Tightrope: My Two Years as Nkrumah's Chief of Staff* (London: Pall Mall Press, 1965), p.vii.
2. Ian Fowler and David Zeitlyn, *African Crossroads*, (Providence, RI: House of Books, 1989), p.39.
3. Carolyn Hamilton, *Terrific Majesty: The Powers of Shaka Zulu and the Limits of Historical Invention* (Cambridge: Harvard University Press, 1998), p.xi.
4. Carolyn Hamilton, *Terrific Majesty*, p.4.
5. F. K. Buah, "*Asante* versus Southern Ghana," in *A History of Ghana* (London: Macmillan Education Limited, 1980), p.83.
6. Ibid., p.85.
7. Ibid., pp.86–87; 96.
8. Harry A. Gailey, Jr., *History of Africa: From Earliest Times to 1800, Volume I* (Malabar, FL: Robert E. Krieger Publishing Company, 1981), pp.81–82.
9. Ibid., pp.98–99.
10. A visit to some of the slave castles or forts in Africa, particularly in present-day Ghana and Senegal, still show mighty canon balls and canons that the slave-trading Europeans used at places like Elmina and Cape Coast castles (in the former Gold Coast), and *Gore* (in Senegal), which were visited by President Bill Clinton during his official visit to several places in Africa.
11. Albert van Dantzig, *Forts and Castles of Ghana* (Accra, Ghana: Sedco Publishing Limited, 1980), introduction.
12. van Dantzig, *Forts and Castles of Ghana*, introduction.
13. Gailey, *History of Africa*, p.184.
14. van Dantzig, *Forts and Castles of Ghana*, introduction.
15. B. G. Martin, "The Spread of Islam," in *Africa*, ed. Phyllis Martin and Patrick O'Meara (Bloomington: Indiana University Press, 1977), p.98.
16. Ibid.
17. Ibid., p.108.
18. Peter J. Parish, *Slavery: History and Historians* (New York: Harper & Row, Publishers, Inc., 1989), pp.11–12.
19. Orlando Patterson, "Slavery," *Annual Reviews of Sociology* 3 (1977), p.407.
20. Ibid., p.432.
21. Ibid.
22. Ibid., p.407.

23. While European traders did vast business in trading human cargo from Africa to the New World, whatever roles indigenous African played were very minimal and inconsequential, contradicting revisionist historians, who often point accusing fingers at Blacks as having played roles in enslaving themselves (or their kith and kin).

24. E. D. A. Turay and A. Abraham, *The Sierra Leonean Army: A Century of History* (London: Macmillan Publishers, 1987), p.1.

25. Ibid., pp.1–2.

26. Ibid., p.2.

27. Ibid., pp.2–3.

28. Ibid., p.3.

29. Ibid., pp.3–4.

30. E. D. Turay and Abraham provide a lively and much more detailed discussion of these historical matters about Sierra Leone in *The Sierra Leonean Army*. Also, a lot of well-organized copious materials about these matters are available in the colonial archives at Kew Gardens, London; our visit there in 1997 was very helpful in comparing notes and acquiring new research materials.

31. Turay and Abraham, *The Sierra Leonean Army*, pp.27–28.

32. Ibid., p.28.

33. A. L. Adu, *The Civil Service in Commonwealth Africa: Development and Transition* (London: George Allen & Unwin Ltd., 1969), p.212.

34. Ibid., p.17.

35. Ibid., p.213.

36. Ibid.

37. Ibid., pp.213–214.

38. Ibid., p. 214.

39. Olatunde Odetola, *Military Regimes and Development: A Comparative Analysis in African Societies* (London: George Allen & Unwin, 1982), p.23.

40. Ibid.

41. Ibid., p.22.

42. Kole Omotoso, ed., *Fellow Nigerians . . . : Famous First Words of Nigerian Coup-Makers, 1966–1985*, (Ile-Ife, Nigeria: House of Books, 1989), un-numbered pages of Major Nzeogwu's three-page speech of January 15, 1966.

43. Emeka Odumegwu-Ojukwu, *Because I Am Involved*, (Ibadan, Nigeria: Spectrum Books Ltd., 1989), p.157. Former Biafran leader and retired colonel, Emeka Odumegwu-Ojukwu writes that his junior brother, Tom Biggar, died together with Major Chukwuma Kaduna Nzeogwu in a patrol led by the latter.

44. Kwame Nkrumah, *Dark Days In Ghana* (New York: International Publishers, 1968), p.20.

45. Ibid., p.22.

46. Ibid., pp.125–128.

47. Kwame Nkrumah, *Autobiography of Kwame Nkrumah*, (London: Thomas Nelson and Sons, 1957), pp.133–134.

48. Ibid., pp.137–138.

49. Ibid., p.139.

50. Ibid., p.212.

51. Alexander, *African Tightrope*, p.vii.

52. For a detailed study of "bureaucratic corruption" and institutional reforms, the reader may take a good look at John Mukum Mbaku, ed., *Corruption and the Crisis of Institutional Reforms In Africa* (Lewiston, N.Y.: The Mellen Press, 1998).

Chapter 3

1. A. B. Assensoh, African Political Leadership: Jomo Kenyatta, Kwame Nkrumah, and Julius K. Nyerere (Malabar, FL: Krieger Publishing Company, 1998), pp.xvii–xviii; originally quoted in Olusegun Obasanjo and Hans d'Orville, eds., *The Leadership Challenge of Economic Reforms in Africa* (New York: Crane Russak, 1991), p.4. The heralded headline was in *Africa Confidential* 40, no. 5 (5 March 1999): 1.

2. The headlines described here include those that African, European, and American newspapers published, several of which have been drawn on in this study for illustrative purposes. Hence particular headlines are not necessarily stressed or immediately identified with the specific publication.

3. Obasanjo and d'Orville, *Leadership Challenge,* pp.4–6.

4. Bernard-Thompson O. Ikegwuoha, Nigeria: An Endless Cycle of Coup D'Etat (Rome: E. Progetto Gutenberg, 1994), p.29.

5. Kwame Nkrumah, *Ghana: The Autobiography of Kwame Nkrumah* (Edinburgh: Thomas Nelson and Sons, 1957), p.164.

6. Yuri Smertin, Kwame Nkrumah (New York: International Publishers, 1987), p.48.

7. The motto of Nkrumah's political party, "Forward ever, backward never," was also enshrined on the front page of the party's newspaper, the *Accra Evening News.* The motto made Nkrumah's fellow Ghanaians see him as an uncompromising leader who could lead them to the promised land, although behind the scenes, he made a lot of compromises with the colonial authorities.

8. Obasanjo and d'Orville, *Leadership Challenge,* p. 4; also, quoted in Assensoh, *African Political Leadership,* 1998, pp. xvii–xviii.

9. Dennis Austin and Robin Luckham, eds., Politicians and Soldiers in Ghana, 1966–1972 (London: Frank Cass, 1975), p.1.

10. Interestingly, in many countries in postcolonial Africa—including Nkrumah's Ghana—George Orwell's books *Animal Farm* and *Nineteen Eighty-Four* were not looked upon favorably, as they clearly depicted the prevailing politics. Some of these countries, in fact, banned these books or stopped testing bodies and institutions from prescribing them for national examinations.

11. P. A. V. Ansah, "Kwame Nkrumah and the Mass Media," in *The Life and Work of Kwame Nkrumah,* Kwame Arhin, ed. (Trenton, NJ: Africa World Press, Inc., 1993), p.87.

12. Assensoh, *African Political Leadership,* p.12.

13. Kwame Kesse-Adu, *The Politics of Political Detention* (Tema, Ghana: Ghana Publishing Corporation, 1971), p.94.

14. Arhin, *Life and Work,* pp.14–15.

15. K. A. Busia, *Africa In Search of Democracy* (London: Routledge and Kegan Paul Ltd., 1967), Preface, p.ix.

16. Ibid., p.x.

17. Assensoh, *African Political Leadership,* p.114.

18. J. D. Esseks, *Politicians and Politicians in Ghana* (London: Frank Cass, 1975), p.37.

19. The article, coauthored by Professors A. B. Assensoh and Yvette Alex-Assensoh, was titled "Black Literature, African and African-American Writers in Socio-Political Contexts," and it appeared in *Indiana PEN* 4–6 (April-June 1997): 6–10.

20. Editors, "Togo: A Test for France," *Economist* (4 July 1998): 40.

21. Ibid., p.40.

22. Ibid.

23. Ibid.

24. Ibid.

25. Ibid.

26. Ibid.

27. Roger Cohen, "A Nigerian Elder Statesman Laments His Tattered Nation," *New York Times,* 15 July 1998, p.A17.

28. Ibid., p.A1, A8.

29. Ibid., p.A1.

30. Ibid., p.A8.

31. Robert D. McFadden, "Nigeria Dictator Dies after 5 Years of Ruthless Rule: Key Aide Sworn in, Heart Attack Said to Be Cause of Death," *New York Times,* 9 June 1998, p.A1.

32. Ibid.

33. Ibid.

34. Assensoh, African Political Leadership, p.153.

35. Adu Boahen, "A Note on the Ghanaian Elections," *African Affairs Journal* 94 (1995): 277; also, in Assensoh, *African Political Leadership,* p.153.

36. Assensoh, *African Political Leadership,* p.153.

37. McFadden, "Nigeria Dictator Dies," p.A1.

38. Ibid.

39. Elaine Scilino, "With Nigeria's Military Ruler Dead, Concern Is Voiced for the Fate of His Jailed Foe," *New York Times,* 9 June 1998, p.A10.
40. Farai Chideya, "Nigeria's Orphan," *Time* (22 June 1998): p.42.
41. Eds., *Eduardo Mondlane* (London: Panaf Books Limited, 1972), p.11.
42. Ibid.
43. Ibid., p.113.

Chapter 4

1. President Nasser, of Egypt, is among the earliest examples of a coup leader who succeeded in ruling like a civilian leader with electoral mandates. Many other military rulers have followed his example in northern and sub-Saharan Africa.
2. Editors, "Nigeria's Future: Can Obasanjo save Nigeria?" *Economist* (6 March 1999), 45.
3. Ibid.
4. Editors, "Oh, Pakistan," *Economist* (16 October 1999): 17.
5. Ibid.
6. Celia W. Dugger, "Pakistan Army Seizes Power Hours After Prime Minister Dismisses His Military Chief: Country Is Calm . . . ," *New York Times,* 13 October 1999, p.A1.
7. Ibid.
8. "Oh, Pakistan," p.17.
9. Barbara Crossette, "A Soldier's Soldier, Not a Political General," *New York Times,* 13 October 1999, A10.
10. "Pakistan Army Seizes Power," A10.
11. Larry Diamond, *Class, Ethnicity and Democracy in Nigeria: The Failure of the First Republic* (London: The Macmillan Press Ltd., 1988), p.324.
12. The death of General Abacha of Nigeria is another case of a "heart attack" death in African politics. The *New York Times* and other credible sources claimed that the general suffered the heart attack in the company some beautiful women who were not his relatives and none was his wife.
13. "Nigeria's Future," p.45.
14. Ibid.
15. Bola Olowo, "Nigeria: Learn from the Past," *West Africa Magazine* (19 October–1 November 1998): 738.
16. Ibid.
17. "Nigeria's Future," p.44.
18. Ibid.
19. Editors, "Nigeria: Virtual Voters," *Economist* 40, no. 5 (5 March 1999): 2.
20. Ibid.
21. Ibid.
22. Ibid.
23. "Nigeria's Future," p.44.
24. "Nigeria: Virtual Voters," p.2.
25. Ibid.
26. Ibid., p.2.
27. "Oh, Pakistan," p.17.
28. Editors, "Ghana: Swiss Property Claims Denied," *West Africa Magazine* (19 October–1 November 1998): 739.
29. Ibid.
30. Editors, "Ghana: Presidential Jet Uproar," *West Africa Magazine*, (19 October–1 November): 739.
31. Ibid.
32. Ibid.
33. Editors, "Togo: A Test for France," *Economist* (4 July 1998): 40.
34. Samuel Decalo, *Coups and Army Rule in Africa* (New Haven: Yale university Press, 1990), pp. 224–25.
35. Ibid., p.225.
36. Ibid.
37. Ibid.
38. Ibid.

39. Interestingly, when some African nations face mounting economic and political difficulties, some of the odd things they do include changing the name of the country, as Dahomey, Upper Volta, and others did, as well as deciding to switch the capital cities and build expensive new ones, as Malawi and Nigeria, have done.
40. Delcalo, *Coups and Army Rules,* p.89.
41. Ibid.
42. Ibid., p.102.
43. Ibid., p.103.
44. Ibid., p.112.
45. Mike Adjei, *Death and Pain: Rawlings' Ghana, The Inside Story,* (London: Black Line Publishing Ltd., 1993), p.7.
46. Decalo, *Coups and Army Rules,* pp.118–119. Also, *West Africa Magazine* of 6 and 29 November 1972 gave extensive coverage of the Dahomean events.
47. Two excellent Ghanaian legal scholars, Dr. Victor K. Essien and Dr. Paul Kuruk, law professors in New York and Alabama, respectively, did their JSD dissertations on different aspects of the renegotiated Ghana contracts. Dr. Essien's study was at New York University Law School, and Dr. Kuruk's was at Stanford University. Readers should take a good look at both studies when renegotiated contracts of post-Nkrumah regimes of Ghana are concerned.
48. Decalo, *Coups and Army Rule,* p.20.
49. Ibid. The issue of corruption in the Acheampong regime has also been well covered in Naomi Chazan, *An Anatomy of Ghanaian Politics: Managing Political Recession* (Boulder, CO: Westview Press, 1983); and Donald Rothchild, "Military Regime Performance: An Appraisal of the Ghana Experience 1972–78," *Comparative Politics* (July 1980).
50. Adjei, *Death and Pain,* p.95. A Ghanaian female lawyer pointed out her father in a picture of a line-up of arrested and paraded *Kalabule* practitioners published in Adjei's book. Although this lawyer was an early supporter of the Rawlings regime, she was supposed to be anti-Rawlings's regime at the time that she pointed out her father's picture to us. She, however, could not deny that her father was being humiliated for corruption.
51. Decalo, *Coups and Army Rule,* p.20.
52. Adjei, *Death and Pain,* p.291.
53. Kofi Batsa, introduction to *The Spark: From Kwame Nkrumah to Limann* (London: Rex Collings, 1985).
54. Adjei, *Death and Pain,* pp.210–211.
55. Ibid., pp.316–317.
56. Ibid., p.317.
57. Editors, "Liberia: Taylorland under Siege," *Africa Confidential* 40, no. 19 (19 February, 1999): 6.
58. Ibid.
59. Ibid., pp.6–7.
60. S. Saccoh, "Kabbah's folly," *New African* (March 1999): p.35.
61. "Liberia," p.6.
62. Adama Gaye, "Charles Taylor talks to *West Africa*," *West Africa Magazine* (6–12 November, 2000): 9.
63. Baffour Ankomah, "Sierra Leone: There Is Hope Yet," *New African* (March 1999): 34.
64. Joseph R. Gregory, "Africa, Sierra Leone: Ex-Rebels Join Government," *New York Times,* 22 October 1999, A6.
65. Assensoh, *African Political Leadership,* (Malabar, FL: Krieger, 1998), p.108.
66. Editors, "Ghana: MPs commend President on US State Visit," *Ghana Review International* (13 March 1999): 1–2.
67. Kwame Nkrumah, *Ghana: The Autobiography of Kwame Nkrumah* (Edinburgh, Eng.: Thomas Nelson and Sons Ltd., 1957), pp.132–135.
68. Editors, "Congo-Kinshasa: Hard Talk in Kinshasa," *African Confidential Journal* (5 March 1999): 6.
69. Decalo, *Coups and Army Rule,* p.256.
70. Ibid., p.261.
71. Editors, "The Politics of Drought," *West Africa Magazine* (22 April 1974); also reported in Decalo, *Coups and Army Rules,* p.264.
72. Assensoh, *African Political Leadership,* p.122.
73. Decalo, *Coups and Army Rules,* p.178.
74. Samuel Finer, "The Morphology of Military Regimes," in *Soldiers, Peasants, and Bureaucrats,* eds. Kolkowicz et al., (London: George Allen & Unwin, 1982), p. 281.

75. Decalo, *Coups & Army Rule in Africa*, p.17.
76. Adjei, *Death and Pain*, p.110.
77. "Oh, Pakistan," p.17.

Chapter 5

1. T. O. Odetola, *Military Regimes and Development: A Comparative Analysis in African Societies* (London: George Allen & Unwin, 1982), p.138.
2. C. Rosberg and J. Nottingham, *The Myth of Ma-Mau* (New York: Praeger, 1966), p.26.
3. Mr. Hannington Ochwada, a Kenyan national, was studying history at the doctoral level at University of Florida, Gainesville, at the time of this interview.
4. In many African countries—especially in former British territories—it was the general assumption that only young men and women who could not enter the universities would opt to enlist in the army and its constituent forces (including the air force and the police). That impression changed when it became clear, after the spate of coups that, indeed, entering the armed forces was both a lucrative and serious business, and that it could become the avenue through which to attain fame and affluence, especially so as several lower-ranked officers shot their way into power.
5. T. O. Odetola, *Military Regimes and Development*, (London: George Allen Ltd, 1982), p.138.
6. Adewale Ademoyega, *Why We Struck: The Story of the First Nigerian Coup* (Ibadan, Nigeria: Evans Brothers, 1981), p.50.
7. John Mukum Mbaku, *Institutions and Reform in Africa* (Westport, CT: Praeger, 1997), p.97. Here Professor Mbaku offers additional information in the discussion of these issues.
8. T. O. Odetola, *Military Regimes and Development*, p.138.
9. Kwame Nkrumah, *Axioms of Kwame Nkrumah* (London: Thomas Nelson and Sons, Ltd., 1967), p.16. The entire speech is available at the Ghana Ministry of Information Archives in Accra, Ghana.
10. Nkrumah, *Axioms of Kwame Nkrumah*, pp.16–17.
11. Peter O. Agbese, "The State versus Human Rights Advocates in Africa: The Case of Nigeria," in *Africa, Human Rights, and the Global System*, edited by Eileen McCarthy-Arnolds, David R. Penna, and Debra Joy Cruz Sobrepena (Westport, CT.: Greenwood Press, 1994), p.147.
12. Agbese, "State versus Human Rights Advocates," p. 147. Some of the measures of the new military regime, headed by then General Ibrahim Babangida, are published in *Portrait of a New Nigeria: Selected Speeches of IBB* (Lagos: Precision Press, no date given), pp. 21–26. Also, the official Nigerian document *Official Gazette (Extraordinary)* of April 4, 1984 reported some of the new measures to correct abuses in the deposed regime of retired General Buhari.
13. Agbese, "State versus Human Rights Advocates," p.148.
14. Ibid.
15. Ibid.
16. Ibid., pp.148–149.
17. George Klay Kieh, Jr., preface to *Ending the Liberian Civil War: Implications for United States Policy toward West Africa* (Washington, D.C.: Transafrica Forum, 1996), p.ix.
18. A. Adu Boahen, foreword to *History, Politics and Early Press in Ghana: The Fictions and the Facts*, edited by K. A. B. Jones-Quartey (Accra-Tema, Ghana: The Assembly Press, 1975), p. xix.
19. Agbese, "States Versus Human Rights Advocates," p.148.
20. Zaya Yeebo, *State of Fear in Paradise: The Military Coup in the Gambia and Its Implications for Democracy* (London: The Africa Research and Information Bureau, ARIB, 1995), p.2.
21. Editors, *The Daily Observer* (Banjul, Gambia, 24 October 1994), p.1; also reported in Yeebo, *State of Fear*, p.92. .
22. Yeebo, *State of Fear*, p.92.
23. Ibid.
24. Ibid.,p.93.
25. Editors, *Gambia News and Report* 2, (Banjul, Gambia, March 1994); also, it is reported in Yeebo, *State of Fear*, p.93.
26. Ibid., p.95.
27. Ibid.
28. Ibid., p.96. Since Yeebo worked for the Rawlings regime in a cabinet-level position, one may assume that he knew well what he discussed, especially if it was true that the American CIA,

which had initial problems with the Rawlings regime, was then backing Rawlings in Accra. The Pinochet scenario, as mentioned by Yeebo, is an interesting one because many of President Allende's friends and supporters, including the late sociology professor Clodomiro Almeyda Medina, were allegedly arrested and tortured by the Pinochet regime after the 1973 "brutal" coup d'etat in Chile. Medina was, for example, imprisoned at Dawson Island together with other Allende regime officials, later transferred to a Santiago jail, and, in 1975, sent into exile in East Germany. He died at the age of 74 in August 1997.

29. Yeebo, *State of Fear,* p.97.
30. Ibid., pp.98.
31. Burgess Car, foreword to *The Roots of Crisis in Southern Africa,* edited by Ann Seidmann, (Trenton, NJ: Africa World Press, 1985), p.xi.
32. James Gibbs, "Reflecting on Five Score (1)," *West Africa Magazine* (14–20 July 1997): 1149.
33. Part of the information about Mr. Mike Adjei used in this chapter can be found at the back of his book, *Death and Pain Rawlings' Ghana: The Inside Story,* (London: Black Line Publishing. Ltd., 1993), in the section marked "Author Details."
34. Ibid, p. 34.
35. Ibid.
36. Ibid., p.30.
37. Ibid., pp.30–31.
38. Tunde Thompson, *Power and the Press* (Lagos, Nigeria: Academy Press Plc., 1988), dedication page.
39. Ibid.; this discussion can be found in chapter 6 of his book.
40. Ibid., p.148.
41. Ibid.
42. Ibid., p.164.
43. Ibid.
44. Ibid.
45. Francis P. Kasoma, *The Press in Zambia* (Lusaka, Zambia: Multimedia Publications, 1986), p. 194.
46. Ibid.
47. A. B. Assensoh, "Justice in Africa: An Overview of Recent Injustice," *Issue: A Journal of Opinion* 15 (1987): 91. This quotation also appeared earlier in *African World News* (October 1984): p.12.
48. Boahen, foreword, p.xix.
49. Ibid.
50. A. B. Assensoh, "Injustice in Africa," in *Issue: A Journal of Opinion* 15 (1984), p.91.
51. Wiseman Khuzwayo, "*The Rand Daily Mail*: The Death of a Crusading Paper," *Concord Weekly,* no. 5, 20 June, 1985, p.13. This information is also contained in Assensoh, *Issue,* pp.91–92.
52. Assensoh, *Issue,* p.92.
53. Terrence Neilan, "Africa: Zambia Espionage Case Advances," *New York Times,* 17 April 1999, p.A4.
54. Wole Soyinka, "Every Dictator's Nightmare," *New York Times Magazine,* (18 April 1999), sec. 6, pp.90–92.
55. Ibid., p.90.
56. Ibid.
57. Wole Soyinka, "On the Trail of Transition: Notes from East Africa," *Transition,* 7, no. 75–76 (1999): 418.
58. Ibid.
59. Ibid., pp.418–419.
60. Coauthor Assensoh was in Nigeria when the Nigeria-Biafra civil war was beginning and, therefore, witnessed some of the documented atrocities that we came across in our research for this publication.
61. Rajat Neogy, "Nigerian War: On Biafra, a Conversation with Chinua Achebe," *Transition* 7, no. 75–76 (1999): p.222. The description of Dr. Achebe as the "unofficial ambassador for the breakaway Republic of Biafra," can be found in this issue of the journal, as shown in the contents.
62. Ibid., p.222.
63. Burgess Carr, foreword, p.ix.
64. Adjei, "Nsawam Prison," in *Death and Pain in Rawlings' Ghana: The Inside Story,* p.95.
65. Ibid.
66. Ibid., p.94.

67. Ibid., pp. 125–136.
68. Ibid.
69. Ibid., p.79.
70. Agency France-Presse and Reuters News Agency, "Africa, Niger: France Suspends Aid," *New York Times,* 4 April 1999, p.A8.
71. Ibid.
72. Kwame Nkrumah, "Army," *Axioms of Kwame Nkrumah,* (London: Panaf Books, 1980), pp.16–17.
73. Associate Press, "Uganda: A New Cabinet," *New York Times,* 7 April 1999, p.A9.
74. George B. N. Ayittey, *Africa Betrayed* (New York: St. Martin's Press, 1992), p.16.
75. Ibid., p.107.
76. Ibid.
77. Editors, "Eritrea/Ethiopia: Pride and Prejudice," *Africa Confidential* 40, no. 4 (19 February 1999): p.4.
78. Ibid.
79. Ibid.
80. Ibid., pp.4–5.
81. Editorial, "Algeria Looks to the Ballot Box," *New York Times,* 14 April 1999, p. A28.
82. Ibid.
83. Agency France-Presse, "Algeria: Rebels Make Election Pick," *New York Times,* 7 April 1999, p.A9.
84. Norimitsu Onishi, "Nigeria's Military Turns Over Power to Elected Leader: Optimism, and Concerns. Newly Sworn in as President, Obasanjo Vows to Follow a Path of Democracy'," *New York Times,* 30 May 1999, pp.A1, A4.
85. Ibid.
86. Ibid.
87. Ibid.
88. Ibid.
89. Ibid.
90. Ibid.
91. Ibid.
92. A. B. Assensoh, *African Political Leadership: Jomo Kenyatta, Kwame Nkrumah, and Julius K. Nyerere* (Malabar, FL: Krieger Publishing Company, 1998), pp.xvii–xviii.

Chapter 6

1. Editors, *Panaf Great Lives: Kwame Nkrumah* (London: Panaf Books Limited, 1974): pp.202–203.
2. Editors, *Webster's Ninth New Collegiate Dictionary,* (Springfield, MA: Merriam-Webster, Inc., 1985), p.997. This definition of "ideology" places an emphasis on socioeconomic but not sociopolitical aspects, although both are relevant within the context of our study.
3. Edmond J. Keller, "Introduction: Toward a New African Political Order," in *Africa in The New International Order : Rethinking State Sovereignty and Regional Security,* edited by Edmond J. Keller and Donald Rothchild, (Boulder, CO: Lynne Rienner Publishing, Inc., 1996), p.1.
4. John Mukum Mbaku, ed., *Corruption and the Crisis of Institutional Reforms in Africa* (Lewiston, NY: The Edwin Mellen Press, 1998), p.15.
5. Keller, "Introduction," p.1.
6. Ibid.
7. Olusegun Obasanjo, "A Balance Sheet of the African Region and the Cold War," in Keller and Rothchild, *Africa in the New International Order,* pp.15–16.
8. Richard Butler, "Bewitched, Bothered, and Bewildered: Repairing the Security Council," *Foreign Affairs* (September-October 1999): 9.
9. Ibid.
10. A. B. Assensoh, *African Political Leadership: Jomo Kenyatta, Kwame Nkrumah and Julius K. Nyerere* (Malabar, FL: Krieger Publishing Company, 1998), p.122.
11. Ibid.
12. Ibid.
13. Ibid., pp.122–123.
14. Kwame Nkrumah, *Dark Days in Ghana* (New York: International Publishers, 1968), p.49.

15. Ibid.
16. Kwame Nkrumah, *Ghana: Autobiography of Kwame Nkrumah* (Edinburgh: Thomas Nelson and Sons Ltd., 1957), p.12.
17. BoLeo Huberman and Paul M. Sweeney, foreword to *Ghana: End of an Illusion,* by Bob Finch and Mary Openheimer (New York: Monthly Review Press, 1966), p.ix.
18. A. B. Assensoh, *Kwame Nkrumah: Six Years in Exile, 1966–1972* (Devon, Eng.: Arthur H. Stockwell, Ltd., 1974). p.51.
19. Ibid.
20. John Stockwell, *In Search of Enemies: A CIA Story* (New York: W.W. Norton, 1978), p. 160.
21. Ibid., p.201n.
22. Ibid.
23. Ibid., p.160.
24. Anver Versi, "The Enigma of Robern Mugabe," *African Business Journal* (1 June 1998): p.6.
25. What is strange is that, since 1966, no Igbo person in Nigeria seemed to know where either General Ironsi or Western Region Governor Fajui (sometimes written as Fajuyi) was buried. A Soviet report indicated that the remains of the Russian Czar and his family, were found and exhumed for reburial. The secrecy behind the burial grounds of the late General Ironsi and his host, Governor Fajui, prompted Igbos to make the wild claim that, when the pro-Northern troops tried to arrest Ironsi, he reportedly turned into a crocodile, a mythical claim that is yet to be authenticated by any credible eyewitness.
26. *Panaf Great Lives,* p.217.
27. Martin van Creveld, *The Encyclopedia of Revolutions and Revolutionaries: From Anarchism to Zhou Enlai* (New York: Facts on File, 1996). The most relevant article is titled "Egypt under Nasser," pp.106–107.
28. Ibid., pp.107–109.
29. Ibid., pp.110.
30. Ibid., pp.110–111.
31. Asafa Jalata, preface to *Geerarsa Folksong as the Oromo National Literature,* by Addisu Tolesa (Lewiston, NY: The Edwin Mellen Press, Ltd., 1999), p.vii.
32. Mbaku, *Corruption and the Crisis,* p.20.
33. Ibid.
34. Afrifa's book *The Ghana Coup* (London: Frank Cass, 1966) is quoted in earlier chapters. In it, he recalls some of these incidents, as he explained the rationale for the coup d'etat of 1966 in Ghana.
35. Robin Cohen and Harry Goulbourne, *Democracy and Socialism in Africa* (Boulder, CO: Westview Press, 1991), p.1.
36. Mbaku, *Corruption and Crisis,* p.xvi.
37. Ibid.
38. Ibid., p.xix.
39. Ibid., p.xxvi.
40. Anthony Akinola, "What Is Going on in Nigeria," *West Africa Magazine,* (3–16 August 1998), p.623.
41. Todd S. Purdum and David Firestone, "A Vote Deadline in Florida Is Set for Today: U.S. Judge Refuses to Block Hand Tallying of Votes," *New York Times,* 14 November 2000, p.A1.

Chapter 7

1. Although several writers have, over the years, held this contention, the most notable is Harold L. Nieburg. Readers may take a look at his published works and, if desired, read more on his discussion of how the reaction of people of a society can begin a revolution that, sometimes, stems from a minor issue. One learned similar lessons from the French Revolution of 1879, when French women marched in the streets to protest and speak out against the exorbitant price of bread and others protested against other forms of injustice and lack of freedom under the "old" order. In African countries, even a violation of a taboo or custom by the ruling elite can spark a violent protest of sorts, which might "force" military adventurers to step in through a coup d'etat. That is why many experts on African (or Third World) politics were saying that if the November 2000 American electoral stalemate had taken place in a developing society, armed soldiers would have taken matters into their own hands, possibly to staging a coup d'etat to bring about "redemption."

2. For a detailed study of the violent nature of these early nineteenth-century protest events in the former Gold Coast, readers are urged to turn to Larry W. Yarak's book, *Asante and the Dutch, 1744–1873* (1990). It is a 316–page study with maps and other illustrations.

3. Professor Walter Rodney's study of the Islamic Jihad and social revolution in the mountains that were known as the Futa Djallon of eighteenth-century Nigeria can be found in *Journal of the Historical Society of Nigeria* 4, no. 2 (1968). Noted for similar studies earlier in his student days in London, Rodney had done part of his doctoral research on the Guinea Coast of West Africa, a revised version of which later became one of his earliest published books.

4. Very often, many people confuse Peter Enahoro, *Daily Times of Nigeria*'s journalist par excellence, whose pen-name was Peter Pan, with his politically astute brother, Anthony, whose book *The Fugitive Offender* detailed his suspected involvement in the very treasonable case that sent Chief Obafemi Awolowo and other political allies to prison. (Chief Awolowo was so well respected that when he died in the mid-1980s, the former secessionist "Biafran" leader, Oxford-educated retired Colonel Odumegwu Ojukwu reportedly described the stalwart Yoruba leader and constitutional lawyer as "the best President Nigeria never had.") Chief Anthony Enahoro was able to elude the Nigerian security forces and left Nigeria for a temporary exile in Ghana. When the Enahoro issue became too "hot" for the regime of President Kwame Nkrumah to handle, the Nigerian fugitive politician left Ghana for London, thinking that he would be safer in the former imperial capital. His celebrated case, for which the Nigerian government of Alhaji Sir Tafawa Balewa sought his extradition, is discussed fully and with candor in *The Fugitive Offender*. A perusal of Enahoro's book on the issue provides an illumination of the facts as he saw them.

5. Whenever a coup d'etat takes place in a country, be it in Africa or in Asia, like the most recent one in Pakistan, the coup leaders make the point of using their maiden radio and television broadcasts to highlight some of the catalogued shortcomings of the deposed leaders. This is a way of continuing to get public support for the new revolution. When Prime Minister Nawaz Sharif of Pakistan was overthrown in the October 12, 1999 coup by Army Chief Pervez Musharraf, it was reported the next day by the world media, including the *New York Times* of October 13, 1999 (pp.A1 and A10), with the reasons for the coup spelled out clearly.

6. Professor Soyinka's escape from Nigeria into exile was widely published, but his interview with the *New York Times*, as reported in the December 7, 1994 issue of the newspaper, was a good lesson for African writers who would dare to critique some of the repressive regimes on the continent. In fact, known for his hunting ability, Dr. Soyinka did not openly reveal how he got out of Nigeria but he intimated that hunters knew how to "vanish" in the bush.

7. Malawi's Professor Mapanje explained to coauthor Assensoh that, under the erstwhile President Kamuzu Banda regime in his country, several opposition politicians were either being murdered or reported missing, including the daring abduction from Zambia and the subsequent imprisonment of the Cherewas, the lawyering couple that led an anti-Banda campaign from exile. Therefore, when Mapanje wrote a poem with "vultures" as the theme, the intolerant Banda regime felt that he was referring to what vultures eat—dead bodies or corpses—as the regime allegedly tortured its opponents and secretly buried its dead victims. Hence his arrest and long detention at Mikuyu Prison without trial. Malawians sighed relief when Banda's several-decade rule ended in an internationally-monitored electoral defeat.

8. Kwame Kesse-Adu, *The Politics of Political Detention* (Accra-Tema: Ghana Publishing Corporation, 1971), p.25.

9. "For the public good" often described the reasons why a dictatorial African regime of the post-colonial period either arrested a political opponent to be detained indefinitely, often without trial, or served a suspected foreign critic within its borders with deportation orders, deeming them persona non grata. Some of these excesses in postcolonial African governance prompted Rene Dumont, the French agronomist, to write his seminal work, *False Start in Africa*, which amply details some of the unusual political, economic, and sociocultural behaviors of the ruling class. Readers may take a look at Dumont's 320–page book, *False Start in Africa* (New York: Frederick A. Praeger, Publishers, 1966). Originally published in French, the book was translated into English in 1966 for Andre Deutsch Limited, publishers, by Phyllis Nauts Ott.

10. President Obasanjo is fondly remembered by this quote, as many of his fellow Africans have wondered how he dared to make such a bold statement to critique indigenous repression and dictatorship. However, his compatriots understood why, as a retired general and former Nigerian head of state, he suffered imprisonment on suspicion of planning a coup d'etat during the alleged corrupt leadership of General Sani Abacha.

11. Coauthor A. B. Assensoh, as the editor of the three Liberian newspapers in Monrovia in the late 1960s, had the privilege of attending President Tubman's Friday press conferences at the Executive Mansion in Monrovia. It was on such occasions that Tubman sometimes lashed out at his critics and vowed not to allow them to undermine or overthrow his True Whig Party government by "the stroke of the pen." When Mr. Tolbert succeeded Tubman as the President of Liberia, he scaled down the weekly press conferences but held them when there were topical issues to announce, including the signing of death warrants for convicted criminals to be prepared for public hanging. The hangings were seen by Tolbert's opponents as activities meant to put fear in would-be Liberian coup makers until April 1980, when his Americo-Liberian government was overthrown and he himself was assassinated in a coup d'etat.

12. Many dictators of postcolonial rule in Africa happily relied on autocratic laws that the departing colonial officials left behind. When queried for using such laws against their own people, such leaders would point accusing fingers at the former leaders, who happened to be Europeans, instead of trying to overhaul or completely do away with such colonial-era laws.

13. Nnamdi Azikiwe, *My Odyssey* (London: C. Hurst & Company, 1970), p.270.

14. Ibid., p.272.

15. According to Nkrumah's supporters and insiders, the CPP regime believed that the acquitted men were guilty, and that Korsah's court should not have acquitted them, or let them go free.

16. Martin van Creveld, *The Encyclopedia of Revolutions and Revolutionaries: From Anarchism to Zhou Enlai*, "Argentina," 1996, p.118.

17. Baffour Agyeman-Duah, "Military Coups, regime Change, and interstate Conflicts in West Africa," *Armed Forces & Society* vol. 16, no. 4 (Summer 1990): p.550.

18. An interesting aspect of Nasser's coup of 1952 was that, unlike coups in Africa today, there was no bloodshed, although some leading officials were placed under house arrest until the coup leaders are sure of the success of their military exercise.

19. van Creveld, *The Encyclopedia*, p. 118.

20. Ibid. p.119.

21. The British reaction to the assassination of Prime Minister Alhaji Sir Tafawa Balewa and some of his regional leaders in the 1966 Nigerian coup prompted radical African leaders to point accusing fingers that, as they always claimed, Nigeria was a neo-colonialist entity. In fact, in an early afternoon broadcast on Ghana radio, in a form of a tribute, Nkrumah described Nigeria, under the late Premier as a colonialist possession, and that Mr. Balewa had died a victim of forces he would never understand. The full text of Nkrumah's broadcast is still available in the Ghana Ministry of Information and Broadcasting in Accra, the capital.

22. Anthony H.M. Kirk-Greene, *"Damnosa Hereditas": Ethnic Ranking and the Martial Races Imperative in Africa*, (London: Unicorn, 1978), p. 405.

23. Professor Ali A. Mazrui has offered a fascinating discussion of the ethnic issues in the Ugandan Army in a 1975 study, *Soldiers and Kinsmen in Uganda: The Making of a Military Ethnocrac*, (Denver, CO: University of Denver: 1975).

24. Michael Bratton and Nicolas van de Walle, "Toward Governance in Africa: popular Demands and state responses," in Goran Hyden and Michael Bratton, eds. *Governance and Politics in Africa* (Boulder, CO: Lynne Rienner Publishers, 1992), p.46.

25. Gregory, *The New York Times*, p.A6.

26. Baffaour Ankomah's well-written and very biting columns, even before he succeeded the veteran journalist Alan Rake as the editor of *New African Magazine*, appeared each month throughout 1999. Interested readers can, as a result, check out the fuller details of the remarks or comments. Sadly, the fragile peace brokered between the elected government of Sierra Leone and the RUF—with U.N., ECOWAS, OAU, American, and European Union (EU) support—broke down, and, as this book was being completed by the coauthors, the RUF leader, Sankoh was arrested and detained for possible trial as a "war criminal." In the interest of peace, however, many well-meaning observers of the Sierra Leonean scene do not favor such a trial, hence there is a seeming stalemate in the arrangements to set up a tribunal or a court for that purpose. But, almost in tears, Ghana-born U.N. Secretary-General Kofi Annan, in a spring 2001 CNN interview at the U.N. in New York, described the atrocities committed against innocent civilian populations, including children, in Sierra Leone as barbaric acts that had no equal in African history.

27. Bratton and van de Walle, "Toward Governance," p.45.

28. Among scholars who discuss reasons for coups d'etat and other forms of rebellions for change is E. Wayne Nafziger, who discusses "relative deprivation" theories very clearly. Readers should

consult E. Wayne Nafziger, *Economics of Political Instability: the Nigerian-Biafran War* (Boulder, CO: Westview Press, 1983) among his other scholarly publications.

29. Baffaour Agyeman-Duah, "Military Coups, Regime Change, and Interstate Conflicts in West Africa," p.547.

30. For a detailed look at reported coup events, including the number of coups that various nations of Africa have seen or suffered, readers may take a look at editors, *The Europa Yearbook*, vol. 1, 2 (London: Europa Publications, 1985).

31. For a further count of the number of coups various African nations have suffered, one may take a look at *The Europa Yearbook*.

32. Again, readers may refer to a fuller study of "civilianized military" regimes and military-cum-civilian regimes in West Africa in *The Europa Year Book*, vol. 1.

33. Paul Nugent, *Big Men, Small Boys and Politics in Ghana: Power, Ideology and the Burden of History, 1982–1984* (New York: Pinter, 1975), p.16.

34. Ibid., pp.17–18.

35. Richard W. Hull, *Southern Africa: Civilizations in Turmoil* (New York: New York University Press, 1984). It is a study worthy of note by today's students of southern African history and politics.

36. T. Balogh, Introduction to *False Start in Africa*, by Rene Dumont, (New York: Proeger, 1966) p.5.

37. Ibid.

38. Ibid.

39. Nkrumah's book *Neo-Colonialism: The Last Stage of Imperialism* (London: Thomas Nelson and Sons, 1965) whose reportedly biting anticapitalist and anti-Western stance prompted American President Lyndon B. Johnson to cancel a projected American economic package of over $35 million to Ghana. Although John Stockwell has shown in his *In Search of Enemies*, (New York: W. W. Norton, 1978) that the American Central Intelligence Agency (CIA) encouraged the anti-Nkrumah military coup plotters, it is also believed that the cancellation of the proposed economic aid for Ghana was part of the economic strangulation that squeezed the last breath left in the final stages of the Nkrumah regime. The Osagyefo's February 1966 overthrow was then a matter of time.

40. Balogh, introduction, p.7.

41. Ibid., pp.7–8.

42. Dumont, *False Start in Africa*, p.239.

43. Ibid., pp.239–240.

44. Ibid., p. 240.

45. Ibid.

46. John Hatch, "A Note on English-Speaking Africa" in Dumont's *False Start in Africa*, p.303.

47. Ibid., p.297.

48. Ibid., p.293.

49. Reportedly, it was Mr. Krobo Edusei, one of Nkrumah's cabinet members who used to be in charge of protocol as well as agriculture and interior, who gave his interpretation of socialism to a post-1966 commission of enquiry.

50. Baffour Osei Akoto, *Struggle against Dictatorship* (Adum, Kumasi Ghana: Payless Printing Press, 1992), p.5.

51. Ibid., p.59.

52. Ngugi wa Thiong'o, *Detained: A Writer's Prison Diary* (London: Heinemann, 1981), p.xi.

53. Editors, "USAID's Approach to Corruption," *African Voices* 7, no. 2 (USAID, Washington, DC, summer/fall 1998): 1.

54. Ibid.

55. Ibid.

56. Eric Schimitt, "Treasury Chief Defends U.S. Aid to Russia, but Calls for Safeguards," *New York Times*, 22 September 1999, p.A3.

57. Ibid.

58. Looking at the fraudulent behavior of the Washington, D.C.-based pro-Africa center, many people wondered if the African continent would have any salvation when its educated citizenry, now economic and voluntary exiles, return to attain national leadership of their respective countries.

59. Although Sekou Toure's Guinea was accused of heinous human rights violations, his soldiers were fiercely loyal to him until his death, when they staged Guinea's first successful coup d'etat. The military, after almost five years, is still ruling Guinea.

60. Editors, "Heir Apparent?" *Weekly Review* (Nairobi, Kenya) 9 April 1999, p.4.

61. Ibid.
62. Ibid.
63. Correspondent, "The Ghost of Ouko Returns," *New African* (May 1999): 19.
64. Ibid.
65. Paul Michaud, "Togo: Eyadema 2, Amnesty 1," *New African,* (September 1999): 9.
66. Editors, "Gambia: Best Sells Out," *New African* (September 1999): 11.
67. Ibid.
68. Ibid.
69. Seth Mydans, "Shock and Sorrow in the Aftermath of Timor's Violence, *New York Times* 26 September 1999, p.8.
70. Philip Shenon, "Protests against Military Shift to Indonesia City of Sumatra," *New York Times* 26 September 1999, p.8.
71. Editorial, "Kofi Anna's Critique," *New York Times* 22 September 1999, p. A26.
72. Ibid.
73. A detailed study of the subject of the monarchical tendency in African politics can be fully read in Ali A. Mazrui, "The Monarchical Tendency in African Political Culture," *British Journal of Sociology* 18, no. 3 (September 1967).
74. Elenore Smith Bowen, *Return to Laughter* (Garden City, NJ: Doubleday & Company, Ltd., Inc., 1964).
75. Economic Commission for Africa (ECA), press release no. 89 of October 1999.
76. Ibid.
77. Ibid.
78. Ibid.
79. Ibid.

Chapter 8

1. Culled from a *West Africa Magazine* of London interview on January 10, 2000 with deposed Ivory Coast leader, retired General Robert Guei.
2. Adama Gaye, "Guei's Words When He Took Power," *West Africa Magazine* (30 October–5 November 2000): 12.
3. Ibid.
4. Adama Gaye, "Cote d'Ivoire: Democracy without War," *West Africa Magazine,* (3 October–5 November 2000): 7.
5. Ibid.
6. Kofi Batsa, *The Spark* (London: Rex Collings Ltd., 1985), p.15.
7. The Ghana-CIA fight was comprehensively covered by the *Washington Post*. In fact, the ruling PNDC regime of Chairman Jerry John Rawlings claimed that a Black female CIA operative in the American Embassy in the Ghanaian capital of Accra had become so "close" to Rawlings's cousin, Susudis, that she leaked part of the CIA plot to him, and hence Rawlings got wind of it. Several locally-recruited CIA operatives in Ghana were either "liquidated" by Ghanaian intelligence squads or were simply forced by the circumstances to escape into exile in America and elsewhere. The accused Black female CIA operative was recalled from her Ghana posting, charged, tried, and jailed by a Virginia court, which specializes in the trial of intelligence cases. Now, the Rawlings regime is very close to America, Britain, and other Western nations, and, as trumpeted in the Western press, it has benefitted from Western aid as well as Western-sponsored loans from the IMF, World bank, and other international sources.
8. John Mukum Mbaku, ed., *Corruption and the Crisis of Institutional Reforms in Africa* (Lewiston, NY: The Edwin Mellen Press, 1998), pp.42–52; and 132–133. This book is worth studying in conjunction with our publication, as its emphases are on political economic problems of Africa.
9. General Alexander's book *African Tight Rope* (London: Pall Mall Press, 1965) is quoted extensively elsewhere in this publication along with the written exhortations of Ghana's Nkrumah and other post-independence African leaders, none of whom wanted the armed forces to dabble in partisan or active politics. Referring to these publications can be helpful to understand most of our arguments and discussions. Also, in *Axioms of Kwame Nkrumah* (London: Panaf Books, 1980), several of his axiomatic statements—including those about the Ghanaian military—have been published.

10. Yvette M. Alex-Assensoh, introduction to *Neighborhoods, Family and Political Behavior in Urban America* (New York: Garland Publishing, 1998), p.3.

11. Editors, "Togo: Choppy Waters," *Africa Confidential* 40, no. 18 (10 September 1999), 6–7.

12. Ibid.

13. Although it is not a written rule that any past or present African leader needs to die in office in order to get a state or an official burial, one can count and see the many national leaders who did hang on in office, even past their eightieth birthdays. Some leaders, indeed, falsified the records, which stated their actual age, so that they could appear younger and carry on ruling some African countries.

14. Uche Ezechukwu, "Corruption Monster Out of Control in Nigeria," *West Africa Magazine* (28 August-3 September 2000): 9.

15. Ibid.

16. Ibid., p.11.

17. Anthony A. Akinola, "A History of Corruption," *West Africa Magazine*, (28 August-3 September 2000): 15.

18. Uche Ezechekwu, "And Where is the Money," *West Africa Magazine*, (28 August-3 September 2000): 13.

19. Gustavo Capdevila, "Human Rights in the Global Arena," *West Africa Magazine*, (28 August-3 September 2000): 22.

20. Ibid.

21. Ibid.

22. Ibid.

23. Associated Press, "Ivory Coast: Support from Deposed General," *New York Times* 14 November 2000, p.A6.

24. Ibid.

25. Ibid.

26. Editor, "Interview: I Have No Regrets," *West Africa Magazine* (2–8 October 2000): 12.

27. Ibid.

28. Ibid.

29. Ibid.

30. Editor, "On Death Row," *West Africa Magazine* (2–8 October 2000): 15.

31. Desmond Davies, "Will Nigerians Ever Learn," *West Africa Magazine* (30 October-5 November 2000): 44.

32. Ibid.

33. Nkrumah, *Autobiography*, (London: Thomas Nelson, 1957), p.164.

34. Assensoh, *African Political Leadership*, (Malabar, FL: Krieger, 1998), p.108.

35. A. B. Assensoh, "Conflict or Cooperation?: Africans and African Americans in Multiracial America," in *Black and Multiracial Politics in America* (New York: New York University Press, 2000), pp.113–130.

36. Ibid., p.126; Dr. Tunde Adeleke's article, "The Colorline as a Confining Restraining Paradigm," appeared in *Western Journal of Black Studies* 23, no. 2 (summer 1999).

BIBLIOGRAPHY

Ademoyega, Adewale. *Why We Struck: The Story of the First Nigerian Coup.* Ibadan, Nigeria: Evans Brothers, 1981.

Adjei, Mike. *Death and Pain in Rawlings' Ghana, The Inside Story.* London: Black Line Publishing Ltd., 1993.

Adu, A. L. *The Civil Service in Commonwealth Africa: Development and Transition.* London: George Allen & Unwin Ltd., 1969.

Adu, Boahen A. *Africa Under Colonial Domination.* Berkeley: University of California Press, 1961.

Afrifa, A. A. *The Ghana Coup.* London: Frank Cass, 1966.

Agbese, Pita Ogaba. "Africa and the Dilemmas of Corruption." In *Corruption and the Crisis of Institutional Reforms in Africa,* edited by John Mukum Mbaku. Lewison, NY: The Edwin Mellen Press, 1998.

Alex-Assensoh, Yvette M. *Neighborhoods, Family, and Political Behavior in Urban America.* New York: Garland Publishing Inc., 1998.

———. and A. B. Assensoh. "The Politics of Cross-Cultural Marriage: An Examination of a Ghanaian/African-American Case," in *Cross-Cultural Marriage: Identity and Choice,* edited by Rosemary Breger Rosanna Hill, Oxford, Eng.: Berg, 1998.

———. and A. B. Assensoh, "The Leadership of the American Civil Rights Movement and African Liberation Movements: Their Connections and Similarities," *Proteus,* spring 1998.

———. and Lawrence J. Hanks. *Black and Multiracial Politics in America.* New York: New York University Press, 2000.

Alexander, H. T., Major-General. *African Tightrope.* London: Pall Mall Press, 1965.

Amin, Samir. *Neo-Colonialism in West Africa.* Middlesex, Eng.: Penguin Books, Ltd., 1973.

Ankomah, Baffour. "A Time for Some Home Truths." *New African,* May 1998.

Arhin, Kwame. *The Life and Work of Kwame Nkrumah.* Trenton, NJ: Africa World Press, 1993.

Assensoh, A. B. *African Political Leadership: Jomo Kenyatta, Kwame Nkrumah and Julius K. Nyerere.* Malabar, FL: Krieger publishing Company, 1998.

———. *Kwame Nkrumah of Africa.* Devon, Eng.: Arthur H. Stockwell Publishers, 1998.

———. *Africa in Retrospect.* Devon, Eng.: Stockwell, 1985.

———. *Rev. Dr. Martin Luther King, Jr., and America's Quest for Racial Integration.* Devon, Eng.: Stockwell, 1987.

———. *Kwame Nkrumah: Six Years in Exile, 1966–1972.* Devon, Eng.: Stockwell, 1976.

Austin, Dennis and Robin Luckham. *Politicians and Soldiers in Ghana, 1966–1972.* London: Frank Cass, 1975.

Ayittey, George B. N. *Africa in Chaos.* New York: St. Martin's Press, 1998.

————. *Africa Betrayed.* New York: St. Martin's Press, 1992.

Azikiwe, Nnamdi. *My Odyssey.* London: C. Hurst and Company, 1970.

————. *Liberia in World Politics.* Westport, CT: Negro University Press, 1970.

Barnes, Andrew, E. "Some Fire Behind the Smoke: The Fraser Report and Its Aftermath in Colonial Northern Nigeria." *Canadian Journal of African Studies,* 31, no. 2, (1997).

Batsa, Kofi. *The Spark: From Kwame Nkrumah to Limann.* London: Rex Collings, 1985.

Bayart, Jean-Francois, Stephen Ellis, Beatrice Hibou. *The Criminalization of the State in Africa.* Bloomington: Indiana University Press, 1999.

Bernasko, Frank G. *Nigeria: The Rise and Fall of the Second Republic, 1979–1983.* Windsor, Berkshire, Eng.: The Short Run Book Company, 2000.

Buah, F. K. *History of Ghana.* London: Macmillan, 1980.

Busia, K. A. *The Challenge of Africa.* New York: Praeger, 1962.

Chazan, Naomi. *An Anatomy of Ghanaian Politics.* Boulder, CO: Westview Press, 1983.

Cohen, Robin and Harry Goulbourne. *Democracy and Socialism in Africa.* Boulder, CO: Westview Press, 1991.

Cole, Ellis. "We Are So Terribly Sorry," *Newsweek Magazine,* April 6, 1998.

Decalo, Samuel. *Coups and Army Rule in Africa.* New Haven: Yale University Press, 1990.

Diamond, Larry. *Ethnicity and Democracy in Nigeria.* London: The Macmillan Press, 1988.

Dike, Kenneth O. *Trade and Politics in the Niger Delta, 1830–1885.* London: Oxford University Press, 1956.

Dumont, René. False Start in Africa. New York: Praeger, 1966.

Editors, *Panaf Great Lives: Kwame Nkrumah.* London: Panaf Books Limited, 1974.

Editors. *Webster's Ninth New Collegiate Dictionary.* Springfield, MA: Merriam-Webster, Inc., 1985.

Elaigwu, J. Iswa. *The Biography of a Soldier-Statesman.* Ibadan, Nigeria: West Books, 1985.

Emerson, Rupert. "Nation-Building in Africa." In *Nation-Building,* edited by Karl W. Deutsch and William J. Foltz. New York: Atherton Press, 1963.

Enahoro, Anthony. *Fugitive Offender.* London: Cassell Publishing Co., 1965.

Esseks, J. D. "Economic Independence in a New African State: Ghana, 1956–1965." Harvard Ph.D. Diss., Harvard University, 1967.

Finch, Bob and Mary Openheimer. *Ghana: End of an Illusion.* New York: Monthly Review Press, 1966.

Franklin, John Hope and Alfred A. Moss, Jr. *From Slavery to Freedom.* 7th ed. New York: McGraw Hill, Inc., 1998.

Fyle, C. Magbaily. *Introduction to the History of African Civilization.* Vol. I: *Precolonial Africa.* Lanham, MD: University Press of America, 1999.

Fyle, Hilton Ebenezer. *The Fighter from Death Row: Testimony of Survival.* Columbus, OH: Hilton Fyle Media Co,. 2000.

Gailey, Jr., Harry A. *History of Africa,* Vol. 1. Malabar, FL: Krieger, 1981.

Haley, Alex. *Roots.* Garden City, NY: Doubleday, 1976.

Hamilton, Carolyn. *Terrific Majesty.* Cambridge: Harvard University Press, 1998.

Hull, Richard W. *Southern Africa: Civilizations in Turmoil.* New York: New York University Press, 1982.

Hyden, Goran and Michael Bratton. *Governance and Politics in Africa.* Boulder, CO: Lynne Rienner Publishers, 1992.

Igbokwe, Joe. *Twenty-Five Years after Biafra.* Lagos, Nigeria: Advent Communications Ltd., 1995.

Ikegwuoha, Bernard-Thompson, O. *Nigeria: An Endless Cycle of Coup d'Etat.* Rome, Italy: E. Progetto Gutenberg, 1994.

Irele, F. Abiola. *In Praise of Alienation: An Inaugural Lecture.* Ibadan, Nigeria: University of Ibadan, 1982.

Jahn, J. *Muntu.* New York: Grove Press, 1961.

Johnston, Harry. *Liberia.* Vol. 2. New York: Dodd and Company, Publishers, 1906.

Keller, Edmond, J. and Donald Rothchild, eds. *The New International Order.* Boulder, CO: Lynne Rienner Publishing , Inc., 1996.

Kenyatta, Jomo. *Facing Mount Kenya: The Tribal Life of The Gikuyu.* New York: Vintage Books, 1965.

Kesse-Adu, Kwame. *The Politics of Political Detention.* Tema, Ghana: Ghana Publishing Corporation, 1971.

Kirk-Greene, Anthony H. M. *Damnosa Hereditas: Ethnic Ranking and the Martial Races Imperative in Africa.* London, Unicorn: 1978.

Kolkowicz, E., et al., eds. *Soldiers, Peasants and Bureaucrats.* London: George Allen & Unwin, 1982.

Lewis, Rupert Charles. *Walter Rodney's Intellectual and Political Thought.* Barbados: The Press University of the West Indies and Detroit, MI: Wayne State University Press, 1998.

Mazrui, Ali A. *Cultural Forces in World Politics.* London: Curry, 1990.

Mbaku, John Mukum. *Corruption and the Crisis of Institutional Reforms in Africa.* Lewiston, NY: The Edwin Mellen Press, 1998.

————. and Julius O Ihonvbere. *Multiparty Democracy and Political Change: Constraints to Democratization in Africa.* Aldershot, Eng.: Ashgate Publishers, 1998.

Mbiti, John S. *African Religions and Philosophy.* Garden City, NY: Anchor Books, 1970.

McCarthy-Arnolds, Eileen, et al. *Africa, Human Rights, and the Global System.* Westport, CT: Greenwood Press, 1994.

Melvem, L. R. *A People Betrayed: The Role of the West in Rwanda's Genocide.* London: Zed Books, 2000.

Milne, June. *Kwame Nkrumah: Autobiography.* London: Panaf, 2000.

Nkrumah, Kwame. *Autobiography.* Edinburgh, U. K.: Thomas Nelson & Sons, 1957.

————. *Axioms.* London: Panaf Books, 1980.

————. *Dark Days in Ghana.* London: Panaf Books, 1968.

————. *Neo-Colonialism: The Last Stage of Imperialism.* London: Thomas Nelson & Sons, Ltd., Publishers, 1965.

Nugent, Paul. *Big Men, Small Boys and Politics in Ghana.* New York, Pinter; 1986.

Nyerere, Julius K. *Freedom and Socialism.* London: Oxford University Press, 1968.

Obasanjo, Olusegun and d'Orville, Hans, eds. *The Leadership Challenge of Economic Reform in Africa.* New York: Crane Russak, Publishers, 1991.

Obichere, Boniface I. *West African States and European Expansion.* New Haven: Yale, 1971.

Odetola, Olatunde. *Military Regimes and Development.* London: George Allen & Unwin Ltd., 1982.

Odumegwu-Ojukwu, Emeka. *Because I Am Involved.* Ibadan, Nigeria: Spectrum Books Ltd., 1989.

Ogunsanwo, Alaba. *The Nigerian Military.* Princeton, NJ: Center of International Study, 1980.

Okion, Ojibo. *Nigeria Returns to Civilian Rule.* Lagos, Nigeria: Tokion, Nigeria, Ltd., 1980.

Omotoso, Kole. *Fellow Nigerians. . . : Famous First Words of Nigerian Coup-Makers, 1966–1985.* Ile Ife, Nigeria: House of Books, 1989.

Onyejekwe, Okey. *The Role of the Military in Economic and Social Development: A Comparative Regime Performance in Nigeria, 1960–1979.* Lanham, MD: University Press of America, 1981.

Osabu-Kle, Daniel T. *Comparative Cultural Democracy: The Key to Development in Africa.* Ontario, Canada: Broadview Press, Ltd., 2000.

Oyeridan, Oyeleye and Adigun Agbaje, eds. *Nigeria: Politics of Transition and Governance, 1986–1996.* Dakar, Senegal: Codesria, 2000.

Patterson, Orlando. *Slavery and Social Death: A Comparative Study.* Cambridge, MA: Harvard University Press, 1982.

Rosberg, C. Nottingham, J. *The Myth of Mau-Mau.* New York: Praeger, 1966.

Saxena, S.C. *Politics in Africa.* New Delhi, India: Kalinga Publications, 1993.

Smertin, Yuri. *Kwame Nkrumah.* New York: International Publishers, 1987.

Smith, Edwin W. *Aggrey of Africa.* London: Student Christian Movement Press, 1929.

Stockwell, John. *In Search of Enemies: A CIA Story.* New York: W.W. Norton, 1978.

Tufuo, J. W. and C. E. Donkor. *Ashantis of Ghana.* Accra, Ghana: Anowuo Educational Publications, 1989.

van Creveld, Martin. *The Encyclopedia of Revolutions and Revolutionaries: From Anarchism to Zhou Enlai.* New York: Facts on File, 1996.

van Dantzig, Albert. *Forts and Castles of Ghana.* Accra, Ghana: Sedo Press, 1980.

wa Thiong'o, Ngugi. *Detained: A Writer's Prison Diary.* London: Heinemann, 1981.

Wastberg, Per, ed. *The Writer in Modern Africa.* Uppsala, Sweden: Scandinavia Institute of African Studies, 1968.

Wreh, Tuan. *Love of Liberty.* London: C. Hurst & Co., 1976.

Yarak, Larry W. *Asante and the Dutch, 1744–1873.* New York: Oxford University Press, 1990.

Yeebo, Zaya. *State of Fear in Paradise.* London: ARIB, 1995.

Young, Crawford. *The African Colonial State in Comparative Perspective.* New Haven: Yale University Press, 1994.

Journals, Magazines, News Agencies and Reports Cited

Agency France-Presse, Paris.

Africa Confidential, London.

African Affairs Journal, London.

African Business Journal, London.

Annual Report of the ACS (Second Edition, 1889).

Armed Forces and Society Journal (1990).

The British Journal of Sociology, London.

Canadian Journal of African Studies, Canada.

Concord Weekly, London (1985).

The Daily Observer, Banjul, Gambia.

The Economist, London.

Gambia News & Report, Banjul, Gambia (1992).

Indian P.E.N. Journal, Bombay, India.

League of Nations Advisory Report on Slavery, Geneva (April 5, 1938).

New African Magazine, London.

The New York Times and *The New York Times Magazine,* New York.

News-Watch, Nigeria

Newsweek, USA.

Nigeria's Official Gazette, Lagos, Nigeria (1984).

Proteus Journal, Shippensburg, PA.

Reuters News Agency, London.

Transition, Cambridge, MA.

The Washington Post, Washington, DC.

West Africa Magazine, London.

INDEX

ABOUT THE AUTHORS

A. B. Assensoh is Professor of Afro-American Studies at Indiana University, Bloomington. Dr. Assensoh has published extensively on African, civil rights and liberation issues. His books include *African Political Leadership: Jomo Kenyatta, Kwame Nkrumah, And Julius K. Nyerere* (1998); *Kwame Nkrumah of Africa* (1989); *Rev. Dr. Martin Luther King, Jr., And America's Quest For Racial Integration* (1986; 1987).

Yvette Alex-Assensoh is an Associate Professor of Political Science at Indiana University, Bloomington. Apart from serving as Book Review Editor for *Urban Affairs Review*, Dr. Alex-Assensoh has also published widely on U.S. urban politics. Her publications include the 1998 book, *Neighborhoods, Family and Political Behavior in Urban America* and a co-edited volume, *Black and Multiracial Politics in America*.

Richard W. Hull, author of the foreword, is Professor of African History at New York University, where he is also the director of the Undergraduate Studies in History. Apart from traveling widely in Africa, Professor Hull is the author of numerous books and scholarly articles on Africa, including *Southern Africa: Civilizations in Turmoil*.

Okey Onyejekwe, who wrote the introduction, is a specialist on African politics. In addition to his academic position as an Associate Professor, Dr. Onyejekwe is the director of Ohio State University's Center for African Studies. Most of his extensive scholarly publications are on African political issues, including the 1981 book, *The Role of the Military in Economic and Social Development: A Comparative Regime Performance in Nigeria, 1960–1979*.

General Sanni Abacha, the Nigerian military dictator who died suddenly under mysterious circumstances. Courtesy of A. G. Kromah. Reprinted with permission.

President Samuel Kanyon Doe, who ruled Liberia after his murderous April 1980 coup d'etat, until he was himself captured and, reportedly, killed in 1990 by his armed opponents. Courtesy of A. G. Kromah. Reprinted with permission.

Retired General A. Abubakar of Nigeria, the last military leader, who honorably returned Nigeria to an elected government after the 1999 elections. Courtesy of A. G. Kromah. Reprinted with permission.

President William R. Tolbert, who was brutally murdered in his executive mansion residence in Monrovia in the April 1980 Liberian coup d'etat led by then Master-Sergeant Samuel Kanyon Doe. He wore a cross that symbolized his status as an ordained Baptist minister. Courtesy of A. G. Kromah. Reprinted with permission.

Alhaji G. V. Kromah, a distinguished Liberian journalist, as the then leader of ULIMO-K, one of the warring factions that fought in the seven-year Liberian civil war. Courtesy of A. G. Kromah. Reprinted with permission.

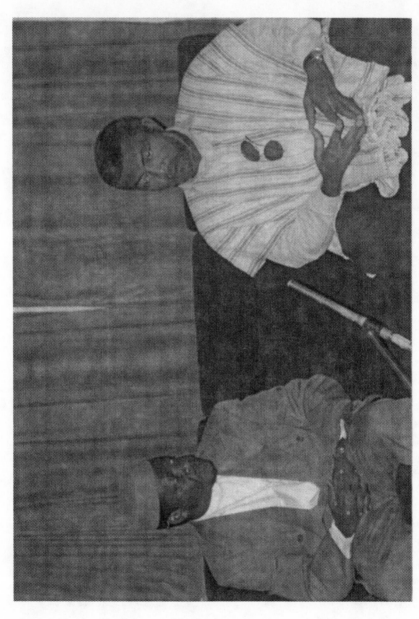

Ghana's former military leader–turned–civilian president, Jerry John Rawlings, speaking with Liberia's former 1995–1997 transitional collective presidency member Alhaji G. V. Kromah. Courtesy of A. G. Kromah. Reprinted with permission.

Sierra Leone's Brigadier Maado Bio, the military leader under whom the former British colony held elections in 1996 to return the nation to civilian rule, with President Ahmed Tejan Kabah as the new leader. Courtesy of A. G. Kromah. Reprinted with permission.

President Ahmed Tejan Kabbah of Sierra Leone, whose government was overthrown by a section of the Sierra Leonean military, stayed in Guinea in exile and returned to power in Sierra Leone by the combined armed ECOMOG forces of the Economic Community of West African States (ECOWAS). Courtesy of A. G. Kromah. Reprinted with permission.